EVERYMAN, I will go with thee,

and be thy guide,

In thy most need to go by thy side

JOHN DRYDEN

Born in Northamptonshire in 1631 and educated
at Westminster School and Trinity College,
Cambridge. Settled in London in 1657 and wrote
complimentary verses on the death of Cromwell
and the Restoration of Charles II (1660). His
first play was acted in 1663, and he wrote many
heroic plays and comedies before 1681, when he
turned to verse satire with *Absalom and Achitophel* (1681–2), *The Medal* (1682) and *Mac
Flecknoe* (1682). Appointed Poet Laureate and
Historiographer Royal in 1670, he became a
Catholic soon after the accession of James II in
1685, and was deprived of both posts with the
Revolution of 1689. For the last decade of his
life he lived in industrious retirement, translating
Juvenal and Persius (1693), Virgil (1697) and
the *Fables* (1700) from Homer, Ovid, Boccaccio
and Chaucer. Died in 1700.

JOHN DRYDEN

Of Dramatic Poesy

AND OTHER CRITICAL ESSAYS

IN TWO VOLUMES · VOLUME ONE

EDITED WITH AN INTRODUCTION BY
GEORGE WATSON

DENT : LONDON
EVERYMAN'S LIBRARY
DUTTON : NEW YORK

© Introduction and editing, J. M. Dent & Sons Ltd, 1962
All rights reserved
Made in Great Britain
at the
Aldine Press · Letchworth · Herts
for
J. M. DENT & SONS LTD
Aldine House · Bedford Street · London
First included in Everyman's Library (abridged edition) 1912
This complete two-volume edition first published 1962
Last reprinted 1971

NO. 568

ISBN: 0 460 00568 5

INTRODUCTION

DRYDEN'S literary criticism must look odd to most who approach it for the first time. Everyone knows that Samuel Johnson called him the Father of English Criticism, and we expect to find him pioneering, in a rough and ready way, techniques which later critics have sophisticated. And this is not quite false: Dryden *is* effectively the first English critic, in the sense of being first in the unbroken evolution of English criticism after the false start made by Elizabethan rhetoricians in the 1570's. Our criticism stems from Dryden. He made Johnson's *Lives of the English Poets* possible, as Johnson knew, and beside Dryden earlier attempts like Sidney's *Apology for Poetry* or Ben Jonson's *Timber* look premature and irrelevant. But the word 'pioneer' summons up all the wrong images. We think of someone vigorous and audacious, a genius crudely and startlingly original, defiant of established values. Nothing Dryden ever wrote in the way of criticism is much like this, least of all his first and most familiar essays. The immense vigour of his mind is deployed to accommodate whatever there may be in his ideas that is original to accepted standards of his age. If he is sometimes a jump ahead of his readers, he usually takes care not to be any further off. At his most characteristic, he is intent upon seeming less original than he is; reverent of precedent and tactfully timorous in intellectual—though not always in personal—controversy; above all, eager to please, 'for I confess my chief endeavours are to delight the age in which I live.'[1] This is not the language of a pioneer. It is the language of a very professional poet zealous to placate his readers and his audiences. And this, at least before the Revolution of 1689, is just what Dryden's criticism is like—the studio-talk of a successful artist who knows how to give away a little, but not much, whose revelations are always likely to be self-recommendations artfully disguised, and who in debate never hesitates to evade or suppress. Of all kinds of criticism, after all, prefaces to one's

---

[1] 'A Defence of *An Essay of Dramatic Poesy*,' p. 116, below.

own works are the most sophisticated and the least ingenuous, and the preface is Dryden's staple form of criticism. His claim to the paternity of English cricism we may concede at once, but it should not encourage us to suppose that what he did as a critic was boldly primitive, or that his successors have refined his crude ore. On the contrary, criticism grew simpler as it grew older. Addison and Johnson seem transparently innocent after Dryden. They acquired techniques of analysis, as in their accounts of *Paradise Lost*, which Dryden was probably incapable of, but the novelty lies not so much in their subtlety as in their disinterestedness. After all, they had no thought of writing epics of their own.

The notion that a poem is worth analysis for its own sake and on its own terms is very modern. Nobody in ancient, medieval, or Renaissance Europe would have understood it. During the half century that divides Dryden's death in 1700 from the advent of Johnson as a critic, such little analysis as there was sought excuses for itself in appeals to general laws. The very profession of criticism was not accepted: nearly all English comment on critics and criticism between the Restoration of 1660 and Johnson is simply hostile. Pope's youthful *Essay on Criticism* (1711), for example, sets up impossibly difficult conditions for a critic to fulfil, and denies in so many words that criticism can ever be a profession:

> Let such teach others who themselves excel,
> And censure freely who have written well (ll. 15-16).

Swift does not even admit as much as that—even poets, in his view, presume too far when they try to justify their own works, and *The Tale of a Tub* (1704) includes a sneer at his elderly cousin Dryden, who 'has often said to me in confidence that the world would never have suspected him to be so great a poet, if he had not assured them so frequently in his prefaces that it was impossible they could either doubt or forget it' (sect. v). And we have solid, if rather neglected, evidence in *The Rehearsal* (1672), a contemporary travesty of Dryden's work as a play-wright, that cultivated opinion in Restoration London denied the poet the right to be a critic too. Like American New Critics between the two World Wars, almost all Englishmen before Johnson believed that a poem or a play is, or ought to be, self-sufficient, and that the poet is somehow cheating unprofessionally in writing an explanation of what he is doing. This is the philistine joke that underlies some of the boisterous fun of *The Rehearsal*, where Buckingham and others ridicule Dryden ('Bayes') as a young and ambitious dramatist. Bayes, when he is told the audience will not be able to follow his play, explains: 'I have printed above a hundred sheets of paper to insinuate the plot into the boxes.'[1] According to the accepted view of Dryden's day, the poet who explains himself condemns himself, and Dryden's decision to supply the run of his own works with critical prefaces was both novel and defiant.[2] It was by this practice that he fathered English criticism, for what we now call criticism—the analysis of the works of other men—takes its rise from the justification of one's own.

In European terms, the true pioneer is not Dryden but Corneille, and it was Corneille's example in providing his own plays with critical prefaces that encouraged Dryden to do the same. The very word that Dryden uses for a critical analysis, *examen*, derives from Corneille, whose three-volume *Théâtre* of 1660 is a clearly original experiment. It was original of Corneille to collect his plays at all. It was startling to head each volume with a *discours* or theoretical treatise, followed by an *examen* of all the plays contained in the volume, sub-divided by play-titles. The order is as follows:

Vol. I: Discours de l'utilité et des parties du poème dramatique, Examen des poèmes [8 plays] contenus en cette première partie;

Vol. II: Discours de la tragédie, Examen des poèmes [8 plays] contenus en cette seconde partie;

Vol. III: Discours des trois unités; Examen des poèmes [7 plays] contenus en ce troisième volume.

Strictly speaking, then, *examen* is something of an abstraction for Corneille—'analysis' rather than 'an analysis'; though modern

---

[1] *The Rehearsal*, ed. Edward Arber (1869), p. 39 (Act I). This may refer to the 'Connection of the *Indian Emperor* to the *Indian Queen*,' which precedes the prologue in the quarto of Dryden's *Indian Emperor* (1667). Dryden explains there that his sequel is set in sixteenth-century Mexico, and describes the intervening action.

[2] For some occasional precursors, cf. preface to *The Tempest*, p. 133n., below.

editors have obscured this usage by dividing Corneille's analyses, as a matter of convenience, into twenty-three play prefaces. Dryden's debt, apart from the general example, is twofold: Corneille showed him in his third *discours* how the pseudo-Aristotelian unities of action, time, and place, insisted upon by the French Academy and by most learned opinion, could be liberalized into practical aids to the popular dramatist; and, in the *examens*, he showed by example how any given play could be analysed according to these rules. Justification-by-analysis is Corneille's object—he is, of course, analysing his own plays; and fifteen of Dryden's are furnished with such analyses in the form of prefaces.[1] Those who ask why Dryden should have spent almost the first twenty years (1664-81) of his critical career upon the drama have their answer here. His success as a playwright never equalled his later triumphs as a satirist and a translator. But dramatic criticism was the only kind of descriptive criticism he knew. All else he was, in principle, forced to invent for himself, and the whole temper of Dryden's mind, as we have seen, was timid of innovation. His object in his plays and poems was to please, his object in his criticism was to prepare an audience for his plays and poems. This leaves his early criticism, at least, strangely without direction: 'He is the best English writer,' it has been said, 'to create no world, no quality, no values of his own.'[2] There are occasional, and minor, acts of defiance, in his middle years, and his quiet, obstinate opposition to Protestantism and William III in the last decade of his life suggests a hardening of the will: but, on the whole, the record is one of accomplished intellectual diplomacy. This is not to deny that Dryden is an original critic. But his originality, in his early years at least, is of the kind admired by M. Jean Cocteau: it consists in an unsuccessful desire to behave like everyone else.

One cardinal difference, however, divides Corneille's prefaces from Dryden. Corneille (1606-84) wrote his in 1660, at the age of fifty-four, his career as a dramatist almost over. Dryden wrote his first preface, to *The Rival Ladies* (1664), only four

---

[1] Others of his plays appeared with prefaces of little or no critical interest, and such prefaces are not included in this edition. They are usually mere appeals to patronage, whereas the fifteen, as well as being dedicatory letters to noble patrons, are made to serve some critical purpose besides.

[2] Stephen Potter, *The Muse in Chains* (1947), p. 55.

years later, when—though already thirty-two years old—he had seen only three of his plays produced, and had no major poem to his credit. Corneille's justifications are of the past, Dryden's of the future: the Englishman is the first European poet to make a habit of so preparing his critical ground in advance. His early prefaces have a youthful, apologetic quality, designed to ingratiate patron and reader. Critical intelligence is there from the beginning, but it is a withdrawn intelligence, reluctant to commit itself. Dryden does not impose ideas, he infiltrates them into the mind of the reader. Some such prudential motive must have inspired him in 1665 when, exiled in the country for eighteen months by the Plague and Fire, he conceived the idea of writing a critical dialogue setting out, in seemingly neutral form, his programme for the English theatre.

The decision was certainly an odd one, and the essay *Of Dramatic Poesy* remains an oddity, the only dialogue on literary criticism in English of any substantial importance. The very form was far from being established in England: Sir Walter Ralegh had written a political dialogue, *The Prerogative of Parliaments* (1628), not long before his execution in 1618; and Hobbes—the only modern philosopher we can be certain Dryden read—had recently produced several very academic dialogues in Latin on problems of mathematics and physics, innocent of characterization (the interlocutors are simply called 'A' and 'B'). Dryden's main technical models for writing a dialogue on the future of the drama were classical, and they fall broadly into three groups: the early Platonic dialogue, such as the *Gorgias*, in which an argumentative genius (Socrates) extracts truth like a midwife—this is Plato's own analogy, put in the mouth of Socrates in *Theaetetus*, 149—from stupid or hostile passers-by; secondly, the late Platonic dialogue, such as the *Laws*, which Plato began writing at about the time when the young Aristotle entered his Academy (367 B.C.),[1] where the early, argumentative, 'obstetric' technique gives place to elaborate exposition by a teacher to obedient pupils; and thirdly, the facetious, autobiographical dialogues of Lucian, more like real conversation than any of Plato's, but unsuited to constructive debate. We must not suppose that these possibilities presented

[1] Cf. Werner Jaeger, *Aristotle*, translated by Richard Robinson (1934), pp. 25f.

themselves clearly to the young Dryden in his father-in-law's mansion in Wiltshire: thirty years later, when he was writing the Life of Lucian as a publisher's commission, he passingly regretted the lack of any treatise on 'the several kinds of dialogue, and the whole art of it,' which he called 'a work long wanted and much desired, of which the Ancients have not sufficiently informed us; and I question whether any man now living can treat it accurately.'[1] And when, in defence of his dialogue against his brother-in-law, Sir Robert Howard, he invoked the traditional right of dialoguists and novelists to dissociate themselves from their own characters, he does so in terms which show he has not grasped the force of these distinctions: 'In vindication of myself,' he insisted in 'The Defence of An Essay' (p. 123, below), 'I must crave leave to say that my whole discourse was sceptical, according to that way of reasoning which was used by Socrates, Plato, and all the Academics of old, which Tully and the best of the Ancients followed, and which is imitated by the modest inquisitions of the Royal Society.' The last point is a fascinating red herring—Dryden had been elected to the Royal Society, then only two years old, in November, 1662, and had been put on two of its committees in 1664, one of them 'for improving the English language,' though he was dropped within two years for failure to attend its 'inquisitions.'[2] Whatever they were like (and one would like to think them Early Platonic rather than Late), they can hardly have been both; and 'Tully,' or Cicero, wrote dialogues in imitation of the lost dialogues of Aristotle, which are thought to have been in the late, expository, professorial manner of Plato's Laws. Certainly Cicero's De oratore, Dryden's likeliest model for Of Dramatic Poesy, is a dialogue of this sort: there is no real argument in it. Cicero's debate, like Dryden's, is conducted among four characters (though in Cicero a fifth character appears in the first part); it is divided, like Dryden's, into three parts; it is set, like Dryden's, in a defined place and time, nearly half a century before (91 B.C.) in the house of Cicero's old tutor Lucinius Crassus at Tusculum, a few days before his death. And Crassus

---

[1] Cf. vol. II, p. 212, below. The history of the dialogue is still unwritten, at least in English; cf. Rudolf Hirzel, Der Dialog (1895).

[2] Cf. Evelyn's letter to Pepys (12 August 1689); Claude Lloyd, 'Dryden and the Royal Society,' PMLA, xlv (1930), with replies, xlvi (1931); and George Watson, 'Dryden and the Scientific Image,' Notes and Records of the Royal Society, xviii (1963).

speaks for Cicero on the art of oratory, with hardly more contradiction than Dryden's Neander. *Of Dramatic Poesy* is certainly a Ciceronian dialogue, one of a school ultimately modelled upon Plato's later works. But Dryden introduces his own characteristic element of non-commitment. Neander, 'the New Man,' represents the young Dryden poised on the brink of a playwright's career, and the other three characters have been identified with fair certainty among other young poets of the day. And yet, in spite of the essentially didactic quality of the Ciceronian dialogue, the whole discourse is sceptical. We are rewarded neither with lively argument nor with much lucid doctrine. Argument, indeed, was never further off: no fire is kindled, no thunder breaks in any of these frigid parliamentary exchanges among four young men of 1665 in a boat on the Thames. The very occasion of their expedition, the naval victory won by the English over the Dutch, seems as much a foil as an analogy: it is consciously like, in that Dryden's (or Neander's) literary programme is patriotic, an assertion of English strength in the theatre in the face of a strong continental challenge; but it is unlike, as Dryden seems half aware, in that the sound of battle is far away. The four young poets 'perceived the air break about them like the noise of distant thunder, or of swallows in a chimney: those little undulations of sound, though almost vanishing before they reached them, yet still seeming to retain somewhat of their first horror which they had betwixt the fleets' (p. 19, below). The debate is conducted amid the faintest of noises off, and it offers hardly more excitement in itself. The opening skirmish, in which alone all four characters take part, is exquisitely contrived to shift the interest from the battle to poetry, and from poetry in general to dramatic poesy in particular; but it only ends in a definition of a play which is bad, which is shown to be bad, and which is none the less accepted (p. 25, below). Our confidence in Dryden's argumentative integrity is never quite re-established. The first of the three exchanges, between Crites and Eugenius on the Ancient-Modern controversy, seems detached almost to the point of indifference, and Dryden himself, as Neander, does not enter into it, only hinting at his own conviction by giving the Moderns the last word. The second, on the superiority of Elizabethan drama over the French, is vitally important for what is embedded in it, Neander's *examen* of Ben Jonson's *Silent Woman*, the first extended example of descriptive criticism in England, where Dryden applies Corneille's techniques of analysis to a classic of the English stage. But, as argument, Neander's case for the English is no better and no worse than that of any patriot in defence of his country. We feel he may well be right in his eulogies of Shakespeare, Jonson, and Beaumont and Fletcher, but we also feel he would say much the same if he were wrong. The third exchange, where Neander defends rhyming plays against Crites's claims for blank verse, is about a critical issue real enough for the working dramatist in Restoration England. But, rich in substance as Neander's speech is, we miss the right of reply, and Dryden's mild joke against his own loquacity at the end does not quite satisfy the reader's sense of fairness. The dialogue is stylistically too accomplished to be dull, and too original in its handling of Jonson's play ever to be neglected: but it is neither conversation, nor argument, nor explicit instruction either. What we miss, amid all the abuse of French civilization we hear from Neander, is any sense of a tradition of cultivated conversation which the French in the 1660's had already acquired. Dryden's francophobe patriotism is rooted in an unspoken sense of inferiority in an age when Paris was confidently the capital of civilized Europe and London a province merely, uncertain of its manners and still struggling to recover and adapt a theatrical tradition broken by twenty years of Puritan sanctions. One critic has suggested that no argument *could* develop in the Essay, because the Restoration gentleman was as likely to fight as to argue—as Dryden painfully discovered a dozen years later, when he was beaten up in Rose Alley in December 1679, perhaps at Rochester's behest—and that, in any real discussion among dramatists about the drama, 'the cut-and-thrust would not have been verbal only.'[1] This is surely right: Dryden himself later proved, in his 'Defence of *An Essay*,' how quickly in Restoration England argument descended into abuse.

For good reason, perhaps, *Of Dramatic Poesy* remains Dryden's only attempt at formal criticism. The rest is almost all prefatorial: Dryden recognized early that the preface fulfilled any purpose he was ever likely to have as a critic. He loved its

[1] Donald A. Davie, 'Dramatic Poetry: Dryden's Conversation Piece,' *Cambridge Journal*, v (1952).

infinite flexibility, 'rambling, never wholly out of the way, nor in it' (vol. II, p. 278, below); and he may have appreciated, too, that in its rambling way it was always to the point—Dryden's point, which is most characteristically an act of self-justification rather than a general manifesto. Writing prefaces may be a French habit, as he complains in the preface to *The Tempest* (1670) (p. 133, below), but it is the perfect instrument for a critic who, like himself, is mainly concerned with defending his place in the sun. Besides, it gave him infinite excuses for changing his mind in public, as in the flagrant change of front in favour of blank verse in the preface to *All for Love* (1678); for we do not expect the artist, in the heat of studio-talk, to expound consistent theories or remain all his life answerable to one set of positions. Dryden found it easy enough to evade the fundamental absurdity of attempting to acclimatize the heroic play to the English theatre, an absurdity which his friend St Evremond had neatly defined: 'The spirit of our religion is directly opposite to that of tragedy: the humility and patience of our saints carry too direct an opposition to those heroical virtues that are so necessary for the theatre.'[1] The incongruity is a moral one, and Dryden's dramatic criticism is about technical, not moral, issues. As the prefatorial habit grew on him, he was only once seriously frightened out of the pose of expansive ease into which, as a middle-aged dramatist, he had readily sunk. Rymer's blast against the Elizabethans, *The Tragedies of the Last Age*, shook him badly when it appeared in the autumn of 1677. It was a book he had intended to write himself;[2] but it was much more learned, and much more scathing, than he had thought possible. Nothing illustrates more clearly the tactical, diplomatic quality of Dryden's critical genius than the way in which he reacted to Rymer's book. On the one hand, he was held fast by deeply instinctive affection for his Elizabethan masters; on the other, he knew the force of neo-classical fashion, and ached to be respectable. The notes he scribbled in his copy of Rymer's book, which he never dared to publish, the so-called 'Heads of an Answer to Rymer', contain in outline the full force of his

[1] St Evremond (1610-1703), 'Of Ancient and Modern Tragedy,' in his posthumous *Works* (1728), II.103. Cf. vol. II, pp. 85f., below.

[2] Cf. 'To the Reader,' prefixed to *Of Dramatic Poesy*, p. 17 and n., below.

convictions, and even presume to attack the most sacred of all critical documents in Renaissance Europe, the *Poetics* of Aristotle, raising questions of hair-raising implications: 'Whether Aristotle has made a just definition of tragedy, of its parts, of its ends, and of its beauties; and whether he, having not seen any others but those of Sophocles, Euripides, etc., had or truly could determine what all the excellencies of tragedy are' (para. 8). Corneille had been willing to bend the rules for his own convenience—this knocks away the lower supports, it reeks of subversion. But 'The Grounds of Criticism in Tragedy' (1679), his principal public reply to Rymer, is a weak dilution of his private notes: slyly forceful, occasionally, if one has learned the art of reading between Dryden's lines, in its demonstration that Greek tragedies were not much more Aristotelian than the Elizabethan, as Rymer defines 'Aristotelian'; but hardly assertive of the native tradition of drama whose champion Dryden had once been. The superiority of the Elizabethans in language and in the theme of love is only hesitatingly advanced; and when Dryden did break with Rymer, a dozen years later, he broke on personal grounds alone.

Dryden's Protestant play, *The Spanish Friar* (1681), with its contemptuous preface against the London audiences he had suffered for eighteen years, marks the end of the first half of his career as a critic—a critic of the drama. The second phase (1680–1700), where his gift for literary history fragmentarily emerges, had already begun. Dryden's historical interests first appear in force in support of his new career as a translator of the classical poets, in the preface to *Ovid's Epistles Translated* (1680). But it is just as likely that he became a translator because of his historical interests. The *examen* of *The Silent Woman*, with its accompanying account—an astonishingly accurate one—of Jonson's theory of humours, is the first hint we have that Dryden's historical sense was unusual for his age. Not many Europeans before the nineteenth century had more than a passing intuition of the assumption we all now share that past ages may have governed their behaviour on principles alien to our own. It is a central neoclassical doctrine, from the sixteenth-century Italians to Samuel Johnson, that (as Dryden obediently echoes it), 'mankind [is] the same in all ages, agitated by the same passions, and moved to action by the same interests' (vol. II, p. 4, below). Dryden never dared to formulate any doctrine to the contrary. His age knew neither literary history nor literary biography—Izaak Walton's *Lives* (1640-78), for example, though certainly biographies of writers, are almost entirely innocent of critical judgments, and the literary life cannot be said to be launched in England before Joseph Warton's *Essay on Pope* (1756-82) and Johnson's *Lives* (1779-81). Dryden very narrowly escaped the honour of naturalizing the form into the English tradition. The inclination was there, but not the leisure or the industry. 'I never read any thing but for pleasure,' he confesses in the Life of Plutarch, but his pleasure, he adds, is history, where precept is reduced to example and 'gently slides into us, is easy and pleasant in its passage' (vol. II, pp. 4, 8, below). His three classical lives— Plutarch, Polybius, and Lucian—approach very near to the literary life by mingling biography with critical analysis. But they are not about English poets, and they are decidedly hackwork. The mass of derivative and undigested information almost buries Dryden's own perceptive asides about historiography and the nature of prose style. Literary history, too, narrowly missed Dryden as a pioneer: in his history of satire in the preface to Juvenal (1693), and in his history of the epic in the preface to the *Aeneis* (1697), he wrote the first extended histories in English of a literary form, if we except only Rymer's *Short View of Tragedy* (1693). But these belong to the last decade, when his critical intelligence, though wonderfully mellowed by experience and indifferent at last to literary fashion, was unable for pressure of work to take trouble with anything. And you cannot be a literary historian without taking trouble. Indeed the history of the epic in the dedication to the *Aeneis* can hardly be called Dryden's at all, so closely does it adhere to the French of Segrais; and the history of satire, though sensible and occasionally brilliant, does not entirely succeed in digesting its sources among the Dutch commentators. Dryden had the talent and instincts to create a school of English literary history, but did not. And when, half a century later, it was finally established by Joseph and Thomas Warton, it found its inspiration not in Dryden's scattered prefaces, but in the careful researches of the literary antiquaries.

Dryden's theory of translation, too, is in fragments. But there is nothing dubious about it, and the loss is to convenience only, for this time Dryden did not change his mind. To study it all, you must pursue it from the 1680 preface to Ovid through the prefaces to Tonson's second and third miscellanies (1685, 1693), the Life of Lucian, and the prefaces to the 1697 Virgil, ending with the opening passages of the preface to the *Fables* (1700). In outline, it is all in the preface to Ovid. For twenty years after, Dryden repeats and consistently develops his theory of a half-way-house of translation called 'paraphrase,' which offends neither in literal awkwardness ('metaphrase') nor in extravagant infidelity ('imitation'). Paraphrase ideally creates works which are both versions and poems too, where the translator is 'a master both of his author's language, and of his own' (p. 271, below). These definitions amount to the most severely useful things in Dryden's criticism: his own translations succeed as examples of his precepts, and together they created the tradition in translation he hoped for. They made Pope's Homer possible. And, unlike his early dramatic criticism, the late essays on translation and literary history are frank and free. In English prose, too, Dryden had found a middle way that suited him in the example of Montaigne, the only mentor in prose style he ever acknowledged: something more restrained than the baroque elaboration of Burton and Browne, heavily outmoded after 1660, and yet more colourful than the severe precepts of the Royal Society strictly required. Thomas Sprat, in his *History of the Royal Society* (1667), had described the linguistic programme of the Society: 'to separate the knowledge of nature from the colours of rhetoric, the devices of fancy, or the delightful deceit of fables' (p. 62). Dryden accommodated himself to much of this programme, but left himself room to turn. Some past richness still lingers in the modern restraint of his mature prose, and such tropes as he admits seem all the more vigorous for their isolation. As he grew older, the cautious stiffness of the sixties and seventies fell away, and a new and exhilarating fluency came upon him—'the tattling quality of age' he calls it with mock modesty in the preface to Juvenal (vol. II, p. 85, below). By the end of his days he is full of old man's pride for his expanding powers: 'Thoughts, such as they are, come crowding in so fast upon me that my only difficulty is to choose or to reject, to run them into verse or to give them the other harmony of prose,' he wrote as he neared seventy (vol. II, p. 272, below). He was lonely and out of favour, but he had won the honest knowledge of what he could and could not do.

The end of a poet's labours lies in such awareness, and Dryden's criticism is a record of his long struggle to win it. As certainty grew, so did candour, until by the end of his life he hardly cared what anybody thought of him, so long as he thought well of himself. It is to these last essays, with all due reservations concerning their avowed and slapdash dependence on foreign sources, that we should turn for best evidence of a mature literary intelligence. Indifferently ordered, it is all there. The comparative evaluations of Persius, Horace, and Juvenal in the 'Discourse Concerning Satire,' or of Homer, Ovid, Chaucer, and Boccaccio in the preface to the *Fables*, prove that descriptive criticism at last exists in England, expansive and deliberate. The stilted, disingenuous self-analyses of the early dramatic prefaces are the apprentice-work in which Dryden learned the critical art: ambitious as he was then, he cannot have had any notion where the prefatorial habit would lead him. 'I have built a house where I intended but a lodge,' he wrote proudly in the last essay of his life. It is a sufficient comment upon an achievement at once untidy and magnificent.

1960   GEORGE WATSON

NOTE ON THE TEXT

THIS EDITION attempts to collect, for the first time, the whole of Dryden's critical writings in whatever form they have survived—prefaces, essays, prologues, epilogues, letters, and private notes—and to annotate them as literary criticism. There are fifty-two items, included entire with four exceptions: the three classical lives of Plutarch (1683), Polybius (1693), and Lucian (1711), and the preface to the *Aeneis* (1697), all of which contained bulky material explicitly translated or adapted from continental treatises and commentaries. A long passage of quotations on painting in 'A Parallel betwixt Painting and

Poetry' (1695) has also been cut. In each case omissions are marked and their contents summarized. Nothing of Dryden's own has been lost, and nothing, in any case, of intrinsic interest. The expulsion of this derivative material has made it possible to include twenty-nine items not in W. P. Ker's edition of the *Essays* (1900), the only previous annotated edition of Dryden's criticism: namely seven letters, the three classical lives, nine more prefaces,[1] seven more prologues and epilogues to plays,[2] the 'Heads of an Answer to Rymer' (written in 1677), the complimentary verses before Roscommon's *Essay on Translated Verse* (1684), and the 'Character' of St Evremond (1692). The order is the probable order of composition. It is never quite possible to say that the whole of Dryden's criticism has been presented, since any of his writings are likely to contain critical asides—some of these have been used in annotation —but no surviving document of any substantial critical interest has been omitted. A few works of almost purely personal concern, such as the abusive *Notes and Observations on the Empress of Morocco* (1674) against Settle, or the attacks on Shadwell in *Mac Flecknoe* (1682) and *The Vindication [of] the Duke of Guise* (1683), have not been considered.

All texts are based upon the first editions. Dryden revised only one of his critical works, the dialogue *Of Dramatic Poesy* (1668, 1684), and in this case the first text has been followed, while revisions made for the second edition are recorded in footnotes. Spelling and punctuation, as in Ker's edition, are modernized, though more conservatively than in Ker. We approach more nearly the world of Restoration compositors by reproducing the chaos of their texts, but it is not clear that we approach more nearly to Dryden's, and it seems pointlessly pedantic (for example) to invite confusion by spelling 'Ben Jonson' as 'Johnson' when Dryden's printers spelled the name indifferently one way or the other. Ker's own reasons for modernization (*Essays*, pp. vi-vii) are still sound in principle; but I have been more fortunate than he in being able to consult first editions in every case, as well as the vast body of twentieth-century Dryden

---

[1] To *Secret Love, The Wild Gallant, The Tempest, Tyrannic Love, The Assignation, Oedipus, Don Sebastian, Eleonora*, and the *Pastorals* in the 1697 Virgil.
[2] Prologues to *The Tempest, Tyrannic Love*, and Congreve's *Double-Dealer*, and both prologues and epilogues to *Aureng-Zebe* and *Oedipus*.

scholarship. Ker's Dryden is one of the classics of English scholarship, and my chief debt lies there; Hugh Macdonald's bibliography of Dryden (1939), and Professor James Kinsley's edition of the poems (1958), follow close behind. It would have been laborious to record in notes every debt to the scholarship of other men: acknowledgment must be general, and it is variously due to all the works cited in the Select Bibliography that follows.

SELECT BIBLIOGRAPHY

PLAYS: *The rival ladies* (1664); *Tyrannic love* (1670); *The conquest of Granada* (1672); *Marriage à-la-mode* (1673); *Aureng-Zebe* (1676); *All for love* (1678); *The Spanish friar* (1681); *Don Sebastian* (1690). Some thirty plays published 1663–94.

POEMS: *Annus mirabilis* (1667); *Ovid's epistles, translated* (1680); *Absalom and Achitophel* (1681–2); *The medal* (1682); *Mac Flecknoe* (1682); *Religio laici* (1682); *The hind and the panther* (1687); *The satires of Juvenalis translated, together with the satires of Persius* (1693); *The works of Virgil translated* (1697); *Fables ancient and modern, translated from Homer, Ovid, Boccace, and Chaucer* (1700). Dryden also contributed heavily to Tonson's four miscellanies: *Miscellany poems* (1684); *Sylvæ* (1685); *Examen poeticum* (1693); and *The annual miscellany* (1694).

PROSE: *Of dramatic poesy: an essay* (1668).

Dryden's prose was first edited by Edmond Malone in 4 vols. (1800), and much of the criticism was re-edited by W. P. Ker in 2 vols. as *Essays* (1900). The *Works* have been edited by Sir Walter Scott in 18 vols. (1808), revised by George Saintsbury (1882–93); a Californian edition is in progress, edited by E. N. Hooker and H. T. Swedenberg (1956–). The poems have been edited by George R. Noyes (1909, 1950), and by James Kinsley in 4 vols. (1958); and the *Letters* by Charles E. Ward (1942).

The first scholarly life of Dryden was Edmond Malone's, in his edition of the *Prose works* (1800), now supplemented by J. M. Osborn's *Dryden: some biographical facts and problems* (1940); the best general studies are Samuel Johnson's Life of Dryden in his *Lives of the English poets* (1779–81), George Saintsbury's *Dryden* (1881) in the English Men of Letters series. D. Nichol Smith's *Dryden* (1950), and Charles E. Ward, *The life of Dryden* (1961). There are notable critical studies by Mark Van Doren, *The poetry of Dryden* (1920, 1946), T. S. Eliot, *Homage to Dryden* (1924), and C. S. Lewis's reply, 'Shelley, Dryden, and Mr. Eliot' in his *Rehabilitations* (1939). Louis I. Bredvold's *The intellectual milieu of Dryden* (1934) analyses his scepticism; see also Philip Harth, *Contexts of Dryden's thought* (1968).

For studies of Dryden as a critic, cf. W. P. Ker's introduction to his edition of the *Essays* (1900); Frank L. Huntley, *The unity of Dryden's dramatic criticism* (1944) and *On Dryden's Essay of dramatic poesy* (1951);

H. T. Swedenberg, *The theory of the epic in England, 1650–1800* (1944);
Barbara M. H. Strang, 'Dryden's innovations in critical vocabulary,'
Durham University Journal, li (1959); H. J. Jensen, *A glossary of Dryden's
critical terms* (1969). For his theory and practice in translating from Latin,
cf. J. M. Bottkol, 'Dryden's Latin scholarship,' *Modern Philology*, xl
(1942–3); H. M. Hooker, 'Dryden's *Georgics* and English predecessors,'
Huntington Library Quarterly, ix (1945); William Frost, *Dryden and the art
of translation* (1955); and L. Proudfoot, *Dryden's Aeneid and its seventeenth-
century predecessors* (1960).

Recent studies of Dryden's critical views include John M. Aden, *The
critical opinions of Dryden: a dictionary* (1963) and Robert D. Hume,
Dryden's criticism (1970).

The authoritative bibliography is Hugh Macdonald's *Dryden: a bibliography of early editions and of Drydeniana* (1939); cf. also Samuel H. Monk,
Dryden: a list of critical studies published from 1895 to 1948 (1950).

ABBREVIATIONS

DNB	*The dictionary of national biography*, 21 vols. (1885-1909)
ed.	edited by
Herford & Simpson	*Ben Jonson*, edited by C. H. Herford, Percy and Evelyn M. Simpson, 11 vols. (1925-52)
Ker	*Essays of John Dryden*, edited by W. P. Ker, 2 vols. (1900)
Kinsley	*The poems of John Dryden*, edited by James Kinsley, 4 vols. (1958)
Malone	*The critical and miscellaneous prose works of John Dryden*, edited by Edmond Malone, 4 vols. (1800)
OED	*The Oxford English Dictionary*, 13 vols. (1933)
Scott-Saintsbury	*The works of John Dryden*, edited by Sir Walter Scott, revised by George Saintsbury, 18 vols. (1882-93)
Spingarn	*Seventeenth-century critical essays*, edited by J. E. Spingarn, 3 vols. (1908-9)
Summers	*The dramatic works of John Dryden*, edited by Montague Summers, 6 vols. (1931-2)
Ward	*The letters of John Dryden*, edited by Charles E. Ward (1942)

CONTENTS

VOLUME I

VOLUME II

TO ROGER, EARL OF ORRERY

Prefixed to *The Rival Ladies* (1664)

DEBT TO ORRERY'S HEROIC PLAYS—A DEFENCE OF RHYME

Text: 4°, 1664.

Dryden's first critical essay, written at the age of thirty-two before he had produced any major poem, strikes a new, psychological
note in its first sentence, but abandons it almost at once to record a
literary debt.

Roger Boyle (1621-79), Earl of Orrery, was the author of the first
heroic play in English, *The General*—if we except Davenant's *The
Siege of Rhodes*, performed in 1656 as an opera—and, indeed, the
first acted Restoration play of any kind to be written. In December
1660, the newly restored Charles II had intervened in an argument
among his courtiers about English plays on the French model, and
suggested to Orrery that he attempt one. Orrery began without delay,
early in 1661, during leisure from his official duties in Ireland forced
on him by attacks of gout, and sent the manuscript of *The General*
to Charles in the spring. It circulated in London for three years,
but was not performed till September 1664, some four months after
Dryden's *Rival Ladies*. Orrery's second play, commissioned by
Davenant in 1661, is now lost, but Davenant may have received
his third play, *Henry the Fifth*, as early as the end of 1662. Cf.
William S. Clark (ed.), *The Dramatic Works of Orrery* (1937),
I.22f.

Dryden is evidently accurate in acknowledging it was Orrery's
example that inspired the heroic plays that followed his comedy
The Wild Gallant. He had plenty of chances of seeing a manuscript of
The General before writing this, his second play to be written and his
first to be printed: his friend and brother-in-law Sir Robert Howard
was not only related to Orrery, but also a chief shareholder in the
King's Company, which eventually performed *The General*. Indeed
it was a collaboration between Dryden and Howard, *The Indian
Queen* (1665), and not Orrery's play, which established the new vogue
when it was performed in January 1664. *The Rival Ladies* followed
in May. By the time Orrery's genuinely experimental play was performed, in September, it must have seemed anything but a revolu-
tionary occasion.

1

My Lord,

This worthless present was designed you long before it was a play; when it was only a confused mass of thoughts, tumbling over one another in the dark; when the fancy was yet in its first work, moving the sleeping images of things towards the light, there to be distinguished, and then either chosen or rejected by the judgment; it was yours, my Lord, before I could call it mine. And I confess, in that first tumult of my thoughts there appeared a disorderly kind of beauty in some of them, which gave me hope something worthy my Lord of Orrery might be drawn from them. But I was then in that eagerness of imagination which, by overpleasing fanciful men, flatters them into the danger of writing; so that, when I had moulded it into that shape it now bears, I looked with such disgust upon it, that the censures of our severest critics are charitable to what I thought (and still think) of it myself: 'tis so far from me to believe this perfect, that I am apt to conclude our best plays are scarcely so. For the stage being the representation of the world, and the actions in it, how can it be imagined that the picture of human life can be more exact than life itself is? He may be allowed sometimes to err who undertakes to move so many characters and humours as are requisite in a play in those narrow channels which are proper to each of them; to conduct his imaginary persons through so many various intrigues and chances as the labouring audience shall think them lost under every billow; and then at length to work them so naturally out of their distresses that when the whole plot is laid open, the spectators may rest satisfied that every cause was powerful enough to produce the effect it had; and that the whole chain of them was with such due order linked together that the first accident would naturally beget the second, till they all rendered the conclusion necessary.

These difficulties, my Lord, may reasonably excuse the errors of my undertaking; but for this confidence of my dedication, I have an argument which is too advantageous for me not to publish it to the world. 'Tis the kindness your lordship has continually shown to all my writings. You have been pleased, my Lord, they should sometimes cross the Irish seas to kiss your hands; which passage (contrary to the experience of others) I have found the least dangerous in the world. Your favour has shone upon me at a remote distance, without the least knowledge of my person; and (like the influence of the heavenly bodies) you have done good without knowing to whom you did it. 'Tis this virtue in your lordship which emboldens me to this attempt; for, did I not consider you as my patron, I have little reason to desire you for my judge; and should appear with as much awe before you in the reading, as I had when the full theatre sat upon the action. For who could so severely judge of faults as he who has given testimony he commits none? Your excellent poems having afforded that knowledge of it to the world, that your enemies are ready to upbraid you with it, as a crime for a man of business to write so well. Neither durst I have justified your Lordship in it, if examples of it had not been in the world before you; if Xenophon had not written a romance, and a certain Roman called Augustus Caesar a tragedy and epigrams.[1] But their writing was the entertainment of their pleasure; yours is only a diversion of your pain. The Muses have seldom employed your thoughts, but when some violent fit of gout has snatched you from affairs of state; and, like the priestess of Apollo, you never come to deliver his oracles, but unwillingly and in torment.[2] So that we are obliged to your Lordship's misery for our delight: you treat us with the cruel pleasure of a Turkish triumph, where those who cut and wound their bodies, sing songs of victory as they pass, and divert others with their own sufferings. Other men endure their diseases; your Lordship only can enjoy them. Plotting and writing in this kind are certainly more troublesome employments than many which signify more, and are of greater moment in the world: the fancy, memory, and judgment, are then extended (like so many limbs) upon the rack; all of them reaching with their utmost stress at nature; a thing so almost infinite and boundless as can never

---

[1] Dryden is invoking two classical precedents for men of action who, like Orrery, were also writers, and Summers is evidently wrong in suggesting Xenophon the Ephesian (second century A.D.), who wrote a Greek love romance but was neither soldier nor statesman. The obvious explanation is the true one: Dryden is referring to Xenophon the Athenian (c. 430-c. 354 B.C.), who not only led an adventurous life as one of Cyrus's Ten Thousand, but wrote *Cyropaedia*, a political romance on the boyhood of Cyrus and his victorious career. Augustus Caesar is known to have written a short poem on Sicily and a book of epigrams, as well as planning a tragedy on Ajax, though all his writings are lost.

[2] Cf. *Aeneid*, VI.77-80.

fully be comprehended but where the images of all things are
always present. Yet I wonder not your Lordship succeeds so
well in this attempt: the knowledge of men is your daily practice
in the world; to work and bend their stubborn minds, which go
not all after the same grain, but each of them so particular a
way that the same common humours, in several persons, must
be wrought upon by several means. Thus, my Lord, your sick-
ness is but the imitation of your health; the poet but subordinate
to the statesman in you; you still govern men with the same
address, and manage business with the same prudence; allowing
it here (as in the world) the due increase and growth, till it
comes to the just height; and then turning it when it is fully ripe,
and Nature calls out, as it were, to be delivered. With this only
advantage of ease to you in your poetry, that you have fortune
here at your command; with which wisdom does often unsuccessfully struggle in the world. Here is no chance which you
have not foreseen; all your heroes are more than your subjects,
they are your creatures. And though they seem to move freely
in all the sallies of their passions, yet you make destinies for
them which they cannot shun. They are moved (if I may dare
to say so) like the rational creatures of the Almighty Poet, who
walk at liberty, in their own opinion, because their fetters are
invisible; when indeed the prison of their will is the more sure
for being large; and instead of an absolute power over their
actions, they have only a wretched desire of doing that which
they cannot choose but do.[1]

I have dwelt, my Lord, thus long upon your writing, not
because you deserve not greater and more noble commendations,
but because I am not equally able to express them in other
subjects. Like an ill swimmer, I have willingly stayed long in
my own depth; and though I am eager of performing more,
yet am loath to venture out beyond my knowledge. For beyond

---

[1] A characteristically sceptical view of free will which may owe something
to Hobbes. Cf. Hobbes's reply to Bishop Bramhall, *Of Liberty and Necessity*
(1654), no. III: 'A wooden top that is lashed by the boys, and runs about,
sometimes to one wall, sometimes to another, sometimes spinning, sometimes
hitting men on the shins, if it were sensible of its own motion, would think it
proceeded from its own will, unless it felt what lashed it. And is a man any
wiser. . . ?' Dryden must have read Hobbes closely in these early years
(cf. pp. 8n., 161n., below); indeed John Aubrey, in his biography of Hobbes,
claims that Dryden 'is his great admirer, and oftentimes makes use of his
doctrine in his plays.'

your poetry, my Lord, all is ocean to me. To speak of you as a soldier, or a statesman, were only to betray my own ignorance; and I could hope no better success from it than that miserable rhetorician[1] had, who solemnly declaimed before Hannibal of the conduct of armies and the art of war. I can only say, in general, that the souls of other men shine out at little crannies; they understand some one thing, perhaps, to admiration, while they are darkened on all the other parts. But your Lordship's soul is an entire globe of light, breaking out on every side; and if I have only discovered one beam of it, 'tis not that the light falls unequally, but because the body which receives it is of unequal parts.

The acknowledgment of which is a fair occasion offered me to retire from the consideration of your Lordship to that of myself. I here present you, my Lord, with that in print which you had the goodness not to dislike upon the stage; and account it happy to have met you here in England; it being, at best, like small wines, to be drunk out upon the place, and has not body enough to endure the sea. I know not whether I have been so careful of the plot and language as I ought; but, for the latter, I have endeavoured to write English, as near as I could distinguish it from the tongue of pedants, and that of affected travellers. Only I am sorry that (speaking so noble a language as we do) we have not a more certain measure of it, as they have in France, where they have an Academy[2] erected for that purpose, and endowed with large privileges by the present king. I wish we might at length leave to borrow words from other nations, which is now a wantonness in us, not a necessity; but so long as some affect to speak them, there will not want others who will have the boldness to write them.

But I fear lest, defending the received words, I shall be accused for following the new way: I mean, of writing scenes in verse. Though, to speak properly, 'tis not so much a new way amongst us, as an old way new revived; for many years before Shakespeare's plays was the tragedy of Queen Gorboduc, in

[1] Phormio, an old philosopher who, according to Cicero (*De oratore*, II. 18, 75), lectured to an unwilling Hannibal at Ephesus on the art of war.

[2] L'Académie Française, founded by Louis XIII in 1635 at Richelieu's instigation, with the express purpose of regulating and purifying the French language.

English verse,[1] written by that famous Lord Buckhurst, afterwards Earl of Dorset, and progenitor to that excellent person who
(as he inherits his soul and title) I wish may inherit his good
fortune. But supposing our countrymen had not received this
writing till of late; shall we oppose ourselves to the most
polished and civilized nations of Europe? Shall we, with the
same singularity, oppose the world in this, as most of us do
in pronouncing Latin? Or do we desire that the brand, which
Barclay has (I hope unjustly) laid upon the English, should still
continue? *Angli suos ac sua omnia impensè mirantur; cœteras
nationes despectui habent.*[2] All the Spanish and Italian tragedies
I have yet seen are writ in rhyme. For the French, I do not
name them, because it is the fate of our countrymen to admit
little of theirs among us but the basest of their men, the extravagancies of their fashions, and the frippery of their merchand-
ise. Shakespeare (who, with some errors not to be avoided in
that age, had undoubtedly a larger soul of poesy than ever any
of our nation) was the first who, to shun the pains of continual
rhyming, invented that kind of writing which we call blank
verse,[3] but the French, more properly, *prose mesurée*; into which
the English tongue so naturally slides that, in writing prose,
'tis hardly to be avoided. And therefore I admire some men
should perpetually stumble in a way so easy, and inverting the
order of their words, constantly close their lines with verbs,
which though commended sometimes in writing Latin, yet we
were whipped at Westminster if we used it twice together. I
know some, who, if they were to write in blank verse, *Sir, I ask
your pardon*, would think it sounded more heroically to write,
Sir, I your pardon ask. I should judge him to have little command of English whom the necessity of a rhyme should force

[1] *The Tragedy of Gorboduc* (1565), by Thomas Sackville (Lord Buckhurst) and Thomas Norton, was of course written in blank verse, except for
the choruses; and Gorboduc was a king of Britain. This, and the reference
below to Shakespeare as the inventor of blank verse in English, are among the
most notorious of Dryden's howlers in literary history, which became less
common with the passing years.

[2] A vague memory of John Barclay's *Icon animorum* (1614), pp. 74-5:
'The English eagerly admire themselves and their own works; they despise
other peoples.'

[3] A graver error than the reversal of Gorboduc's sex, above. The first
extended blank verse in English was Surrey's translation of the second and
fourth books of the *Aeneid* (1557), and a number of Elizabethan playwrights,
notably Marlowe, had employed blank verse before Shakespeare.

often upon this rock; though sometimes it cannot easily be avoided; and indeed this is the only inconvenience with which rhyme can be charged. This is that which makes them say rhyme is not natural, it being only so when the poet either makes a vicious choice of words, or places them, for rhyme sake, so unnaturally as no man would in ordinary speaking; but when 'tis so judiciously ordered that the first word in the verse seems to beget the second, and that the next, till that becomes the last word in the line which, in the negligence of prose, would be so; it must then be granted, rhyme has all the advantages of prose besides its own. But the excellence and dignity of it were never fully known till Mr Waller taught it; he first made writing easily an art; first showed us to conclude the sense most commonly in distichs; which, in the verse of those before him, runs on for so many lines together that the reader is out of breath to overtake it. This sweetness of Mr Waller's lyric poesy was afterwards followed in the epic by Sir John Denham, in his *Cooper's Hill*,[1] a poem which, your Lordship knows, for the majesty of the style is, and ever will be, the exact standard of good writing. But if we owe the invention of it to Mr Waller, we are acknowledging for the noblest use of it to Sir William Davenant, who at once brought it upon the stage, and made it perfect, in the *Siege of Rhodes*.[2]

The advantages which rhyme has over blank verse are so many that it were lost time to name them. Sir Philip Sidney, in his defence of poesy,[3] gives us one which, in my opinion, is not

---

[1] The first of many references by Dryden and his neo-classical successors to Waller and Denham as the founders of the Augustan tradition in verse. Dryden never changed his opinion of Waller's achievement. In his preface to Walsh's *Dialogue Concerning Women* (1691), he called Waller 'the father of our English numbers.' 'I am desirous of laying hold on his memory on all occasions, and thereby acknowledging to the world that unless he had written, none of us could write.'

Dryden's sense of precedence is probably correct. Waller's poems, though not published till 1645, were no doubt in circulation before the first and pirated edition of Denham's *Cooper's Hill* (1642), a long moral-descriptive poem in heroic couplets which Dryden oddly calls an 'epic.'

[2] Davenant had contrived to produce his heroic play in 1656 as an opera, in spite of the closing of the theatres between 1642 and 1660. It was not p iblished till 1663.

[3] *Apology for Poetry* (1595), 37: 'Now that verse far exceedeth prose in tne knitting up of the memory, the reason is manifest: the words . . . being so set as one cannot be lost but the whole work fails, which accusing itself, calleth the remembrance back to itself, and so most strongly confirmeth it.' But Sidney is comparing verse with prose, not rhyme with blank verse.

the least considerable: I mean the help it brings to memory,
which rhyme so knits up by the affinity of sounds that, by
remembering the last word in one line, we often call to mind
both the verses. Then, in the quickness of repartees (which in
discoursive scenes fall very often), it has so particular a grace,
and is so aptly suited to them, that the sudden smartness of the
answer and the sweetness of the rhyme set off the beauty of each
other. But that benefit which I consider most in it, because I
have not seldom found it, is that it bounds and circumscribes the
fancy.[1] For imagination in a poet is a faculty so wild and lawless
that like an high-ranging spaniel it must have clogs tied to it,
lest it outrun the judgment.[2] The great easiness of blank verse
renders the poet too luxuriant; he is tempted to say many things
which might better be omitted, or at least shut up in fewer
words; but when the difficulty of artful rhyming is interposed,
where the poet commonly confines his sense to his couplet, and
must contrive that sense into such words that the rhyme shall
naturally follow them, not they the rhyme; the fancy then gives
leisure to the judgment to come in; which, seeing so heavy a tax
imposed, is ready to cut off all unnecessary expenses. This last
consideration has already answered an objection which some
have made, that rhyme is only an embroidery of sense, to make

[1] The first hint, much elaborated in *Of Dramatic Poesy* and later prefaces,
of Dryden's key concept of the poet's double talent, 'judgment' controlling
'fancy.' His source is certainly Hobbesian psychology; cf. Hobbes's account
of poetic creation in his *Answer to Davenant* (1650): 'Time and education
begets experience; experience begets memory; memory begets judgment
and fancy; judgment begets strength and structure, and fancy begets the
ornaments of a poem. . . . For memory is the world (yet not really, yet so
as in a looking glass) in which Judgment, the severer sister, busieth herself
in a grave and rigid examination of all the parts of Nature, and in registering
by letters their order, causes, uses, differences, and resemblances; whereby
the Fancy, when any work of art is to be performed, finds her materials at
hand and prepared for use, and needs no more than a swift motion over
them' (*Spingarn*, II.59).

[2] The analogy was something of a commonplace in Renaissance psychology and criticism. Juan Huarte (1531?-91?), the Spanish medico, whose
Examen de ingenios (1575) had been translated as *The Examination of Men's
Wits* by R.C. (Richard Carew) in 1594, named 'a very swift imagination' as
the second necessary talent of the orator, 'and that the same supply (as it
were) the place of a brach [*perro ventor*], to hunt and bring the game to his
hand' (ch. x). Hobbes's use of the same figure is better known, and may be
Dryden's immediate source: 'Sometimes a man knows a place determinate,
within the compass whereof he is to seek; and then his thoughts run over
all the parts thereof, . . . as a spaniel ranges the field till he find a scent'
(*Leviathan*, I.iii). Dryden repeats the simile in the prefaces to *Annus
Mirabilis* and *Fables*, p. 98, and vol. II, p. 284, below.

that which is ordinary in itself pass for excellent with less examination. But certainly that which most regulates the fancy, and gives the judgment its busiest employment, is like to bring forth the richest and clearest thoughts. The poet examines that most which he produceth with the greatest leisure, and which he knows must pass the severest test of the audience, because they are aptest to have it ever in their memory; as the stomach makes the best concoction when it strictly embraces the nourishment, and takes account of every little particle as it passes through. But as the best medicines may lose their virtue by being ill applied, so is it with verse, if a fit subject be not chosen for it. Neither must the argument alone, but the characters and persons be great and noble; otherwise (as Scaliger says of Claudian) the poet will be *ignobiliore materiâ depressus*.[1] The scenes which in my opinion most commend it, are those of argumentation and discourse, on the result of which the doing or not doing some considerable action should depend.

But, my Lord, though I have more to say upon this subject, yet I must remember 'tis your Lordship to whom I speak; who have much better commended this way by your writing in it, than I can do by writing for it. Where my reasons cannot prevail, I am sure your Lordship's example must. Your rhetoric has gained my cause; at least the greatest part of my design has already succeeded to my wish, which was to interest so noble a person in the quarrel, and withal to testify to the world how happy I esteem myself in the honour of being,

MY LORD,
Your Lordship's most
humble, and most
obedient servant,

JOHN DRIDEN.

[1] From J. C. Scaliger (1484-1558), *Poetices* (1561), bk vi, 5: 'depressed by unworthy material.'

OF DRAMATIC POESY: AN ESSAY (1668)

—fungar vice cotis, acutum
reddere quae ferrum valet, exsors ipsa secandi.

Horat. De arte poet.[1]

DEFINITION OF A PLAY—ANCIENTS *v.* MODERNS— FRENCH *v.* ENGLISH—BLANK VERSE *v.* RHYME

Text: 4°, 1668, 1684, 1693. The second edition is a largely grammatical revision of the first: Dryden corrects some pronouns and relatives, abolishes certain vigorous colloquial usages, and eliminates the use of final prepositions, to conform to the stricter usages of Restoration prose. The third edition is a reprint of the second. Like Ker (1900) and D. D. Arundell (in his edition *Dryden and Howard, 1664-1668* (1929)), I have preferred the first edition as livelier than *1684-93*, which was preferred by Malone (1800) and D. Nichol Smith (1900); but verbal variants have all been noted, and corrections to quotations made in *1684* have been adopted.

The Essay, according to Dryden himself, was written during his enforced absence of eighteen months (June 1665—December 1666) from the London Plague, spent at his father-in-law's home at Charlton Park, near Malmesbury. Wiltshire gave Dryden the only leisure he ever allowed himself to write a formal work of criticism, and the Essay is the only critical work he ever troubled to revise. During the same period in the country, the poem *Annus Mirabilis* (1667) and probably the play *Secret Love* (1668) were also written, but the Essay was almost certainly begun and perhaps finished first of the three. Its occasion, after all, is the naval victory over the Dutch of 3rd June 1665, whereas *Annus Mirabilis* is also concerned with the Great Fire of fifteen months later. Besides, the preface to *Annus Mirabilis*, addressed to Sir Robert Howard (the Crites of the Essay), looks like a pendant to the Essay, and extends the debate beyond the drama to the issue of the language of poetry in general. And the Essay is just the sort of task that an ambitious young dramatist might reserve for an unexpected holiday far from theatres.

Its publication, however, was delayed for nearly two years, until August 1667, some six months after *Annus Mirabilis*, when it appeared

[1] Ll. 304-5: 'I shall play the part of a whetstone, which sharpens steel, though itself incapable of cutting.'

with '1668' on the title-page. It is difficult to swallow Dryden's excuse, in the dedicatory letter to Buckhurst, that he had forgotten about the Essay and then rediscovered it, months after his return to London, among his 'loose papers'—the Essay is too deliberate, too carefully articulated a work to be pigeon-holed for anything less than a calculated reason. And it was surely false modesty to pretend, in the 'Defence' (p. 112, below), that the Essay was no more than 'a little discourse in dialogue, for the most part borrowed from the observations of others.'[1] Dryden may have guessed that the portrait of Crites would antagonize his brother-in-law, and perhaps held the Essay over until the complimentary preface to *Annus Mirabilis* could appear. If so, the stratagem did not save him from a family quarrel.

The Essay marks a phase in an international controversy as well as a crisis in a family circle. In 1664 Samuel Sorbière, a French member of the newly formed Royal Society, had attacked English drama for its neglect of rhyme and of the three unities in his *Relation d'un voyage en Angleterre*, to which Thomas Sprat, already busy on *The History of the Royal Society* (1667), was stung to reply in his *Observations on M. de Sorbier's Voyage into England* (1665). Sprat's defence of English drama anticipates Dryden's in part,[2] notably in its self-contradictory vindication of English irregularities. 'For the last fifty years,' wrote Sprat, 'our stage has been as regular in those circumstances [i.e. the three unities] as the best in Europe'—but he later, like Dryden, defends the licence of English dramatists on naturalistic grounds: 'By the liberty of prose they render their speech and pronunciation more natural, and are never put to make contention between the rhyme and the sense,' and he adds that a mixture of plots makes English plays 'more lively and diverting than the precepts of philosophers, or the grave delight of heroic poetry, which the French tragedies do resemble.' Sprat, too, defends low-life characters, 'men of mean condition,' and praises the rich tradition of the English in comedy: 'The French,' he complains, 'have always seemed almost ashamed of the true comedy.' There can be no doubt that Dryden found encouragement in Sprat for the cultural nationalism of the Essay.

In the controversy over rhyme with Howard, the Essay represents the third of five stages: first, Dryden's preface to his *Rival Ladies* (1664), above, where he defends the use of rhyme; second, Howard's reply in the preface to his *Four New Plays* (1665) where—unlike the Crites of the Essay—he finds the Ancients lacking both in their plots and in their wit, though he also condemns tragi-comedy and rhyme in English drama; third, the last of the three principal exchanges in the present Essay, between Crites and Neander, where Dryden defends rhyme; fourth, Howard's angry retort to the Essay in his preface to *The Great Favourite* (1668); and fifth, Dryden's 'Defence,' below. But this double controversy must not be allowed to make the Essay

[1] Cf. 'Discourse concerning Satire,' vol. II, p. 74, below.

[2] Cf. George Williamson, 'The Occasion of *An Essay of Dramatic Poesy*,' *Modern Philology*, xliv (1946), reprinted in his *Seventeenth-Century Contexts* (1960).

look more radical than it is. Apart from the issue of rhyme, Dryden is at one with Sprat and Howard in his preference for the English dramatists over the French as the worthier heirs to the classical tradition. The dialogue form makes it unusually difficult to be certain where he stands. But it is surely a fair inference to suppose that, with Neander, he supports the English drama against the French, and rhyme against blank verse, and there is no need to suppose, with Professor Nichol Smith, that the Essay is the work of a literary innocent, or that Dryden 'states contradictory views, and very fairly, as they are all tenable.'[1] Neander has a way of getting the last word. Nor is it sensible to pretend that 'the Essay has the vivacity of good conversation'[2]—after the first few pages, where a naturalistic conversation fizzles out in a loose definition of drama, the Essay consists not of conversation but of three pairs of set speeches among the four characters, and there is nothing searching or Socratic about so inflexible a proceeding. Any comparison with the dialogues of Plato, such as T. S. Eliot has suggested,[3] is wildly out of place, though no praise of Dryden's prose seems extravagant: always, 'as in his verse, in perfect training; there is nowhere an ounce of superfluous fat; he is neither anaemic nor apoplectic; every blow delivered has just the right force behind it.'[4] In the Essay, however ambiguous and sly the technique of dialogue, Dryden's contrivance never fails. The evasions, as well as the assertions, are all deliberated.

To the Right Honourable

CHARLES, LORD BUCKHURST[5]

My Lord,

As I was lately reviewing my loose papers, amongst the rest I found this Essay, the writing which, in this rude and indigested

[1] *Dryden* (1950), p. 13.   [2] *Ibid.*, p. 21.
[3] 'I can think of no essay in dialogue form in English, which on its own plane—less sublime, less profound in thought—compares more favourably with the dialogues of Plato.' From 'Dryden the Critic, Defender of Sanity,' *Listener*, v (1931), p. 724.
[4] *Ibid.*
[5] Charles Sackville (1638-1706) was created Earl of Middlesex in 1675, and succeeded his father as sixth Earl of Dorset in 1677; the two earldoms, omitted by an oversight from the second edition of 1684, were inserted in 1693. His political ambitions were gratified in a way which Dryden can hardly have welcomed: he was William III's Lord Chamberlain of the Household from 1689 to 1697. He took part in the battle of 3 June 1665, the ostensible occasion of the following dialogue, but the character of Eugenius has nevertheless been attributed with fair certainty to him. He had a reputation, which outlived him, as a poet and man of taste (cf. Addison, *Spectator*, no. 85).

manner wherein your Lordship now sees it, served as an amuse-
ment to me in the country, when the violence of the last
plague[1] had driven me from the town. Seeing then our theatres
shut up, I was engaged in these kind of thoughts with the same
delight with which men think upon their absent mistresses: I
confess I find many things in this discourse which I do not now
approve; my judgment being a little altered[2] since the writing of
it, but whether for the better or the worse, I know not: neither
indeed is it much material in an Essay where all I have said is
problematical. For the way of writing plays in verse which I
have seemed to favour, I have since that time laid the practice
of it aside, till I have more leisure, because I find it troublesome
and slow. But I am no way altered from my opinion of it, at least
with any reasons which have opposed it. For your Lordship
may easily observe that none are very violent against it but
those who either have not attempted it, or who have succeeded
ill in their attempt. 'Tis enough for me to have your Lordship's
example for my excuse in that little which I have done in it;
and I am sure my adversaries can bring no such arguments
against verse as the fourth act of *Pompey* will furnish me with[3]
in its defence. Yet, my Lord, you must suffer me a little to complain of you that you too soon withdraw from us a contentment
of which we expected the continuance, because you gave it us
so early. 'Tis a revolt without occasion from your party, where
your merits had already raised you to the highest commands,
and where you have not the excuse of other men that you have
been ill used and therefore laid down arms. I know no other
quarrel you can have to verse than that which Spurina had to his
beauty, when he tore and mangled the features of his face only

[1] The Great Plague of 1665, which occasioned the closing of the London
theatres from May 1665 till November 1666. Dryden spent most or all of the
period with his father-in-law, the Earl of Berkshire, at his Jacobean mansion
Charlton Park, near Malmesbury, Wiltshire.

[2] 'not a little alter'd,' *1684, 1693*, to allow for the verbal and grammatical
changes of the later editions. If, as seems likely, the Essay appeared in the
autumn of 1667 (with '1668' on the title-page), then two years at the most
elapsed between composition and publication.

[3] 'as those with which the fourth act of *Pompey* will furnish me,' *1684,
1693*.
Pierre Corneille, *La mort de Pompée* (1644), had recently been translated
by Buckhurst, with Godolphin, Edmund Waller, and Sir Charles Sedley, as
Pompey the Great: a Tragedy (1664). The implication is that Buckhurst was
especially responsible for the translation of Act IV.

because they pleased too well the lookers on.[1] It was an honour which seemed to wait for you to lead out a new colony of writers from the mother nation; and upon the first spreading of your ensigns there had been many in a readiness to have followed so fortunate a leader; if not all, yet the better part of writers:[2]

> pars, indocili melior grege; mollis et exspes
> inominata perprimat cubilia.[3]

I am almost of opinion that we should force you to accept of the command, as sometimes the Praetorian bands have compelled their captains to receive the Empire. The Court, which is the best and surest judge of writing, has generally allowed of verse; and in the town it has found favourers of wit and quality. As for your own particular, my Lord, you have yet youth and time enough to give part of it[4] to the divertisement of the public, before you enter into the serious and more unpleasant business of the world. That which the French poet said of the Temple of Love may be as well applied to the Temple of the Muses. The words, as near as I can remember them, were these:

> Le jeune homme a mauvaise grâce,
> N'ayant pas adoré dans le Temple d'Amour;
> Il faut qu'il entre; et pour le sage,
> Si ce n'est pas son vray séjour,
> C'est un giste sur son passage.[5]

I leave the words to work their effect upon your Lordship in their own language, because no other can so well express the nobleness of the thought; and wish you may be soon called to bear a part in the affairs of the nation, where I know the world expects you, and wonders why you have been so long forgotten; there being no person amongst our young nobility on whom the eyes of all men are so much bent. But in the mean time your Lordship may imitate the course of Nature, who gives us

---

[1] 'the sight,' *1684, 1693*. For Spurina, cf. Valerius Maximus, IV, 5.

[2] 'poets,' *1684, 1693*.

[3] Horace, *Epodes*, xvi.37-8: 'the part better than the ignorant herd; let the feeble and hopeless lie on their unlucky beds.'

[4] 'them,' *1684, 1693*.

[5] Quotation untraced—perhaps from a miscellany of society verse. This is the version as it appears in *1684*, apparently corrected by Dryden in two details. 'A young man is in ill humour for not having worshipped in the Temple of Love. He has to go in; and as for the wise man, if it is not his true home, it is at least a place of refuge on his journey.'

the flower before the fruit: that I may speak to you in the language of the Muses, which I have taken from an excellent poem to the King:

> As Nature, when she fruit designs, thinks fit
> By beauteous blossoms to proceed to it;
> And while she does accomplish all the spring,
> Birds to her secret operations sing.[1]

I confess I have no greater reason in addressing this Essay to your Lordship, than that it might awaken in you the desire of writing something, in whatever kind it be, which might be an honour to our age and country. And me thinks it might have the same effect on you which Homer tells us the fight of the Greeks and Trojans before the fleet had on the spirit of Achilles who, though he had resolved not to engage, yet found a martial warmth to steal upon him at the sight of blows, the sound of trumpets, and the cries of fighting men. For my own part, if in treating of this subject I sometimes dissent from the opinion of better wits, I declare it is not so much to combat their opinions as to defend my own, which were first made public. Sometimes, like a scholar in a fencing-school, I put forth myself, and show my own ill play, on purpose to be better taught. Sometimes I stand desperately to my arms, like the foot when deserted by their horse, not in hope to overcome, but only to yield on more honourable terms. And yet, my Lord, this war of opinions, you well know, has fallen out among the writers of all ages, and sometimes betwixt friends. Only it has been prosecuted by some like pedants, with violence of words, and managed by others like gentlemen, with candour[2] and civility. Even Tully had a controversy with his dear Atticus; and in one of his Dialogues[3] makes him sustain the part of an enemy in philosophy who, in his letters, is his confident of state, and made privy to the most weighty affairs of the Roman Senate. And the same respect which was paid by Tully to Atticus, we find returned to him afterwards by Caesar on a like occasion who, answering his book in praise of Cato, made it not so much his business to condemn Cato, as to praise Cicero.[4] But that I may decline some part of

---

[1] Sir William Davenant, *Poem to the King's Most Sacred Majesty* (1663).
[2] I.e. purity, integrity, as in Elizabethan usage. The modern sense (frankness, outspokenness) is not recorded by *OED* before 1769.
[3] Cicero, *De legibus*.
[4] Cicero, *Ad Atticum*, xii.40; Plutarch, 'Julius Caesar.' Cf. vol. II pp. 74, 75.

the encounter with my adversaries, whom I am neither willing to combat, nor well able to resist, I will give your Lordship the relation of a dispute betwixt some of our wits upon this subject[1], in which they did not only speak of plays in verse, but mingled, in the freedom of discourse, some things of the ancient, many of the modern ways of writing; comparing those with these, and the wits of our nation with those of others: 'tis true they differed in their opinions, as 'tis probable they would; neither do I take upon me to reconcile, but to relate them; and that as Tacitus professes of himself, *sine studio partium aut irâ*,[2] without passion or interest; leaving your Lordship to decide it in favour of which part you shall judge most reasonable, and withal, to pardon the many errors of

Your Lordship's most obedient humble servant,

JOHN DRYDEN.

[1] 'on the same subject,' *1684, 1693.*

[2] 'Sine ira et studio, quorum causas procul habeo' (*Annals*, I.i): 'without anger or partiality, motives both distant from me.' Cf. vol. II, p. 118.

TO THE READER

THE drift of the ensuing discourse was chiefly to vindicate the honour of our English writers from the censure of those who unjustly prefer the French before them. This I intimate, lest any should think me so exceeding vain as to teach others an art which they understand much better than myself.[1] But if this incorrect Essay, written in the country without the help of books, or advice of friends, shall find any acceptance in the world, I promise to myself a better success of the second part, wherein the virtues and faults of the English poets who have written either in this, the epic, or the lyric way, will be more fully treated of, and their several styles impartially imitated.[2]

[1] An outright disclaimer of legislative intent which the Essay hardly justifies, in spite of Dryden's care in casting it in dialogue form and stating, with a show of impartiality, both sides to every question. Neander is allowed to have the last word in the second and third of the three exchanges, and there can be no doubt the balance of argument lies on his side, especially in his advocacy of rhyming plays. Cf. p. 124, below.

[2] 'wherein I shall more fully treat of the virtues and faults of the English poets who have written either in this, the epic, or the lyric way,' *1684, 1693*. This promise of a second essay, perhaps in literary-historical form, on the past achievements of the English poets was never formally realized, probably because Rymer anticipated it in part in his *The Tragedies of the Last Age* (1678). Dryden's criticism as a whole reveals only scattered remarks on the lyric, though his Dedication to the *Aeneis* (1697) may be considered as a late fulfilment of his promise to examine the epic.

AN ESSAY OF DRAMATIC POESY

IT was that memorable day,[1] in the first summer of the late war, when our navy engaged the Dutch: a day wherein the two most mighty and best appointed fleets which any age had ever seen disputed the command of the greater half of the globe, the commerce of nations, and the riches of the universe. While these vast floating bodies, on either side, moved against each other in parallel lines, and our countrymen, under the happy conduct of his Royal Highness,[2] went breaking, by little and little, into the line of the enemies; the noise of the cannon from both navies reached our ears about the City; so that all men being alarmed with it, and in a dreadful suspense of the event which we[3] knew was then deciding, every one went following the sound as his fancy led him; and leaving the town almost empty, some took towards the park,[4] some cross the river, others down it; all seeking the noise in the depth of silence.

Among the rest, it was the fortune of Eugenius,[5] Crites,[6]

[1] 3 June 1665. The 'late war' between England and the Netherlands was concluded by the Treaty of Breda in July 1667, a few weeks before the publication of the Essay, so that the opening was evidently written, or at least revised, late.

[2] The Duke of York, Charles II's younger brother and later James II, who commanded the English fleet in the action off the Suffolk coast at Lowestoft.

[3] 'they,' *1684, 1693.   [4] St James's Park.

[5] Malone's identification of the four characters has only recently been questioned. Eugenius (i.e. the well-born one), the advocate for the Moderns, he identified as Charles Sackville, Lord Buckhurst (p. 12n., above), to whom the Essay is dedicated, following Matthew Prior's assertion in the dedication to his own *Poems* of 1709. If so, Dryden's dedication of the Essay to Buckhurst is a deliberate red herring—he avoids every opportunity to hint at any such attribution. It is certain, too, that Buckhurst was actually engaged in the battle, but then there is no reason to suppose that the circumstances of the dialogue were other than imaginary.

[6] I.e. the critical or censorious, who defends the Ancients and opposes rhyme, is evidently a recognizable portrait of Dryden's brother-in-law and collaborator Sir Robert Howard (1626-98): it was recognized, resented, and replied to by Howard in his preface to *The Duke of Lerma* (1668). G. R. Noyes (*Modern Language Notes*, xxxviii, 1923) has pointed out that the cap only fits in parts: Howard in his earlier preface to *Four New Plays* (1665) had opposed rhyme, indeed, but inclined rather to the Moderns than to the Ancients. The fact underlines the largely fictional quality of the 'persons

Lisideius,[1] and Neander[2] to be in company together: three of them persons whom their wit and quality have made known to all the town; and whom I have chose to hide under these borrowed names that they may not suffer by so ill a relation as I am going to make of their discourse.

Taking then a barge which a servant of Lisideius had provided for them, they made haste to shoot the bridge, and left behind them that great fall of waters which hindered them from hearing what they desired: after which, having disengaged themselves from many vessels which rode at anchor in the Thames, and almost blocked up the passage towards Greenwich, they ordered the watermen to let fall their oars more gently; and then, every one favouring his own curiosity with a strict silence, it was not long ere they perceived the air break[3] about them like the noise of distant thunder, or of swallows in a chimney: those little undulations of sound, though almost vanishing before they reached them, yet still seeming to retain somewhat of their first horror which they had betwixt the fleets. After they had attentively listened till such time as the sound by little and little went from them, Eugenius, lifting up his head, and taking notice of it, was the first who congratulated to the rest that happy omen of our nation's victory: adding, we had[4] but this to desire in confirmation of it, that we might hear no more of that noise which was now leaving the English coast. When the rest had concurred in the same opinion, Crites, a person of a sharp judgment, and somewhat too delicate a taste in wit, which the world have mistaken in him for ill nature, said, smiling to us, that if the concernment of this battle had not been so exceeding great, he could scarce have wished the victory at the price he

whom their wit and quality have made known to all the town,' but Dryden's distinctly disagreeable portrait of Crites fits the Howard whom Evelyn found 'unsufferably boasting' (*Diary*, 16 February 1685) and whom Shadwell satirized in the *Sullen Lovers* (1668) as Sir Positive At-All.

[1] According to Malone, a Latinized anagram of Sir Charles Sedley or Sidley (1639?-1701), poet, dramatist, and courtier. In view of Lisideius's rôle as advocate for the French drama, F. L. Huntley (*On Dryden's Essay of Dramatic Poesy* (1951), p. 11) has suggested his name may be a pun on Corneille's *Le Cid*.

[2] I.e. the new man, the parvenu, representing Dryden himself—hence the modest denial of his own gentility in the following sentence. But in his defence of English drama and of rhyming plays Dryden may also be hinting at his own position as a rising playwright.

[3] 'to break,' *1684, 1693*.   [4] 'that we had,' *1684, 1693*.

knew he must pay for it, in being subject to the reading and
hearing of so many ill verses as he was sure would be made
upon it;[1] adding that no argument could scape some of those
eternal rhymers, who watch a battle with more diligence than
the ravens and birds of prey; and the worst of them surest to be
first in upon the quarry, while the better able, either out of
modesty writ not at all, or set that due value upon their poems
as to let them be often called for[2] and long expected. 'There are
some of those impertinent people you speak of,'[3] answered
Lisideius, 'who to my knowledge are already so provided, either
way, that they can produce not only a panegyric upon the victory
but, if need be, a funeral elegy upon the Duke; and[4] after they
have crowned his valour with many laurels, at last[5] deplore the
odds under which he fell, concluding that his courage deserved
a better destiny.' All the company smiled at the conceit of
Lisideius; but Crites, more eager than before, began to make
particular exceptions against some writers, and said the public
magistrate ought to send betimes to forbid them; and that it
concerned the peace and quiet of all honest people that ill poets
should be as well silenced as seditious preachers. 'In my
opinion,' replied Eugenius, 'you pursue your point too far; for
as to my own particular, I am so great a lover of poesy that I
could wish them all rewarded who attempt but to do well;
at least, I would not have them worse used than Sylla the
Dictator[6] did one of their brethren heretofore: *quem in concione
vidimus* (says Tully speaking of him)[7] *cum ei libellum malus
poeta de populo subjecisset, quod epigramma in eum fecisset
tantummodo alternis versibus longiusculis, statim ex iis rebus quas tunc
vendebat jubere ei præmium tribui, sub ea conditione ne quid
postea scriberet.*[8] 'I could wish with all my heart,' replied Crites,
'that many whom we know were as bountifully thanked upon
the same condition, that they would never trouble us again.
For amongst others, I have a mortal apprehension of two

---

[1] 'on that subject,' *1684, 1693*.   [2] 'desired,' *1684, 1693*.
[3] 'of whom you speak,' *1684, 1693*.   [4] 'wherein,' *1684, 1693*.
[5] 'they will at last,' *1684, 1693*.
[6] 'than one of their brethren was by Sylla the Dictator,' *1684, 1693*.
[7] 'says Tully,' *1684, 1693*.
[8] Cicero, *Pro Archia poeta*, x: 'We have seen him at a public meeting,
when a bad poet handed up from the crowd an epigram on himself, written
in rather unmetrical elegiacs. Sulla at once ordered him to be paid out of the
proceeds of the sale, on the condition that he never write again.'

poets[1] whom this victory, with the help of both her wings, will never be able to escape.' ''Tis easy to guess whom you intend,' said Lisideius; 'and without naming them, I ask you if one of them does not perpetually pay us with clenches[2] upon words, and a certain clownish kind of raillery? if now and then he does not offer at a catachresis or Clevelandism,[3] wresting and torturing a word into another meaning: in fine, if he be not one of those whom the French would call *un mauvais buffon*; one that[4] is so much a well-willer to the satire that he spares[5] no man; and though he cannot strike a blow to hurt any, yet ought[6] to be punished for the malice of the action, as our witches are justly hanged because they think themselves so;[7] and suffer deservedly for believing they did mischief, because they meant it.' 'You have described him,' said Crites, 'so exactly, that I am afraid to come after you with my other extremity of poetry. He is one of those who, having had some advantage of education and converse, knows better than the other what a poet should be, but puts it into practice more unluckily than any man; his style and matter are everywhere alike; he is the most calm, peaceable writer you ever read; he never disquiets your passions with the least concernment, but still leaves you in as even a temper as he found you; he is a very Leveller in poetry, he creeps along with ten little words in every line[8] and helps out his numbers with *for to* and *unto*, and all the pretty expletives he can find, till he drags them to the end of another line; while the sense is left tired half way behind it; he doubly starves all his verses, first for want of thought, and then of expression; his poetry

---

[1] Probably a *post facto* jibe at two poetasters who had in fact written poems in celebration of the battle: Robert Wild (1609-79) in a poem entitled *An Essay upon the Late Victory* (licensed 16 June 1665); and Richard Flecknoe (d. 1678) who for reasons unknown excited Dryden's especial scorn, and who as a well-travelled priest may be thought to fit Crites's description (below).
[2] I.e. puns.
[3] John Cleveland (1613-58), a royalist poet of Cambridge whose *Poems* (1651) ran into many editions and represented, even more clearly than Cowley's, the last extravagance of the dying Metaphysical style. Catachresis, or the misuse of terms (Puttenham calls it 'the figure of abuse') may be an unsympathetic reference to the violence of Cleveland's metaphors.
[4] 'who,' *1684, 1693*.   [5] 'intends at least to spare,' *1684, 1693*.
[6] 'he ought,' *1684, 1693*.   [7] 'think themselves to be such,' *1684, 1693*.
[8] Perhaps the source of Pope, *Essay on Criticism* (1711), ll. 346-7:
    While expletives their feeble aid do join,
    And ten low words oft creep in one dull line.

neither has wit in it, nor seems to have it; like him in Martial:

pauper videri Cinna vult, et est pauper.[1]

'He affects plainness, to cover his want of imagination: when
he writes the serious way, the highest flight of his fancy is some
miserable antithesis, or seeming contradiction; and in the comic
he is still reaching at some thin conceit, the ghost of a jest, and
that too flies before him, never to be caught; these swallows
which we see before us on the Thames are the just resemblance
of his wit: you may observe how near the water they stoop,
how many proffers they make to dip, and yet how seldom they
touch it; and when they do, 'tis but the surface: they skim
over it but to catch a gnat, and then mount into the air and
leave it.'

'Well, gentlemen,' said Eugenius, 'you may speak your
pleasure of these authors; but though I and some few more
about the town may give you a peaceable hearing, yet, assure
yourselves, there are multitudes who would think you malicious
and them injured: especially him whom you first described; he
is the very Withers[2] of the city: they have bought more editions
of his works than would serve to lay under all their pies at the
Lord Mayor's Christmas. When his famous poem first came
out in the year 1660, I have seen them reading it in the midst of
'Change time; nay, so vehement they were at it, that they lost
their bargain by the candles' ends;[3] but what will you say if he
has been received amongst the great ones?[4] I can assure you
he is, this day, the envy of a great person[5] who is lord in the art
of quibbling; and who does not take it well that any man should
intrude so far into his province.' 'All I would wish,' replied
Crites, 'is that they who love his writings may still admire
him, and his fellow poet: *qui Bavium non odit, &c.*,[6] is curse
sufficient.' 'And farther,' added Lisideius, 'I believe there is no

---

[1] *Epigrams*, VIII.19: 'Cinna wants to look poor, and so he is' (i.e. no one
can afford to affect poverty).
[2] George Wither (1588-1667), an old Parliamentary poet still alive when
the Essay was written, and by then a butt because of the abundance of his
doggerel verse.
[3] I.e. at auction sales, where bids stopped when the candle went out.
[4] 'amongst great persons,' *1684, 1693*. Cf. p. 175 and n., below.
[5] 'one,' *1684, 1693*.
[6] Virgil, *Eclogues*, III.90 ('. . . amet tua carmina, Maevi'): 'Let him who
does not hate Baevius love your songs, Maevius.'

man who writes well, but would think himself very hardly dealt with,[1] if their admirers should praise anything of his: *nam quos contemnimus, eorum quoque laudes contemnimus.*'[2] 'There are so few who write well in this age,' says Crites, 'that methinks any praises should be welcome; they neither rise to the dignity of the last age, nor to any of the Ancients: and we may cry out of the writers of this time, with more reason than Petronius of his, *pace vestra liceat dixisse, primi omnium eloquentiam perdidistis:*[3] you have debauched the true old poetry so far, that nature, which is the soul of it, is not in any of your writings.'

'If your quarrel,' said Eugenius, 'to those who now write, be grounded only on your reverence to antiquity, there is no man more ready to adore those great Greeks and Romans than I am: but on the other side, I cannot think so contemptibly of the age I live in,[4] or so dishonourably of my own country, as not to judge we equal the Ancients in most kinds of poesy, and in some surpass them; neither know I any reason why I may not be as zealous for the reputation of our age, as we find the Ancients themselves[5] in reference to those who lived before them. For you hear your Horace saying,

> indignor quicquam reprehendi, non quia crasse
> compositum, illepidève putetur, sed quia nuper.[6]

And after:

> si meliora dies, ut vina, poemata reddit,
> scire velim, pretium chartis quotus arroget annus?[7]

'But I see I am engaging in a wide dispute, where the arguments are not like to reach close on either side; for poesy is of so large an extent, and so many both of the Ancients and Moderns have done well in all kinds of it, that in citing one against the

---

[1] 'think he had hard measure,' *1684, 1693.*

[2] Quotation untraced: 'For we despise those who admire such as we despise.'

[3] *Satyricon*, 2: 'With your permission, let me say that you [rhetoricians] have been the death of eloquence.'

[4] 'in which I live,' *1684, 1693.*

[5] 'themselves were,' *1684, 1693.*

[6] *Epistles*, II.i.76-7: 'It angers me when anything is blamed, not for being ill written or inelegant, but for being new.'

[7] *Ibid.*, 34-5: 'If poems, like wine, improved with every passing day, I should like to know which year is best for literature.'

other we shall take up more time this evening than each man's
occasions will allow him: therefore I would ask Crites to what
part of poesy he would confine his arguments, and whether he
would defend the general cause of the Ancients against the
Moderns, or oppose any page of the Moderns against this of
ours?'

Crites, a little while considering upon this demand, told
Eugenius he approved his propositions and, if he pleased,[1] he
would limit their dispute to dramatic poesy; in which he thought
it not difficult to prove either that the Ancients were superior
to the Moderns,[2] or the last age to this of ours.

Eugenius was somewhat surprised when he heard Crites
make choice of that subject. 'For aught I see,' said he, 'I have
undertaken a harder province than I imagined; for though I
never judged the plays of the Greek or Roman poets comparable
to ours; yet on the other side those we now see acted come short
of many which were written in the last age: but my comfort is,
if we are o'ercome, it will be only by our own countrymen; and
if we yield to them in this one part of poesy, we more surpass
them in all the other; for in the epic or lyric way it will be hard
for them to show us one such amongst them, as we have many
now living, or who lately were so.[3] They can produce nothing so
courtly writ, or which expresses so much the conversation of
a gentleman, as Sir John Suckling; nothing so even, sweet, and
flowing, as Mr Waller; nothing so majestic, so correct as Sir
John Denham; nothing so elevated, so copious, and full of
spirit, as Mr Cowley; as for the Italian, French and Spanish
plays, I can make it evident that those who now write surpass
them; and that the drama is wholly ours.'

All of them were thus far of Eugenius his opinion that the
sweetness of English verse was never understood or practised by
our fathers; even Crites himself did not much oppose it: and
every one was willing to acknowledge how much our poesy is
improved by the happiness of some writers yet living,[4] who first

---

[1] 'told Eugenius that if he pleased,' *1684, 1693*.

[2] Here Howard is made to argue out of character. In his preface to *Four
New Plays* (1665) he had taken his stand for the Moderns, claiming that 'our
English plays justly challenge the pre-eminence' over those of the Ancients.

[3] 'or who lately were,' *1684, 1693*.

[4] Suckling had died in 1642, and Cowley chanced to die in July 1667, a
few weeks before the Essay appeared, but Denham lived till 1669, and Waller
till 1687.

taught us to mould our thoughts into easy and significant words, to retrench the superfluities of expression, and to make our rhyme so properly a part of the verse that it should never mislead the sense, but itself be led and governed by it.

Eugenius was going to continue this discourse, when Lisideius told him it was[1] necessary, before they proceeded further, to take a standing measure of their controversy; for how was it possible to be decided who writ the best plays, before we know what a play should be? But, this once agreed on by both parties, each might have recourse to it, either to prove his own advantages, or to discover the failings of his adversary.

He had no sooner said this, but all desired the favour of him to give the definition of a play; and they were the more importunate, because neither Aristotle, nor Horace, nor any other who writ[2] of that subject, had ever done it.

Lisideius, after some modest denials, at last confessed he had a rude notion of it; indeed rather a description than a definition; but which served to guide him in his private thoughts, when he was to make a judgment of what others writ: that he conceived a play ought to be *A just and lively image of human nature, representing its passions and humours, and the changes of fortune to which it is subject, for the delight and instruction of mankind.*

This definition, though Crites raised a logical objection against it, that it was only *a genere et fine*,[3] and so not altogether perfect, was yet well received by the rest: and after they had given order to the watermen to turn their barge, and row softly, that they might take the cool of the evening in their return, Crites, being desired by the company to begin, spoke on behalf of the Ancients, in this manner:

'If confidence presage a victory, Eugenius, in his own opinion, has already triumphed over the Ancients: nothing seems more easy to him than to overcome those whom it is our greatest praise to have imitated well; for we do not only build upon their foundation,[4] but by their models. Dramatic poesy had time enough, reckoning from Thespis (who first invented it) to

---

[1] 'that it was,' *1684, 1693.*
[2] 'had writ,' *1684, 1693.* The claim seems to be a just one, so far as the classical and English critics are concerned.
[3] I.e. included other literary forms besides drama.
[4] 'foundations,' *1684, 1693.*

Aristophanes, to be born, to grow up, and to flourish in maturity. It has been observed of arts and sciences, that in one and the same century they have arrived to a great[1] perfection; and no wonder, since every age has a kind of universal genius which inclines those that live in it to some particular studies: the work then being pushed on by many hands, must of necessity go forward.

'Is it not evident in these last hundred years (when the study of philosophy has been the business of all the virtuosi in Christendom), that almost a new nature has been revealed to us? that more errors of the school have been detected, more useful experiments in philosophy have been made, more noble secrets in optics, medicine, anatomy, astronomy discovered, than in all those credulous and doting ages from Aristotle to us? so true it is, that nothing spreads more fast than science, when rightly and generally cultivated.

'Add to this the more than common emulation that was in those times of writing well; which though it be found in all ages and all persons that pretend to the same reputation, yet poesy, being then in more esteem than now it is, had greater honours decreed to the professors of it, and consequently the rivalship was more high between them; they had judges ordained to decide their merit, and prizes to reward it; and historians have been diligent to record of Æschylus, Eurupides, Sophocles, Lycophron, and the rest of them, both who they were that vanquished in these wars of the theatre, and how often they were crowned: while the Asian kings and Grecian commonwealths scarce afforded them a nobler subject than the unmanly luxuries of a debauched court, or giddy intrigues of a factious city. *Alit æmulatio ingenia* (says Paterculus), *et nunc invidia, nunc admiratio incitationem accendit:*[2] emulation is the spur of wit; and sometimes envy, sometimes admiration, quickens our endeavours.

'But now, since the rewards of honour are taken away, that virtuous emulation is turned into direct malice; yet so slothful, that it contents itself to condemn and cry down others, without attempting to do better: 'tis a reputation too unprofitable, to take the necessary pains for it; yet wishing they had it[3] is

---

[1] 'to great,' *1684, 1693*.   [2] *Historia romana*, I.17.
[3] 'wishing they had it, that desire,' *1684, 1693*.

incitement enough to hinder others from it. And this, in short, Eugenius, is the reason why you have now so few good poets, and so many severe judges. Certainly, to imitate the Ancients well, much labour and long study is required; which pains, I have already shown, our poets would want encouragement to take, if yet they had ability to go through with it.[1] Those Ancients have been faithful imitators and wise observers of that nature which is so torn and ill represented in our plays; they have handed down to us a perfect resemblance of her; which we, like ill copiers, neglecting to look on, have rendered monstrous and disfigured. But, that you may know how much you are indebted to those your masters, and be ashamed to have so ill requited them, I must remember you that all the rules by which we practise the drama at this day, either such as relate to the justness and symmetry of the plot, or the episodical ornaments, such as descriptions, narrations, and other beauties, which are not essential to the play, were delivered to us from the observations which Aristotle made of those poets, which[2] either lived before him, or were his contemporaries:[3] we have added nothing of our own, except we have the confidence to say our wit is better; of which none boast in this our age, but such as understand not theirs. Of that book which Aristotle has left us, περὶ τῆς Ποιητικῆς, Horace his *Art of Poetry* is an excellent comment and, I believe, restores to us that second book of his concerning comedy, which is wanting in him.

'Out of these two has[4] been extracted the famous rules

[1] 'through the work,' *1684, 1693*.   [2] 'who,' *1684, 1693*.

[3] The *Poetics* of Aristotle opens with a proposal to treat all poetry 'in its various kinds,' but only the section on tragedy has survived.

[4] 'have,' *1684, 1693*. The extraction of the three dramatic unities from Aristotle—Horace is an irrelevant figure in this story—was effected by Castelvetro in the commentary to his Italian translation of the *Poetics*. The misreading, though blatant, was current for some two centuries, until Johnson in his preface to Shakespeare (1765) dismissed it as a logical absurdity in a few vigorous paragraphs ('It is false that any representation is mistaken for reality'). In its slightly liberalized form as stated by Corneille and Dryden, who both insisted that the doctrine must be considered an aid to the dramatist rather than a master, it was accepted by Rymer, Dennis, and Pope.

In terms of Aristotle, the error is a double one: first, though Aristotle names the unity of action, and commits himself to unity of time to the extent of 'a single revolution of the sun, or slightly longer', he nowhere mentions the unity of place at all; second, the unities of action and time appear in the *Poetics* not as rules, but as facts observed in Greek tragedy. Cf. p. 36 and n., below.

which the French call *des trois unités*,[1] or the Three Unities,
which ought to be observed in every regular play: namely, of
time, place, and action.

'The unity of time they comprehend in twenty-four hours,
the compass of a natural day, or as near as it can be contrived;
and the reason of it is obvious to every one, that the time of the
feigned action, or fable of the play, should be proportioned as
near as can be to the duration of that time in which it is represented; since, therefore, all plays are acted on the theatre in a
space of time much within the compass of twenty-four hours,
that play is to be thought the nearest imitation of nature whose
plot or action is confined within that time; and, by the same rule
which concludes this general proportion of time, it follows that
all the parts of it are[2] to be equally subdivided; as namely,[3]
that one act take not up the supposed time of half a day, which
is out of proportion to the rest; since the other four are then to
be straitened within the compass of the remaining half: for it is
unnatural that one act, which being spoke or written is not
longer than the rest, should be supposed longer by the audience;
'tis therefore the poet's duty to take care that no act should be
imagined to exceed the time in which it is represented on the
stage; and that the intervals and inequalities of time be supposed to fall out between the acts.

'This rule of time, how well it has been observed by the
Ancients, most of their plays will witness; you see them in their
tragedies (wherein to follow this rule is certainly most difficult)
from the very beginning of their plays, falling close into that
part of the story which they intend for the action or principal
object of it, leaving the former part to be delivered by narration:
so that they set the audience, as it were, at the post where the
race is to be concluded; and, saving them the tedious expectation of seeing the poet set out and ride the beginning of the
course, you behold him not[4] till he is in sight of the goal, and
just upon you.

[1] From the title of Corneille's third *discours* of 1660, 'Discours des trois
unités.' The use of 'des' for 'les' is oddly literal. The 'Aristotelian' rules had
been under discussion by English critics for a century, but this is the first
recorded application of the word 'unity' to the rules—a usage instantly
adopted by English neo-classical critics.
[2] 'are (as near as may be),' *1684, 1693*.
[3] 'subdivided; namely,' *1684, 1693*.
[4] 'they suffer you not to behold him,' *1684, 1693*.

'For the second unity, which is that of place, the Ancients meant by it that the scene ought to be continued through the play, in the same place where it was laid in the beginning: for the stage on which it is represented being but one and the same place, it is unnatural to conceive it many, and those far distant from one another. I will not deny but, by the variation of painted scenes, the fancy (which in these cases will contribute to its own deceit) may sometimes imagine it several places, with some appearance of probability; yet it still carries the greater likelihood of truth if those places be supposed so near each other, as in the same town or city; which may all be comprehended under the larger denomination of one place; for a greater distance will bear no proportion to the shortness of time which is allotted in the acting, to pass from one of them to another; for the observation of this, next to the Ancients, the French are to be most commended. They tie themselves so strictly to the unity of place that you never see in any of their plays a scene changed in the middle of an act: if the act begins in a garden, a street, or chamber, 'tis ended in the same place; and that you may know it to be the same, the stage is so supplied with persons that it is never empty all the time: he that enters the second[1] has business with him who was on before; and before the second quits the stage, a third appears who has business with him. This Corneille calls *la liaison des scènes*,[2] the continuity or joining of the scenes; and 'tis a good mark of a well contrived play when all the persons are known to each other, and every one of them has some affairs with all the rest.

'As for the third unity, which is that of action, the Ancients meant no other by it than what the logicians do by their *finis*, the end or scope of any action; that which is the first in intention, and last in execution: now the poet is to aim at one great and complete action, to the carrying on of which all things in his play, even the very obstacles, are to be subservient; and the reason of this is as evident as any of the former.

'For two actions, equally laboured and driven on by the writer, would destroy the unity of the poem; it would be no longer one play, but two: not but that there may be many actions

---

[1] 'who enters second,' *1684, 1693*.
[2] In the 'Discours des trois unités,' and in the *examen* of *La suivante*.

in a play, as Ben Jonson has observed in his *Discoveries;*[1] but
they must be all subservient to the great one, which our language
happily expresses in the name of *under-plots*: such as in
Terence's *Eunuch* is the difference and reconcilement of Thais
and Phædria, which is not the chief business of the play, but
promotes the marriage of Chærea and Chremes's sister, principally intended by the poet. There ought to be but one action,
says Corneille,[2] that is, one complete action which leaves the
mind of the audience in a full repose; but this cannot be brought
to pass but by many other imperfect ones which conduce to
it, and hold the audience in a delightful suspense of what
will be.

'If by these rules (to omit many other drawn from the precepts
and practice of the Ancients) we should judge our modern
plays, 'tis probable that few of them would endure the trial:
that which should be the business of a day, takes up in some of
them an age; instead of one action, they are the epitomes of a
man's life; and for one spot of ground (which the stage should
represent) we are sometimes in more countries than the map
can show us.

'But if we will allow the Ancients to have contrived well, we
must acknowledge them to have writ[3] better; questionless we
are deprived of a great stock of wit in the loss of Menander
among the Greek poets, and of Cæcilius, Afranus, and Varius
among the Romans; we may guess of[4] Menander's excellency by
the plays of Terence, who translated some of his;[5] and yet
wanted so much of him that he was called by C. Caesar the
half-Menander;[6] and of Varius,[7] by the testimonies of Horace,
Martial, and Velleius Paterculus. 'Tis probable that these, could
they be recovered, would decide the controversy; but so long as
Aristophanes in the old comedy and Plautus in the new[8] are

[1] *Timber: or Discoveries* (1640), in Herford & Simpson, vol. viii (1947),
p. 647: 'Now, that it should be one, and entire. "One" is considerable two
ways: either, as it is only separate and by itself or, as being composed of
many parts, it begins to be one as those parts grow, or are wrought, together.'
[2] 'Il n'y doit avoir qu'une action complète, qui laisse l'esprit de l'auditeur
dans le calme; mais elle ne peut le devenir que par plusieurs autres im-
parfaites qui lui servent d'acheminements, et tiennent cet auditeur dans une
agréable suspension' ('Discours des trois unités').
[3] 'written,' *1684, 1693.*   [4] 'at,' *1684, 1693.*   [5] 'them,' *1684, 1693.*
[6] Cf. Suetonius, *Vita Terentii.*
[7] 'and may judge of Varius,' *1684, 1693.*
[8] 'as Aristophanes and Plautus are extant,' *1684, 1693.*

extant, while the tragedies of Euripides, Sophocles, and Seneca, are to be had,[1] I can never see one of those plays which are now written but it increases my admiration of the Ancients. And yet I must acknowledge further that, to admire them as we ought, we should understand them better than we do. Doubtless many things appear flat to us, whose wit[2] depended on some custom or story which never came to our knowledge; or perhaps upon some criticism in their language, which being so long dead, and only remaining in their books, 'tis not possible they should make us know it perfectly. To read Macrobius[3] explaining the propriety and elegancy of many words in Virgil which I had before passed over without consideration as common things, is enough to assure me that I ought to think the same of Terence; and that in the purity of his style (which Tully so much valued that he ever carried his works about him) there is yet left in him great room for admiration, if I knew but where to place it. In the mean time I must desire you to take notice that the greatest man of the last age (Ben Jonson) was willing to give place to them in all things: he was not only a professed imitator of Horace,[4] but a learned plagiary of all the others; you track him every where in their snow: if Horace, Lucan, Petronius Arbiter, Seneca, and Juvenal had their own from him, there are few serious thoughts which are new in him: you will pardon me, therefore, if I presume he loved their fashion, when he wore their clothes. But since I have otherwise a great veneration for him, and you, Eugenius, prefer him above all other poets, I will use no farther argument to you than his example: I will produce Father Ben to you,[5] dressed in all the ornaments and colours of the Ancients; you will need no other guide to our party, if you follow him; and whether you consider the bad plays of our age, or regard the good ones[6] of the last, both the best and worst of the modern poets will equally instruct you to esteem[7] the Ancients.'

---

[1] 'are in our hands,' *1684, 1693*.   [2] 'the wit of which,' *1684, 1693*.

[3] Macrobius (*fl.c.* A.D. 400), *Conviviorum Saturnaliorum libri septem*, bk IV.

[4] Cf. *Timber, op. cit.*, p. 642, where Jonson calls Horace 'the best master both of virtue and wisdom; and excellent and true judge upon cause and reason.' Jonson's translation of the *Ars poetica* appeared posthumously in 1640.

[5] 'before you Father Ben,' *1684, 1693*. Buckhurst had recently praised Jonson in a prologue written for a Restoration production of *Every Man in His Humour*.

[6] 'good plays,' *1684, 1693*.   [7] 'admire,' *1684, 1693*.

Crites had no sooner left speaking, but Eugenius, who
waited[1] with some impatience for it, thus began:

'I have observed in your speech that the former part of it is
convincing as to what the Moderns have profited by the rules
of the Ancients; but in the latter you are careful to conceal how
much they have excelled them. We own all the helps we have
from them, and want neither veneration nor gratitude while we
acknowledge that to overcome them we must make use of the
advantages we have received from them: but to these assistances
we have joined our own industry; for (had we sat down with a
dull imitation of them) we might then have lost somewhat of
the old perfection, but never acquired any that was new. We
draw not therefore after their lines, but those of nature; and
having the life before us, besides the experience of all they knew,
it is no wonder if we hit some airs and features which they have
missed. I deny not what you urge of arts and sciences, that they
have flourished in some ages more than others; but your instance
in philosophy makes for me: for if natural causes be more
known now than in the time of Aristotle, because more studied,
it follows that poesy and other arts may, with the same pains,
arrive still nearer to perfection; and, that granted, it will rest
for you to prove that they wrought more perfect images of
human life than we; which, seeing in your discourse you have
avoided to make good, it shall now be my task to show you some
part of their defects, and some few excellencies of the Moderns.
And I think there is none among us can imagine I do it enviously,
or with purpose to detract from them; for what interest of fame
or profit can the living lose by the reputation of the dead?
On the other side, it is a great truth which Velleius Paterculus
affirms: *audita visis libentius laudamus; et præsentia invidia,
præterita admiratione prosequimur; et his nos obrui, illis instrui
credimus,*[2] that praise or censure is certainly the most sincere
which unbribed posterity shall give us.

'Be pleased then in the first place to take notice that the
Greek poesy, which Crites has affirmed to have arrived to perfection in the reign of the Old Comedy, was so far from it that

---

[1] 'had waited,' *1684, 1693.*

[2] *Historia romana,* II.92 (for *admiratione* read *veneratione*): 'We are more
inclined to praise what we have heard than what we have seen; we look
upon the present with envy, the past with admiration, and believe ourselves
eclipsed by the one while we learn from the other.'

the distinction of it into acts was not known to them; or if it were, it is yet so darkly delivered to us that we cannot make it out.

'All we know of it is from the singing of their Chorus; and that too is so uncertain that in some of their plays we have reason to conjecture they sung more than five times. Aristotle indeed divides the integral parts of a play into four.[1] First, the *protasis*, or entrance, which gives light only to the characters of the persons, and proceeds very little into any part of the action. Secondly, the *epitasis*, or working up of the plot, where the play grows warmer, the design or action of it is drawing on, and you see something promising that it will come to pass. Thirdly, the *catastasis*, or counterturn,[2] which destroys that expectation, imbroils the action in new difficulties, and leaves you far distant from that hope in which it found you; as you may have observed in a violent stream resisted by a narrow passage: it runs round to an eddy, and carries back the waters with more swiftness than it brought them on. Lastly, the *catastrophe*, which the Grecians called λύσις,[3] the French *le dénouement*, and we the discovery or unravelling of the plot; there you see all things settling again upon their first foundations, and the obstacles which hindered the design or action of the play once removed, it ends with that resemblance of truth and nature that the audience are satisfied with the conduct of it. Thus this great man delivered to us the image of a play; and I must confess it is so lively that from thence much light has been derived to the forming it more perfectly into acts and scenes: but what poet first limited to five the number of the acts, I know not,[4] only we see it so firmly established

---

[1] *Poetics*, ch. xii, where Aristotle identifies the four parts of tragedy as prologue, episode, exodos, and choric song. Dryden's source for the four elements as he enumerates them is not Aristotle but J. C. Scaliger (1484-1558), *Poetices* (1561), I.ix, who added 'catastasis' to the other three as they are listed by Aelius Donatus (*fl. c.* A.D. 350) in his commentary on Terence. Cf. Ben Jonson, *Magnetic Lady* (acted 1632), I, Chorus, who borrows the four terms for comic effect from Thomas Godwyn, *Romanae historiae anthologia* (1614), pp. 70-1.

[2] 'Thirdly, the *catastasis*, called by the Romans *status*, the height and full growth of the play: we may call it properly the counter-turn,' *1684, 1693*. The term 'status' derives from Scaliger, whom Dryden may have read between the first and second editions of the Essay.

[3] 'unravelling'—so corrected in *1684, 1693*. *1668* has δεσις, 'complication.'

[4] The question is still unanswered. Early editors and commentators such as Donatus on Terence divided Roman comedies into five acts, in obedience to Horace. Cf. T. W. Baldwin, *Shakespere's Five-Act Structure* (1947).

in the time of Horace that he gives it for a rule in comedy: *neu brevior quinto, neu sit productior actu.*[1] So that you see the Grecians cannot be said to have consummated this art; writing rather by entrances than by acts, and having rather a general indigested notion of a play, than knowing how and where to bestow the particular graces of it.

'But since the Spaniards at this day allow but three acts, which they call *jornadas*,[2] to a play, and the Italians in many of theirs follow them, when I condemn the Ancients, I declare it is not altogether because they have not five acts to every play, but because they have not confined themselves to one certain number: 'tis building an house without a model; and when they succeeded in such undertakings, they ought to have sacrificed to Fortune, not to the Muses.

'Next, for the plot, which Aristotle called τὸ μῦθος,[3] and often τῶν πραγμάτων σύνθεσις,[4] and from him the Romans *fabula*, it has already been judiciously observed by a late writer[5] that in their tragedies it was only some tale derived from Thebes or Troy, or at least something that happened in those two ages, which was worn so threadbare by the pens of all the epic poets, and even by tradition itself of the talkative Greeklings (as Ben Jonson calls them) that before it came upon the stage it was already known to all the audience: and the people, so soon as ever they heard the name of Oedipus, knew as well as the poet that he had killed his father by a mistake, and committed incest with his mother, before the play; that they were now to hear of a great plague, an oracle, and the ghost of Laius: so that they sat with a yawning kind of expectation, till he was to come with his eyes pulled out, and speak a hundred or two of verses[6] in a tragic tone, in complaint of his misfortunes. But one Oedipus, Hercules, or Medea had been tolerable: poor people, they

[1] 'Neve minor neu sit quinto productior actu,' *Ars poetica*, l. 189: 'Let no play be shorter or longer than five acts.'

[2] A custom established in the early years of the century by Lope de Vega (1562–1635). Cf. his verse epistle *Arte nuevo de hacer comedias en este tiempo* (1609), where Lope justifies his tripartite division of plays into introduction, crisis, and *dénouement*. But he regularly uses the term 'acto'; 'jornada' is preferred by Calderón.

[3] I.e. ὁ μῦθος, an error passed by Dryden in *1684* and *1693*.

[4] I.e. the arrangement of events.

[5] Sir Robert Howard, preface to *Four New Plays* (1665): 'The subjects they [the Greek and Latin dramatists] chose drove them upon the necessity, which were usually the most known stories and fables.'

[6] 'a hundred or more verses,' *1684, 1693*.

scaped not so good cheap; they had still the *chapon bouillé* set before them, till their appetites were cloyed with the same dish, and the novelty being gone, the pleasure vanished; so that one main end of dramatic poesy in its definition, which was to cause delight, was of consequence destroyed.

'In their comedies, the Romans generally borrowed their plots from the Greek poets; and theirs was commonly a little girl stolen or wandered from her parents, brought back unknown to the same city,[1] there got with child by some lewd young fellow who, by the help of his servant, cheats his father; and when her time comes to cry *Juno Lucina, fer opem*,[2] one or other sees a little box or cabinet which was carried away with her, and so discovers her to her friends, if some god do not prevent it by coming down in a machine,[3] and take[4] the thanks of it to himself.

'By the plot you may guess much of the characters of the persons. An old father who would willingly, before he dies, see his son well married; his debauched son, kind in his nature to his wench,[5] but miserably in want of money; a servant or slave, who has so much wit to strike in with him, and help to dupe his father; a braggadochio captain, a parasite, and a lady of pleasure.

'As for the poor honest maid, whom all the story is built upon,[6] and who ought to be one of the principal actors in the play, she is commonly a mute in it: she has the breeding of the old Elizabeth way,[7] for maids to be seen and not to be heard; and it is enough you know she is willing to be married when the fifth act requires it.

'These are plots built after the Italian mode of houses: you see through them all at once. The characters are indeed the imitations of nature, but so narrow as if they had imitated only an eye or an hand, and did not dare to venture on the lines of a face, or the proportion of a body.

'But in how strait a compass soever they have bounded their plots and characters, we will pass it by if they have regularly pursued them, and perfectly observed those three unities of time, place, and action; the knowledge of which you say is derived to us from them. But in the first place give me leave to

---

[1] 'to the city,' *1684, 1693*.   [2] Terence, *Andria*, III.i.15.
[3] Cf. p. 160 and n., below.   [4] 'taking,' *1684, 1693*.
[5] 'mistress,' *1684, 1693*.   [6] 'on whom the story is built,' *1684, 1693*.
[7] 'way, which was,' *1684, 1693*.

tell you that the unity of place, however it might be practised by them, was never any of their rules: we neither find it in Aristotle, Horace, or any who have written of it, till in our age the French poets[1] first made it a precept of the stage. The unity of time even Terence himself (who was the best and most regular of them) has neglected: his *Heautontimorumenos*, or *Self-Punisher*, takes up visibly two days; therefore, says Scaliger,[2] the two first acts concluding the first day were acted overnight; the three last on the ensuing day; and Euripides, in tying himself to one day, has committed an absurdity never to be forgiven him; for in one of his tragedies he has made Theseus go from Athens to Thebes, which was about forty English miles, under the walls of it to give battle, and appear victorious in the next act; and yet, from the time of his departure to the return of the Nuntius, who gives the relation of his victory, Æthra and the Chorus have but thirty-six verses; that[3] is not for every mile a verse.[4]

'The like error is as evident in Terence his *Eunuch*, when Laches, the old man, enters in a mistake the house[5] of Thais; where, betwixt his exit and the entrance of Pythias, who comes to give an ample relation of the garboyles[6] he has raised within, Parmeno, who was left upon the stage, has not above five lines to speak. *C'est bien employer[7] un temps si court,* says the French

---

[1] In fact the Italian Castelvetro invented the rule. It is characteristic of Dryden's reluctance to admit all his intellectual debts that this very sneer at the French playwrights is a translation from Corneille's third 'Discours': 'Quant à l'unité de lieu, je n'en trouve aucun précepte ni dans Aristote, ni dans Horace.' The three unities are said to have been established in France by Jean Chapelain (1595-1674), who in about 1636 encouraged Cardinal Richelieu to impose them upon French drama; but they had already been adopted by Englishmen with recourse to Italian and classical sources, e.g. Sir Philip Sidney in the *Apology for Poetry* (1595) and Ben Jonson in the Prologue to *Every Man in his Humour* (acted 1598).

[2] *Poetices*, VI.iii. *1684* and *1693* have 'two days, says Scaliger, the two first acts concluding the first day, the three last the day ensuing.'

[3] 'which,' *1684*, *1693*.

[4] The passage is avowedly based on Corneille's third 'Discours': 'Euripide, dans *Les Suppliantes*, fait partir Thésée d'Athènes avec une armée, donner une bataille devant les murs de Thèbes, qui en étaient éloignés de douze ou quinze lieues, et revenir victorieux en l'acte suivant; et depuis qu'il est parti jusqu'à l'arrivée du messager qui vient faire le récit de sa victoire, Ethra et le chœur n'ont que trente-six vers à dire. C'est assez bien employé un temps si court.' Cf. Scaliger, *Poetices*, III.xcvii.

[5] 'by mistake into the house,' *1684*, *1693*.

[6] 'give ample relation of the disorders,' *1684*, *1693*.

[7] So corrected in *1684*, *1693*. The first edition has 'employé.'

poet[1] who furnished me with one of the observations: and
almost all their tragedies will afford us examples of the like
nature.

' 'Tis true, they have kept the continuity or, as you called it,
liaison des scènes, somewhat better: two do not perpetually
come in together, talk, and go out together; and other two
succeed them, and do the same throughout the act, which the
English call by the name of single scenes; but the reason is,
because they have seldom above two or three scenes, properly
so called, in every act; for it is to be accounted a new scene, not
every time[2] the stage is empty, but every person who enters,
though to others, makes it so; because he introduces a new
business. Now the plots of their plays being narrow, and the
persons few, one of their acts was written in a less compass
than one of our well wrought scenes; and yet they are often
deficient even in this. To go no further than Terence, you find
in the *Eunuch* Antipho entering single in the midst of the third
act, after Cremes and Pythias were gone off;[3] in the same play
you have likewise Dorias beginning the fourth act alone; and
after she has made a relation of what was done at the soldier's
entertainment[4] (which by the way was very inartificial[5] to do,
because she was presumed to speak directly to the audience, and to
acquaint them with what was necessary to be known, but yet
should have been so contrived by the poet as to have been told
by persons of the drama to one another, and so by them to have
come to the knowledge of the people), she quits the stage, and
Phædria enters next, alone likewise: he also gives you an account
of himself, and of his returning from the country, in monologue;
to which unnatural way of narration Terence is subject in
all his plays. In his *Adelphi*, or *Brothers*, Syrus and Demea

---

[1] Corneille. Cf. p. 36n. above.   [2] 'not only every time,' *1684*, *1693*.
[3] Also based on Corneille's third 'Discours': 'Les anciens ne s'y sont pas
toujours assujettis, bien que la plupart de leurs actes ne soient chargés
que de deux ou trois scènes; ce qui la rendait bien plus facile pour eux que
pour nous, qui leur en donnons, quelquefois jusqu'à neuf ou dix.' Corneille
offers one example from the *Ajax* of Sophocles, and goes on: 'l'autre
[exemple] est du troisième acte de l'*Eunuque* de Térence, où celle
d'Antiphon seul n'a aucune communication avec Chrémès et Pythias, qui
sortent du théâtre quand il y entre.' But the following instances are Dryden's
own, and show an immediate knowledge of Terence.
[4] *Eunuch*, IV. i. Cf. p. 53 and n., below.
[5] I.e. inartistic, clumsy.

enter after the scene was broken by the departure of Sostrata, Geta, and Canthara; and indeed you can scarce look into any of his comedies, where you will not presently discover the same interruption.

'But as they have failed both in laying of their plots, and managing of them,[1] swerving from the rules of their own art by misrepresenting nature to us, in which they have ill satisfied one intention of a play, which was delight; so in the instructive part they have erred worse: instead of punishing vice and rewarding virtue, they have often shown a prosperous wickedness, and an unhappy piety: they have set before us a bloody image of revenge in Medea,[2] and given her dragons to convey her safe from punishment; a Priam and Astyanax murdered, and Cassandra ravished, and the lust and murder ending in the victory of him who acted them: in short, there is no indecorum in any of our modern plays which, if I would excuse, I could not shadow with some authority from the Ancients.

'And one farther note of them let me leave you: tragedies and comedies were not writ then as they are now, promiscuously, by the same person; but he who found his genius bending to the one, never attempted the other way. This is so plain, that I need not instance to you that Aristophanes, Plautus, Terence, never any of them writ a tragedy; Æschylus, Euripides,[3] Sophocles, and Seneca, never meddled with comedy: the sock and buskin[4] were not worn by the same poet. Having then so much care to excel in one kind, very little is to be pardoned them if they miscarried in it; and this would lead me to the consideration of their wit, had not Crites given me sufficient warning not to be too bold in my judgment of it; because the languages being dead, and many of the customs and little accidents on which it depended lost to us, we are not competent judges of it. But though I grant that here and there we may miss the application of a proverb or a custom, yet a thing well said will be wit in all languages; and though it may lose something in the translation,

---

[1] 'in the management,' *1684, 1693*.
[2] I.e. the *Medea* of Euripides. Seneca's play has also survived.
[3] In fact Euripides meddled with comedy at least once, in the *Cyclops*, where he tells of Odysseus's escape, and Sophocles is known to have written a satirical *Ichneutai*.
[4] Latin *soccus* and *cothurnus*, symbols of comedy and tragedy on the Roman stage.

yet to him who reads it in the original, 'tis still the same: he has an idea of its excellency, though it cannot pass from his mind into any other expression or words than those in which he finds it. When Phædria, in the *Eunuch*, had a command from his mistress to be absent two days, and, encouraging himself to go through with it, said, *tandem ego non illa caream, si opus sit, vel totum triduum*?[1]—Parmeno, to mock the softness of his master, lifting up his hands and eyes, cries out, as it were in admiration, *hui! universum triduum!* the elegancy of which *universum*, though it cannot be rendered in our language, yet leaves an impression of the wit upon our souls: but this happens seldom in him; in Plautus oftener, who is infinitely too bold in his metaphors and coining words, out of which many times his wit is nothing; which questionless was one reason why Horace falls upon him so severely in those verses:

> sed proavi nostri Plautinos et numeros et
> laudavere sales, nimium patienter utrumque,
> ne dicam stolidè[2]

For Horace himself was cautious to obtrude a new word upon his readers, and makes custom and common use the best measure of receiving it into our writings:

> multa renascentur quae nunc cecidere, cadentque
> quae nunc sunt in honore vocabula, si volet usus,
> quem penes arbitrium est, et jus, et norma loquendi.[3]

'The not observing this rule is that which the world has blamed in our satirist, Cleveland: to express a thing hard and unnaturally, in his new way of elocution. 'Tis true, no poet but may sometimes use a catachresis; Virgil does it:

> mixtaque ridenti colocasia fundet acantho,[4]

in his eclogue of Pollio; and in his 7th Æneid.

---

[1] *Eunuch*, II.i.17-18: 'But am I to do without her, if I must, for all of three days?' to which his servant answers: "Three whole days!'

[2] *Ars poetica*, ll. 270-2 ('At vestri proavi Plautinos . . . ne dicam stulte'): 'Yet our fathers praised Plautus's verse and his wit, being too tolerant, not to say stupid.'

[3] *Ibid.*, 70-2: 'Many terms fallen out of use shall be reborn, and others now in repute shall fall, if usage wills it so, in whose power lies the judging and the law and the rule of speech.'

[4] *Eclogues*, IV.20, perhaps to the son of C. Asinius Pollio: '[For thee the earth] shall pour forth the Egyptian bean blended with the smiling acanthus.'

> mirantur et undae,
> miratur nemus insuetum fulgentia longe
> scuta virum fluvio pictasque innare carinas.[1]

And Ovid once so modestly, that he asks leave to do it:

> si verbo audacia detur,
> haud metuam summi dixisse Palatia caeli,[2]

calling the court of Jupiter by the name of Augustus his palace, though in another place he is more bold, where he says *et longas visent Capitolia pompas*.[3] But to do this always, and never be able to write a line without it, though it may be admired by some few pedants, will not pass upon those who know that wit is best conveyed to us in the most easy language; and is most to be admired when a great thought comes dressed in words so commonly received that it is understood by the meanest apprehensions, as the best meat is the most easily digested: but we cannot read a verse of Cleveland's without making a face at it, as if every word were a pill to swallow: he gives us many times a hard nut to break our teeth, without a kernel for our pains. So that there is this difference betwixt his satires and Doctor Donne's, that the one gives us deep thoughts in common language, though rough cadence; the other gives us common thoughts in abstruse words.[4] 'Tis true, in some places his wit is independent of his words, as in that of the *Rebel Scot*:

> Had *Cain* been *Scot*, God would have chang'd his doom;
> Not forc'd him wander, but confin'd him home.[5]

'*Si sic omnia dixisset!*[6] This is wit in all languages: 'tis like mercury, never to be lost or killed: and so that other:

---

[1] *Aeneid*, VIII, 91-3: 'The very waves and unaccustomed woods admire the warriors' gleaming shields and the painted hulls.'

[2] *Metamorphoses*, I.175-6 (for *metuam* read *timeam*): 'If I may make so bold as to say it, I would not fear to call it the Palatia of Heaven itself.'

[3] *Ibid.*, I.561: 'and Capitols view long processions.'

[4] A comparison perhaps echoed by Coleridge (*Biographia Literaria*, ch. xix) in his contrast between the Metaphysical and Romantic poets: 'the one conveying the most fantastic thoughts in the most correct and natural language; the other in the most fantastic language conveying the most trivial thoughts.' Dryden's later comments on Donne as a poet (vol. II, pp. 75, 144, below) are more reserved than here.

[5] Cleveland, 'Rebel Scot', ll. 63-4.

[6] Juvenal, *Satires*, X.123-4: 'If only he had always spoken so!'

> For beauty like white-powder makes no noise,
> And yet the silent hypocrite destroys.[1]

You see, the last line is highly metaphorical, but it is so soft and gentle that it does not shock us as we read it.

'But, to return from whence I have digressed to the consideration of the Ancients' writing and their wit (of which by this time you will grant us in some measure to be fit judges), though I see many excellent thoughts in Seneca, yet he of them who had genius most proper for the stage was Ovid; he had a way of writing so fit to stir up a pleasing admiration and concernment, which are the objects of a tragedy, and to show the various movements of a soul combating betwixt two different passions that, had he lived in our age, or in his own could have writ with our advantages, no man but must have yielded to him; and therefore I am confident the *Medea* is none of his: for, though I esteem it for the gravity and sententiousness of it, which he himself concludes to be suitable to a tragedy, *omne genus scripti gravitate tragaedia vincit*,[2] yet it moves not my soul enough to judge that he who in the epic way wrote things so near the drama as the story of Myrrha, of Caunus and Biblis, and the rest, should stir up no more concernment where he most endeavoured it.[3] The master-piece of Seneca I hold to be that scene in the *Troades*[4] where Ulysses is seeking for Astyanax to kill him; there you see the tenderness of a mother so represented in Andromache that it raises compassion to a high degree in the reader, and bears the nearest resemblance of any thing in their tragedies[5] to the excellent scenes of passion in Shakespeare, or in Fletcher: for love-scenes, you will find few among them, their tragic poets dealt not with that soft passion but with lust, cruelty, revenge, ambition, and those bloody actions they produced; which were more capable of raising horror than compassion

---

[1] 'Rupertismus,' ll. 39-40. 'White-powder' is arsenic.

[2] *Tristia*, II.381: 'Tragedy surpasses every other kind of writing in gravity.'

[3] Johnson justly censures the clumsy history of this passage in his Life of Dryden (1779): 'He might have determined the question upon surer evidence; for it [the *Medea*] is quoted by Quintilian as the work of Seneca; and the only line which remains of Ovid's play, for one line is left us, is not there to be found. There was therefore no need of the gravity of conjecture, or the discussion of plot or sentiment, to find what was already known upon higher authority than such discussions can ever reach.'

[4] Ll. 533f.   [5] 'in the tragedies of the Ancients,' *1684, 1693*.

in an audience: leaving love untouched, whose gentleness would have tempered them, which is the most frequent of all the passions, and which, being the private concernment of every person, is soothed by viewing its own image in a public entertainment.

'Among their comedies, we find a scene or two of tenderness, and that where you would least expect it, in Plautus; but to speak generally, their lovers say little, when they see each other, but *anima mea, vita mea; ζωὴ καὶ ψυχή*,[1] as the women in Juvenal's time used to cry out in the fury of their kindness: then indeed to speak sense were an offence.[2] Any sudden gust of passion (as an ecstasy of love in an unexpected meeting) cannot better be expressed than in a word and a sigh, breaking one another. Nature is dumb on such occasions, and to make her speak would be to represent her unlike herself. But there are a thousand other concernments of lovers, as jealousies, complaints, contrivances, and the like, where not to open their minds at large to each other were to be wanting to their own love, and to the expectation of the audience; who watch the movements of their minds, as much as the changes of their fortunes. For the imaging of the first is properly the work of a poet; the latter he borrows of[3] the historian.'

Eugenius was proceeding in that part of his discourse, when Crites interrupted him. 'I see,' said he, 'Eugenius and I are never like to have this question decided betwixt us; for he maintains the Moderns have acquired a new perfection in writing, I can only grant they have altered the mode of it. Homer described his heroes men of great appetites, lovers of beef broiled upon the coals, and good fellows; contrary to the practice of the French romances, whose heroes neither eat, nor drink, nor sleep, for love. Virgil makes Æneas a bold avower of his own virtues:

sum pius Æneas, fama super aethera notus;[4]

which in the civility of our poets is the character of a Fanfaron or Hector: for with us the knight takes occasion to walk out, or sleep, to avoid the vanity of telling his own story, which the

---

[1] Juvenal, *Satires*, VI.195: 'my life and my soul.'
[2] 'then indeed . . . offence' omitted in *1684, 1693.*
[3] 'from,' *1684, 1693.*
[4] *Aeneid*, I.378-9 (compressed): 'I am the dutiful Aeneas, known by report through all the world.'

trusty squire is ever to perform for him. So in their love-scenes, of which Eugenius spoke last, the Ancients were more hearty, we more talkative: they writ love as it was then the mode to make it; and I will grant thus much to Eugenius, that perhaps one of their poets, had he lived in our age,

si foret hoc nostrum fato delapsus in ævum[1]

(as Horace says of Lucilius), he had altered many things; not that they were not as natural[2] before, but that he might accommodate himself to the age he lived in.[3] Yet in the mean time, we are not to conclude any thing rashly against those great men, but preserve to them the dignity of masters, and give that honour to their memories (*quos Libitina sacravit*)[4] part of which we expect may be paid to us in future times.'

This moderation of Crites, as it was pleasing to all the company, so it put an end to that dispute; which Eugenius, who seemed to have the better of the argument,[5] would urge no farther: but Lisideius, after he had acknowledged himself of Eugenius his opinion concerning the Ancients, yet told him he had forborne, till his discourse were ended, to ask him why he preferred the English plays above those of other nations; and whether we ought not to submit our stage to the exactness of our next neighbours.

'Though,' said Eugenius, 'I am at all times ready to defend the honour of my country against the French, and to maintain we are as well able to vanquish them with our pens as our ancestors have been with their swords; yet, if you please,' added he, looking upon Neander, 'I will commit this cause to my friend's management; his opinion of our plays is the same with mine: and besides, there is no reason that Crites and I, who

---

[1] Horace, *Satires*, I.10.68 (for *delapsus* read *dilatus*): 'if Fate had deferred his birth to this age of ours.'

[2] 'not natural,' *1684*, *1693*.   [3] 'age in which he lived,' *1684*, *1693*.

[4] Horace, *Epistles*, II.i.49: 'whom the Funeral Goddess has consecrated.'

[5] Dryden ranges himself on the side of the Moderns by giving Eugenius the last word. This first exchange in the Essay represents the chief English contribution to the Ancient-Modern debate between the Modernism of Francis Bacon and of George Hakewill in his *Apology* (1627), on the one hand, and the Temple-Bentley-Swift debate of the 1690's on the other. The controversy, which begins in English with Bacon, was in Italy as old as the fifteenth century. Cf. Hans Baron, '*Querelle* of Ancients and Moderns,' *Journal of History of Ideas*, **xx** (1959).

have now left the stage, should re-enter so suddenly upon it; which is against the laws of comedy.'

'If the question had been stated,' replied Lisideius, 'who had writ best, the French or English, forty years ago, I should have been of your opinion, and adjudged the honour to our own nation; but since that time', said he (turning towards Neander) 'we have been so long together bad Englishmen, that we had not leisure to be good poets. Beaumont, Fletcher, and Jonson (who were only capable of bringing us to that degree of perfection which we have) were just then leaving the world,[1] as if in an age of so much horror, wit, and those milder studies of humanity, had no farther business among us. But the Muses, who ever follow peace, went to plant in another country: it was then that the great Cardinal of Richelieu began to take them into his protection; and that, by his encouragement, Corneille and some other Frenchmen reformed their theatre,[2] which before was as much below ours, as it now surpasses it and the rest of Europe. But because Crites in his discourse for the Ancients has prevented me, by touching upon[3] many rules of the stage which the Moderns have borrowed from them, I shall only, in short, demand of you whether you are not convinced that of all nations the French have best observed them. In the unity of time you find them so scrupulous that it yet remains a dispute among their poets whether the artificial day of twelve hours, more or less, be not meant by Aristotle, rather than the natural one of twenty-four; and consequently, whether all plays ought not to be reduced into that compass.[4] This I can testify, that in

[1] All three died some years before the outbreak of the Civil War in 1642: Beaumont in 1616, John Fletcher in 1625, and Jonson in 1637.

[2] In about 1636 Richelieu, on Chapelain's advice, imposed the three unities upon the French dramatists and charged the French Academy with the duty of seeing they were observed. But Corneille's *Le Cid* (1636) soon fell under the disapproval of the Academy for its failure to observe the rules.

[3] 'observing,' *1684, 1693*.

[4] Cf. Corneille, 'Discours des trois unités': 'Ces paroles [d'Aristote] donnent lieu à cette dispute fameuse, si elles doivent être entendues d'un jour naturel de vingt-quatre heures, ou d'un jour artificiel de douze; ce sont deux opinions dont chacune a des partisans considérables: et, pour moi, je trouve qu'il y a des sujets si malaisés à renfermer en si peu de temps, que non seulement je leur accorderais les vingt-quatre heures entières, mais je me servirais même de la licence que donne ce philosophe de les excéder un peu, et les pousserais sans scrupule jusqu'à trente.' Scaliger, and La Mesnardière in his *Poétique*, had argued for twenty-four hours or even more, as Corneille does; but d'Aubignac, in his *Pratique du théâtre* (1657), had insisted on twelve (II.7).

all their dramas writ within these last twenty years and upwards, I have not observed any that have extended the time to thirty hours: in the unity of place they are full as scrupulous; for many of their critics limit it to that very spot of ground where the play is supposed to begin; none of them exceed the compass of the same town or city.

"The unity of action in all plays is yet more conspicuous, for they do not burden them with under-plots, as the English do; which is the reason why many scenes of our tragi-comedies carry on a design that is nothing of kin to the main plot; and that we see two distinct webs in a play, like those in ill wrought stuffs; and two actions, that is, two plays, carried on together, to the confounding of the audience; who, before they are warm in their concernments for one part, are diverted to another; and by that means espouse the interest of neither. From hence likewise it arises that the one half of our actors are not known to the other. They keep their distances, as if they were Montagues and Capulets, and seldom begin an acquaintance till the last scene of the fifth act, when they are all to meet upon the stage. There is no theatre in the world has any thing so absurd as the English tragi-comedy;[1] 'tis a drama of our own invention, and the fashion of it is enough to proclaim it so; here a course of mirth, there another of sadness and passion, a third of honour, and fourth a duel:[2] thus, in two hours and a half we run through all the fits of Bedlam. The French affords you as much variety on the same day, but they do it not so unseasonably, or *mal à propos*,[3] as we: our poets present you the play and the farce

---

[1] A censure which Dryden disallows in the person of Neander, in his own practice as a dramatist and, in later life, in critical pronouncement. Cf. the preface to *Don Sebastian* (1690), vol. II, p. 49, below. Sir Robert Howard, who like Lisideius had condemned tragi-comedy in the preface to his *Four New Plays*, is again under attack. Milton, if he ever read the Essay, was evidently unimpressed with Dryden's defence of tragi-comedy, which he dismissed in his preface to *Samson Agonistes* (1671) as 'the poet's error of intermixing comic stuff with tragic sadness and gravity, or introducing trivial and vulgar persons.' Dryden did not recant his view that tragi-comedy is allowable until his dramatic career was over; cf. 'Parallel,' vol. II, p. 202, below.

[2] 'and a third of honour, and a duel,' *1684, 1693*.

[3] One of the earliest of some forty French borrowings attributed to Dryden as the first to use them in print, though French usages were evidently fashionable in Restoration London. Cf. E. A. Horsman, 'Dryden's French Borrowings', *Review of English Studies*, new ser. I (1950). Most have been subsequently taken into the language, in spite of Johnson's hostile prediction that they 'continue only where they stood first, perpetual warnings to

together; and our stages still retain somewhat of the original
civility of the Red Bull.[1]

> atque ursum et pugiles media inter carmina poscunt.[2]

The end of tragedies or serious plays, says Aristotle, is to beget
admiration, compassion, or concernment;[3] but are not mirth
and compassion things incompatible? and is it not evident that
the poet must of necessity destroy the former by intermingling
of the latter? that is, he must ruin the sole end and object of his
tragedy to introduce somewhat that is forced in,[4] and is not of
the body of it. Would you not think that physician mad who,
having prescribed a purge, should immediately order you to
take restringents upon it?[5]

'But to leave our plays, and return to theirs, I have noted one
great advantage they have had in the plotting of their tragedies:
that is, they are always grounded upon some known history;
according to that of Horace, *ex noto fictum carmen sequar*;[6] and
in that they have so imitated the Ancients that they have surpassed them. For the Ancients, as was observed before, took
for the foundation of their plays some poetical fiction such as
under that consideration could move but little concernment in
the audience, because they already knew the event of it. But the
French goes farther:

> atque ita mentitur, sic veris falsa remiscet,
> primo ne medium, medio ne discrepet imum.[7]

future innovators' (Life of Dryden). The present phrase re-occurs in
Marriage a-la-mode (1673), V.i. Lisideius, as the defender of the French,
appropriately uses five of the six French borrowings to appear in the Essay.

[1] A popular open-air theatre built in about 1605 in Upper St John St,
Clerkenwell, noted for its blood-and-thunder productions. Pepys, on his visit
of 23 March 1661, reported 'confusion and disorder' behind the scenes
among the actors, who seemed 'but common fellows.' After a very few years
of renewed activity after the Restoration, it seems to have fallen into disuse.

[2] Horace, *Epistles*, II.1.185-6 ('media inter carmina poscunt/aut ursum
aut pugilis'): 'and [the groundlings] are capable, in the middle of the play, of
calling for a bear-fight or a boxing-match.'

[3] In fact Aristotle in his *Poetics* (ch. vi) mentions only 'compassion' (or
pity) and 'concernment' (or fear). But sixteenth-century critics had added
'admiration' to the list; Sidney, indeed, in his *Apology*, replaces 'fear' with
'admiration,' and the heroic play presupposes such a definition. Cf. Addison,
Spectator, no. 42.

[4] 'into it,' *1684, 1693*.   [5] 'to take restringents,' *1684, 1693*.

[6] *Ars poetica*, l. 240: 'I shall create out of familiar matter.'

[7] *Ibid.*, 151-2: 'And so [Homer] fabricates, so mingling the false with
the true that the middle is never out of harmony with the beginning, nor the
end with the middle.'

He so interweaves truth with probable fiction, that he puts a pleasing fallacy upon us; mends the intrigues of fate, and dispenses with the severity of history, to reward that virtue which has been rendered to us there unfortunate. Sometimes the story has left the success so doubtful, that the writer is free, by the privilege of a poet, to take that which of two or more relations will best suit with his design: as, for example, the[1] death of Cyrus, whom Justin and some others report to have perished in the Scythian war, but Xenophon affirms to have died in his bed of extreme old age.[2] Nay more, when the event is past dispute, even then we are willing to be deceived, and the poet, if he contrives it with appearance of truth, has all the audience of his party; at least during the time his play is acting: so naturally we are kind to virtue, when our own interest is not in question, that we take it up as the general concernment of mankind. On the other side, if you consider the historical plays of Shakespeare, they are rather so many chronicles of kings, or the business many times of thirty or forty years, cramped into a representation of two hours and an half, which is not to imitate or paint nature, but rather to draw her in miniature, to take her in little; to look upon her through the wrong end of a perspective,[3] and receive her images not only much less, but infinitely more imperfect than the life: this, instead of making a play delightful, renders it ridiculous.

> quodcumque ostendis mihi sic, incredulus odi.[4]

For the spirit of man cannot be satisfied but with truth, or at least verisimility; and a poem is to contain, if not τὰ ἔτυμα, yet ἐτύμοισιν ὁμοῖα,[5] as one of the Greek poets has expressed it.

'Another thing in which the French differ from us and from

---

[1] 'in the death,' *1684, 1693.

[2] Justinus, 1.8.ii.3 and xxxvii.3, and Xenophon, *Cyropaedia*, VIII, 7.

[3] I.e. telescope. The passage may be an echo from Corneille's third Discours: 'Ne passons pas de beaucoup les vingt-quatre, de peur de tomber dans le déréglement, et de réduire tellement le portrait en petit, qu'il n'aye plus ses dimensions proportionnées, et ne soit qu'imperfection.' Cf. Pierre Legouis, 'Corneille and Dryden as Dramatic Critics,' in *Seventeenth-Century Studies Presented to Sir Herbert Grierson* (1938). But the scientific analogy is characteristically Dryden's.

[4] Horace, *Ars poetica*, l. 188: 'Whatever you show me thus, I unbelieving hate.'

[5] Hesiod, *Theogony*, l. 27: 'the truth,' 'the likeness of truth.'

the Spaniards is that they do not embarrass[1] or cumber themselves with too much plot; they only represent so much of a
story as will constitute one whole and great action sufficient for a
play; we, who undertake more, do but multiply adventures;
which, not being produced from one another, as effects from
causes, but barely following, constitute many actions in the
drama, and consequently make it many plays.

'But by pursuing close[2] one argument, which is not cloyed
with many turns, the French have gained more liberty for verse,
in which they write; they have leisure to dwell on a subject which
deserves it; and to represent the passions (which we have
acknowledged to be the poet's work), without being hurried
from one thing to another, as we are in the plays of Calderón,
which we have seen lately upon our theatres under the name of
Spanish plots.[3] I have taken notice but of one tragedy of ours,
whose plot has that uniformity and unity of design in it which I
have commended in the French; and that is *Rollo*, or rather,
under the name of *Rollo*,[4] the story of Bassianus and Geta in
Herodian: there indeed the plot is neither large nor intricate,
but just enough to fill the minds of the audience, not to cloy
them. Besides, you see it founded upon the truth of history,
only the time of the action is not reduceable to the strictness of
the rules; and you see in some places a little farce mingled,[5]
which is below the dignity of the other parts; and in this all our

---

[1] A French borrowing—hence the immediate explanation—and the earliest
recorded use of the verb in English, though Pepys in his *Diary* (15 July
1664) had recently used the noun *embarras*.

[2] 'closely,' *1684, 1693*.

[3] Several adaptations from the plays of Calderón (1600-8) had been
performed since the Restoration. Dryden's *An Evening's Love* (1671),
by an odd irony, was first performed in June 1668, only some months after
the publication of the Essay: it is derived from Calderón's *Astrologo fingido*
by way of Thomas Corneille's French adaptation *Le feint astrologue*.

[4] A sensational melodrama first published in 1639 under the title *The
Bloody Brother*, and probably the joint work of Chapman, John Fletcher,
Ben Jonson, and Massinger, who transferred Herodian's story from Imperial
Rome to Normandy. Cf. Herodian, bks. iii-iv. Rymer seizes upon the point
in *The Tragedies of the Last Age* (1678), where he condemns a change 'to
bring these cut-throats and poisoners from the other side of the Alps.'
Cf. *Rollo*, ed. J. D. Jump (1948).

[5] Especially in II.ii. (the kitchen scene) and IV.ii, where a group of
scoundrels meet in an astrologer's house. Dryden had probably seen the play
recently at Covent Garden; cf. Pepys, *Diary*, 28 March 1661, 17 April 1667,
and 17 September 1668.

poets are extremely peccant. Even Ben Jonson himself in
Sejanus and *Catiline* has given us this oleo[1] of a play, this
unnatural mixture of comedy and tragedy, which to me sounds
just as ridiculously as the history of David with the merry
humours of Golias.[2] In *Sejanus* you may take notice of the
scene betwixt Livia and the physician, which is a pleasant satire
upon the artificial helps of beauty; in *Catiline* you may see the
parliament of women, the little envies of them to one another;
and all that passes betwixt Curio and Fulvia:[3] scenes admirable
in their kind, but of an ill mingle with the rest.

'But I return again to the French writers who, as I have said,
do not burden themselves too much with plot, which has been
reproached to them by an ingenious person[4] of our nation as a
fault, for he says they commonly make but one person considerable in a play; they dwell on him, and his concernments,
while the rest of the persons are only subservient to set him off.
If he intends this by it, that there is one person in the play who
is of greater dignity than the rest, he must tax not only theirs,
but those of the Ancients, and which he would be loth to do,
the best of ours; for 'tis impossible but that one person must
be more conspicuous in it than any other, and consequently the
greatest share in the action must devolve on him. We see it so in
the management of all affairs; even in the most equal aristoc-
racy, the balance cannot be so justly poised but some one will be
superior to the rest, either in parts, fortune, interest, or the
consideration of some glorious exploit; which will reduce the
greatest part of business into his hands.

'But if he would have us to imagine that in exalting one

---

[1] *Olla podrida*, a Spanish stew of meat and vegetables. Ben Jonson uses
the term in *Neptune's Triumph*, l. 240, but Dryden probably picked the word
out of *Rollo* itself, from the Cook's speech on poisoning Otto in one of the
very farcical scenes he here condemns:

> Here stands my broths: my finger slips a little,
> Down drops a dose, I stir him with my ladle,
> And there's a dish for a Duke: *olla podrida*
>   (II.ii.144-6).

[2] A merry character in popular medieval literature. Cf. *Confessio Goliae*,
doubtfully attributed to Walter Map (1137?-1209?). The reference was too
much for the printers, who print 'Golia's' in *1668* and *1684*, and 'Goliah's'
in *1693*.

[3] *Sejanus*, II.i; *Catiline*, III.ix, II.iii.

[4] Thomas Sprat: 'The French, for the most part, take only one or two
great men, and chiefly insist on some remarkable accident of their story'
(*Observations on M. de Sorbier's 'Voyage into England,'* 1665).

character the rest of them are neglected, and that all of them have not some share or other in the action of the play, I desire him to produce any of Corneille's tragedies, wherein every person (like so many servants in a well governed family) has not some employment, and who is not necessary to the carrying on of the plot, or at least to your understanding it.

"There are indeed some protatic[1] persons in the Ancients, whom they make use of in their plays, either to hear or give the relation: but the French avoid this with great address, making their narrations only to, or by, such who are some way interested in the main design. And now I am speaking of relations, I cannot take a fitter opportunity to add this in favour of the French, that they often use them with better judgment and more à propos[2] than the English do. Not that I commend narrations in general, but there are two sorts of them: one, of those things which are antecedent to the play, and are related to make the conduct of it more clear to us; but 'tis a fault to choose such subjects for the stage which will inforce us on that rock,[3] because we see they are seldom listened to by the audience, and that is many times the ruin of the play. For, being once let pass without attention, the audience can never recover themselves to understand the plot; and indeed it is somewhat unreasonable that they should be put to so much trouble as, that to comprehend what passes in their sight, they must have recourse to what was done, perhaps, ten or twenty years ago.

'But there is another sort of relations, that is, of things happening in the action of the play, and supposed to be done behind the scenes; and this is many times both convenient and beautiful; for by it the French avoid the tumult which we are subject to[4] in England by representing duels, battles, and the like; which renders our stage too like the theatres where they

---

[1] I.e. relating to the *protasis*—a French borrowing, and almost the only recorded usage of the word, as well as the earliest, in English. Corneille uses the word in the 'Discours du poème dramatique' ('Térence . . . a introduit une nouvelle sorte de personnages qu'on a appelés protatiques') and in the *examen* for *Rodogune*. Cf. Donatus on Terence, *Andria*, Prologue 1, and Scaliger, *Poetices*, I.xiii.

[2] A French borrowing, and the earliest recorded use in English. Cf. *mal à propos*, p. 45 and n., above.

[3] 'as will force us on that rock,' *1684, 1693*.

[4] 'to which we are subject,' *1684, 1693*.

fight prizes. For what is more ridiculous than to represent an army with a drum and five men behind it,[1] all which the hero of the other side is to drive in before him; or to see a duel fought, and one slain with two or three thrusts of the foils, which we know are so blunted that we might give a man an hour to kill another in good earnest with them.

'I have observed that, in all our tragedies, the audience cannot forbear laughing when the actors are to die; 'tis the most comic part of the whole play. All *passions* may be lively represented on the stage, if to the well-writing of them the actor supplies a good commanded voice, and limbs that move easily, and without stiffness; but there are many *actions* which can never be imitated to a just height: dying especially is a thing which none but a Roman gladiator could naturally perform on the stage, when he did not imitate or represent, but naturally do it;[2] and therefore it is better to omit the representation of it.

"The words of a good writer, which describe it lively, will make a deeper impression of belief in us than all the actor can persuade us to[3] when he seems to fall dead before us; as a poet in the description of a beautiful garden, or a meadow, will please our imagination more than the place itself can please our sight. When we see death represented, we are convinced it is but fiction; but when we hear it related, our eyes (the strongest witnesses) are wanting, which might have undeceived us,[4] and we are all willing to favour the sleight when the poet does not too grossly impose on us. They, therefore, who imagine these relations would make no concernment in the audience, are deceived by confounding them with the other, which are of things antecedent to the play: those are made often in cold blood (as I may say) to the audience; but these are warmed with

---

[1] Cf. Shakespeare, *Henry V*, IV, Prologue, ll. 49-52:

> When, O for pity! we shall much disgrace
> With four or five most vile and ragged foils,
> Right ill-disposed in brawl ridiculous,
> The name of Agincourt.

Shakespeare's awareness of the contrivances of his own stage takes much of the sting out of Dryden's complaint.

[2] 'but do it,' *1684, 1693*.   [3] 'insinuate into us,' *1684, 1693*.

[4] Almost a prediction of Johnson's insistence on dramatic illusion in his preface to Shakespeare (1765)—but with the vital difference that the unbelief or 'alienation' of audiences, which Johnson recognizes as necessary in the theatre, is for Dryden an avoidable evil.

our concernments, which are before awakened in the play.
What the philosophers say of motion, that when it is once begun
it continues of itself, and will do so to eternity without some stop
put to it,[1] is clearly true on this occasion: the soul, being already
moved with the characters and fortunes of those imaginary
persons, continues going of its own accord; and we are no more
weary to hear what becomes of them when they are not on the
stage than we are to listen to the news of an absent mistress.
But it is objected that if one part of the play may be related,
then why not all? I answer, some parts of the action are more
fit to be represented, some to be related. Corneille says judiciously that the poet is not obliged to expose to view all particular
actions which conduce to the principal: he ought to select such
of them to be seen which will appear with the greatest beauty,
either by the magnificence of the show, or the vehemence of
passions which they produce, or some other charm which they
have in them, and let the rest arrive to the audience by narration.[2] 'Tis a great mistake in us to believe the French present
no part of the action on the stage: every alteration or crossing
of a design, every new-sprung passion, and turn of it, is a part
of the action, and much the noblest, except we conceive nothing
to be action till they[3] come to blows; as if the painting of the
hero's mind were not more properly the poet's work than the
strength of his body. Nor does this anything contradict the
opinion of Horace, where he tells us,

---

[1] A principle of Cartesian physics. The first English edition of Descartes's
Principia philosophiae (1644), in which it first appears, had recently appeared
in London in 1664: 'The first [law of nature], that each individual thing
continues as it is, and never changes except by encountering other things. . . .
Once it begins to move, we have no reason to think it will ever cease to move
with the same force, so long as it encounters nothing to retard or stop it'
(II.37). Dryden's scientific interests were amateur and catholic, useful to
him mainly for aesthetic analogies such as this. A few members of the Royal
Society, of which he was a founder-member, were Cartesians, but Sprat in
his *History of the Royal Society* (1667) praises the native, experimental
tradition of Francis Bacon and practically ignores Descartes's mechanical
philosophy. Cf. R. F. Jones, *Ancients and Moderns* (1936).

[2] Cf. 'Discours des trois unités': 'Le poète n'est pas tenu d'exposer à la
vue toutes les actions particulières qui amènent à la principale: il doit
choisir celles qui lui sont les plus avantageuses à faire voir, soit par la beauté
du spectacle, soit par l'éclat et la véhémence des passions qu'elles produisent,
soit par quelque autre agrément qui leur soit attaché, et cacher les autres
derrière la scène, pour les faire connaître au spectateur, ou par une narration,
ou par quelque autre adresse de l'art.'

[3] 'the players,' *1684, 1693*.

segnius irritant animos demissa per aurem,
quam quæ sunt oculis subjecta fidelibus.

For he says immediately after,

non tamen intus
digna geri promes in sænam; multaque tolles
ex oculis, quæ mox narret facundia præsens.

Among which many he recounts some:

nec pueros coram populo Medea trucidet,
aut in avem Procne mutetur, Cadmus in anguem, &c.[1]

That is, those actions which by reason of their cruelty will
cause aversion in us or, by reason of their impossibility, unbelief, ought either wholly to be avoided by a poet, or only
delivered by narration. To which we may have leave to add such
as to avoid tumult (as was before hinted), or to reduce the plot
into a more reasonable compass of time, or for defect of beauty
in them, are rather to be related than presented to the eye.
Examples of all these kinds are frequent, not only among all the
Ancients, but in the best received of our English poets. We find
Ben Jonson using them in his *Magnetic Lady*,[2] where one comes
out from dinner, and relates the quarrels and disorders of it to
save the undecent appearance of them on the stage, and to
abbreviate the story; and this in express imitation of Terence,
who had done the same before him in his *Eunuch*,[3] where
Pythias makes the like relation of what had happened within at
the soldiers' entertainment. The relations likewise of Sejanus's
death, and the prodigies before it, are remarkable;[4] the one of

[1] Horace, *Ars poetica*, ll. 180-7: 'The mind is stirred less by what enters
through the ears than by what lies before its faithful eyes, and by what the
spectator sees for himself. But do not bring on stage what should be performed off, and keep much from our eyes to be told by the actor's ready
tongue. Medea must not butcher her boys before the audience, or evil
Atreus cook human flesh on the stage, or Procne be turned into a bird, or
Cadmus into a serpent.'
[2] III.ii. In fact two characters, Mr Compasse and Capt. Ironside, burst
out on stage after 'a noise within,' and Compasse accuses Ironside of having
started a drunken brawl.
[3] IV.iii, where Pythias, the cunning maidservant, reports a rape.
[4] Ben Jonson, *Sejanus* (1605), V.ix, the last scene of the tragedy, where
Terentius tells how the mob have seized the trunk of the beheaded Sejanus
and torn it to pieces, and Nuntius follows with an account of the rape and
strangling of Sejanus's young daughter and the execution of her brother.
The 'prodigies before' death include the sacrifice of an ox and the destruction
of the disgraced leader's images.

which was hid from sight, to avoid the horror and tumult of the representation; the other, to shun the introducing of things impossible to be believed. In that excellent play the *King and No King*,[1] Fletcher goes yet farther; for the whole unravelling of the plot is done by narration in the fifth act, after the manner of the Ancients; and it moves great concernment in the audience, though it be only a relation of what was done many years before the play. I could multiply other instances, but these are sufficient to prove that there is no error in choosing a subject which requires this sort of narrations; in the ill managing[2] of them, there may.

'But I find I have been too long in this discourse, since the French have many other excellencies not common to us, as that you never see any of their plays end with a conversion, or simple change of will, which is the ordinary way which our poets use to end theirs. It shows little art in the conclusion of a dramatic poem when they, who have hindered the felicity during the four acts, desist from it in the fifth, without some powerful cause to take them off;[3] and though I deny not but such reasons may be found, yet it is a path that is cautiously to be trod, and the poet is to be sure he convinces the audience that the motive is strong enough. As for example, the conversion of the usurer in *The Scornful Lady*[4] seems to me a little forced; for, being an

---

[1] By Beaumont and Fletcher, performed in 1611 and published in 1619, where the plot is resolved in the last scene by the long narration of the Protector Gobrias, who reveals himself as the true father of King Arbaces and so releases him to marry Panthea, hitherto supposed to be his sister. Dryden's esteem for Beaumont and Fletcher's artistic and commercial success was already based on theatrical experience: after the reopening of the theatres, in the early years before Dryden and others created a Restoration drama, the plays of Shakespeare, Jonson, and Beaumont and Fletcher (in their tragi-comedies and comedies), and rarely of any other pre-war dramatist, were frequently revived in London theatres, and Beaumont and Fletcher revivals surpassed all others in frequency. Cf. J. H. Wilson, *The Influence of Beaumont and Fletcher on Restoration Drama* (1928). Dryden had already borrowed ideas from them for *The Rival Ladies*, and three later plays at least—*An Evening's Love, Love Triumphant*, and *The Spanish Friar*—owe something to them.

[2] 'management,' *1684, 1693*.   [3] 'off their design,' *1684, 1693*.

[4] Another collaboration by Beaumont and Fletcher, performed in 1609 and published in 1616. In V.i, Morecraft, the usurer, declares his conversion: 'I purchased, wrung, and wierdrawed for my wealth, and was cozened: for which I make a vow to try all the ways above ground, but I'll find a constant means to riches without curses,' and proceeds to give away his wealth—a spectacle that the young prodigal Loveless finds 'stranger than an Afric monster.'

usurer, which implies a lover of money to the highest degree of covetousness (and such the poet has represented him), the account he gives for the sudden change is, that he has been duped[1] by the wild young fellow, which in reason might render him more wary another time, and make him punish himself with harder fare and coarser clothes to get it up again;[2] but that he should look on it as a judgment, and so repent, we may expect to hear of in a sermon,[3] but I should never endure it in a play.

'I pass by this; neither will I insist on the care they take that no person after his first entrance shall ever appear but the business which brings him upon the stage shall be evident; which,[4] if observed, must needs render all the events in the play more natural; for there you see the probability of every accident, in the cause that produced it; and that which appears chance in the play, will seem so reasonable to you that you will there find it almost necessary; so that in the exits of the actors[5] you have a clear account of their[6] purpose and design in the next entrance (though, if the scene be well wrought, the event will commonly deceive you), for there is nothing so absurd, says Corneille, as for an actor to leave the stage only because he has no more to say.[7]

'I should now speak of the beauty of their rhyme, and the just reason I have to prefer that way of writing in tragedies before ours in blank verse; but because it is partly received by us,[8] and therefore not altogether peculiar to them, I will say no more of it in relation to their plays. For our own, I doubt not but it will exceedingly beautify them, and I can see but one reason why it should not generally obtain, that is, because our poets write so ill in it. This, indeed, may prove a more prevailing argument than all others which are used to destroy it, and therefore I am only troubled when great and judicious poets, and

---

[1] A French borrowing, the earliest recorded use in English.
[2] 'to get up again what he had lost,' *1684, 1693*.
[3] 'to hear in a sermon,' *1684, 1693*.   [4] 'which rule,' *1684, 1693*.
[5] 'exit of the actor,' *1684, 1693*.   [6] 'his,' *1684, 1693*.
[7] 'Discours des trois unités': 'Il faut, s'il se peut, y rendre raison de l'entrée et de la sortie de chaque acteur; surtout pour la sortie, je tiens cette règle indispensable, et il n'y a rien de si mauvaise grâce qu'un acteur qui se retire du théâtre seulement parce qu'il n'a plus de vers à dire.'
[8] *The Rival Ladies* (1664) had been partly in rhyme, and *The Indian Emperor* (1665) entirely so; and Orrery and other Restoration dramatists had also produced a few rhyming plays before the Plague closed the theatres. For Crites's refutation, see pp. 77-81, below.

those who are acknowledged such, have writ or spoke against it; as for others, they are to be answered by that one sentence of an ancient author: '*sed ut primo ad consequendos eos quos priores ducimus, accendimur, ita ubi aut præteriri, aut æquari eos posse desperavimus, studium cum spe senescit: quod, scilicet, assequi non potest, sequi desinit; . . . præteritoque eo in quo eminere non possumus, aliquid in quo nitamur, conquirimus.*'[1]

Lisideius concluded in this manner; and Neander, after a little pause, thus answered him:

'I shall grant Lisideius, without much dispute, a great part of what he has urged against us, for I acknowledge the French contrive their plots more regularly, observe the laws of comedy, and decorum of the stage (to speak generally), with more exactness than the English. Farther, I deny not but he has taxed us justly in some irregularities of ours which he has mentioned; yet, after all, I am of opinion that neither our faults nor their virtues are considerable enough to place them above us.

'For the lively imitation of nature being in the definition of a play, those which best fulfil that law ought to be esteemed superior to the others. 'Tis true, those beauties of the French poesy are such as will raise perfection higher where it is, but are not sufficient to give it where it is not: they are indeed the beauties of a statue, but not of a man, because not animated with the soul of poesy, which is imitation of humour and passions; and this Lisideius himself, or any other, however biassed to their party, cannot but acknowledge, if he will either compare the humours of our comedies, or the characters of our serious plays, with theirs. He that[2] will look upon theirs which have been written till these last ten years, or thereabouts, will find it an hard matter to pick out two or three passable humours amongst them. Corneille himself, their arch-poet, what has he produced except *The Liar*, and you know how it was cried up in France; but when it came upon the English stage, though well translated,

[1] Vellius Paterculus, *Historia romana*, I.17: 'But, as we at first burn to surpass those whom we consider the greatest, so, when we have despaired either of being able to surpass or equal them, our zeal cools with our hopes: no doubt what one cannot pursue with success, one ceases to pursue; . . . and leaving aside those things in which we cannot excel, we seek for something in which we can advance.'

[2] 'He who,' *1684, 1693*.

and that part of Dorant acted to so much advantage by Mr Hart[1] as I am confident it never received in its own country, the most favourable to it would not put it[2] in competition with many of Fletcher's or Ben Jonson's. In the rest of Corneille's comedies you have little humour; he tells you himself his way is, first to show two lovers in good intelligence with each other; in the working up of the play to embroil them by some mistake, and in the latter end to clear it up.[3]

'But of late years Molière,[4] the younger Corneille,[5] Quinault,[6] and some others, have been imitating afar off[7] the quick turns and graces of the English stage. They have mixed their serious plays with mirth, like our tragi-comedies, since the death of Cardinal Richelieu; which Lisideius and many others not observing, have commended that in them for a virtue which they themselves no longer practise. Most of their new plays are, like some of ours, derived from the Spanish novels.[8] There is scarce one of them without a veil, and a trusty Diego, who drolls much after the rate of the *Adventures*.[9] But their humours, if I may grace them with that name, are so thin sown that never above one of them comes up in any play. I dare take upon me to find more variety of them in some one play of Ben Jonson's than in all theirs together; as he who has seen *The Alchemist*,

---

[1] Charles Hart (d. 1683), a leading actor of the Restoration who later played in Dryden's *Secret Love*. Corneille's *Le menteur* (1642) seems to have been translated and performed soon after the reopening of the theatres in 1660, and published in 1685 as *The Mistaken Beauty: or the Liar*. The phrase 'by Mr Hart' is omitted in *1684* and *1693*, following the actor's death.

[2] 'it' omitted by an oversight in *1668*, restored in *1684, 1693*.

[3] 'Discours du poème dramatique': 'Ainsi, dans les comédies, j'ai presque toujours établi deux amants en bonne intelligence, je les ai brouillés ensemble par quelque fourbe, et les ai réunis par l'éclaircissement de cette même fourbe qui les séparait.' *1684* and *1693* read 'to clear it and reconcile them.'

[4] 'de Molière' in *1668*.

[5] Thomas Corneille (1625-1709), the younger brother of Pierre.

[6] Philippe Quinault (1635-88), then a highly popular dramatist in Paris, though Racine's reputation after 1670 turned him from the drama to the opera. His *Les rivales* (1661) is a probable source for *The Rival Ladies*.

[7] 'of afar off,' *1668*. Dryden's patriotism has led him to attribute to the English dramatists an influence in France for which there is not the slightest evidence. Nor was the death of Richelieu in 1642 a signal for liberalizing French drama, as he claims.

[8] Several Beaumont and Fletcher plays have Spanish sources, as well as Dryden's *The Wild Gallant* and *The Rival Ladies*, and many of Thomas Corneille's plays.

[9] Sir Samuel Tuke, *Adventures of Five Hours* (1663), adapted from Coello's *Los empeños de seis horas* (attributed to Calderón), in which Diego is the comic servant.

The Silent Woman, or *Bartholomew-Fair*, cannot but acknowledge with me.

'I grant the French have performed what was possible on the ground-work of the Spanish plays; what was pleasant before, they have made regular; but there is not above one good play to be writ upon all those plots; they are too much alike to please often, which we need not the experience of our own stage to justify. As for their new way of mingling mirth with serious plot, I do not with Lisideius condemn the thing, though I cannot approve their manner of doing it. He tells us we cannot so speedily recollect ourselves after a scene of great passion and concernment as to pass to another of mirth and humour, and to enjoy it with any relish: but why should he imagine the soul of man more heavy than his senses? Does not the eye pass from an unpleasant object to a pleasant in a much shorter time than is required to this? and does not the unpleasantness of the first commend the beauty of the latter? The old rule of logic might have convinced him that contraries, when placed near, set off each other.[1] A continued gravity keeps the spirit too much bent; we must refresh it sometimes, as we bait[2] upon a journey, that we may go on with greater ease. A scene of mirth mixed with tragedy has the same effect upon us which our music has betwixt the acts; and that[3] we find a relief to us from the best plots and language of the stage, if the discourses have been long. I must therefore have stronger arguments ere I am convinced that compassion and mirth in the same subject destroy each other; and in the mean time cannot but conclude, to the honour of our nation, that we have invented, increased, and perfected a more pleasant way of writing for the stage than was ever known to the ancients or moderns of any nation, which is tragi-comedy.

'And this leads me to wonder why Lisideius and many

---

[1] Cf. Franco Burgersdijck, *Institutionum logicarum libri duo* (1626), I.xxii, 'De oppositione rerum', Theorem v: 'Opposita juxta se posita, magis elucescunt' ('Contraries, when placed together, shine the more'). Burgersdicius (1590-1635), the Dutch philosopher and logician, must have been well known for his handbook of logic in Cambridge during Dryden's undergraduate years there (1650-5); the Latin text was published by the Cambridge University Press in 1637 and reprinted in 1644 and 1647. Dryden quotes the Latin tag in the 'Parallel,' vol. II, p. 203, below.

[2] I.e. bate, abate, to fall off, calm down (hence, very rare) to rest.

[3] 'which,' *1684, 1693.*

others should cry up the barrenness of the French plots above the variety and copiousness of the English. Their plots are single, they carry on one design which is pushed forward by all the actors, every scene in the play contributing and moving towards it: ours[1], besides the main design, have under-plots or by-concernments of less considerable persons and intrigues, which are carried on with the motion of the main plot; just as[2] they say the orb of the fixed stars, and those of the planets, though they have motions of their own, are whirled about by the motion of the *primum mobile*,[3] in which they are contained. That similitude expresses much of the English state; for if contrary motions may be found in nature to agree, if a planet can go east and west at the same time, one way by virtue of his own motion, the other by the force of the First Mover, it will not be difficult to imagine how the under-plot, which is only different, not contrary to the great design, may naturally be conducted along with it.

'Eugenius[4] has already shewn us, from the confession of the French poets, that the unity of action is sufficiently preserved if all the imperfect actions of the play are conducing to the main design; but when those petty intrigues of a play are so ill ordered that they have no coherence with the other, I must grant[5] Lisideius has reason to tax that want of due connexion; for co-ordination[6] in a play is as dangerous and unnatural as in a State. In the mean time he must acknowledge our variety, if well ordered, will afford a greater pleasure to the audience.

'As for his other argument, that by pursuing one single theme they gain an advantage to express and work up the passions, I wish any example he could bring from them would make it good: for I confess their verses are to me the coldest I have ever read. Neither, indeed, is it possible for them, in the way they take, so to express passion as that the effects of it should appear in the concernment of an audience: their speeches being so many declamations, which tire us with the length; so

---

[1] 'our plays,' *1684, 1693*.   [2] 'as,' *1684, 1693*.

[3] The ninth sphere beyond the central earth of the Ptolemaic system which gives motion to the rest. Dryden, like Milton in *Paradise Lost.* uses the older astronomy for effect. For allusions to the new astronomy of Copernicus, which he no doubt accepted, cf. vol II. pp. 145, 199, below.

[4] An error for 'Crites.' Cf. p. 30, above.   [5] 'grant that,' *1684, 1693*.

[6] I.e. equality of rank, as opposed to 'subordination'

that instead of persuading us to grieve for their imaginary
heroes, we are concerned for our own trouble, as we are in the
tedious visits[1] of bad company; we are in pain till they are gone.
When the French stage came to be reformed by Cardinal
Richelieu, those long harangues were introduced to comply
with the gravity of a churchman. Look upon the *Cinna* and the
Pompey; they are not so properly to be called plays as long discourses of reason of State; and *Polyeucte*[2] in matters of religion
is as solemn as the long stops upon our organs. Since that time
it is grown into a custom, and their actors speak by the hour-
glass, as our parsons do;[3] nay, they account it the grace of their
parts, and think themselves disparaged by the poet, if they may
not twice or thrice in a play entertain the audience with a
speech of an hundred or two hundred lines.[4] I deny not but
this may suit well enough with the French; for as we, who are a
more sullen people, come to be diverted at our plays; they, who
are of an airy and gay temper, come thither to make themselves
more serious; and this I conceive to be one reason why comedy
is[5] more pleasing to us, and tragedies to them. But to speak
generally, it cannot be denied that short speeches and replies
are more apt to move the passions and beget concernment in us
than the other: for it is unnatural for any one in a gust of passion
to speak long together, or for another in the same condition to
suffer him without interruption. Grief and passion are like
floods raised in little brooks by a sudden rain; they are quickly
up; and if the concernment be poured unexpectedly in upon
us, it overflows us: but a long, sober shower gives them leisure
to run out as they came in, without troubling the ordinary
current. As for comedy, repartee is one of its chiefest graces;
the greatest pleasure of the audience is a chase of wit kept up
on both sides, and swiftly managed. And this our forefathers, if

[1] 'in tedious visits,' *1684, 1693*.

[2] Three of Corneille's early plays. *La mort de Pompée* (1644) had recently
been translated by Buckhurst in collaboration with Godolphin, Sedley, and
Waller as *Pompey the Great* (1664).

[3] 'like our parsons,' *1684, 1693*. Cf. note by Sir Walter Scott in his
edition of Dryden's *Works* (1808): 'The custom of placing an hour-glass
before the clergyman was then common in England. It is still the furniture
of a country pulpit in Scotland. A facetious preacher used to press his
audience to take *another glass with him*.' Cf. Samuel Butler, *Hudibras*,
pt 1 (1663), iii.1061f.

[4] 'an hundred lines,' *1684, 1693*.   [5] 'comedies are,' *1684, 1693*.

not we, have had in Fletcher's plays, to a much higher degree of perfection than the French poets can arrive at.[1]

'There is another part of Lisideius his discourse, in which he has rather excused our neighbours than commended them; that is, for aiming only to make one person considerable in their plays. 'Tis very true what he has urged, that one character in all plays, even without the poet's care, will have advantage of all the others; and that the design of the whole drama will chiefly depend on it. But this hinders not that there may be more shining characters in the play: many persons of a second magnitude, nay, some so very near, so almost equal to the first, that greatness may be opposed to greatness, and all the persons be made considerable, not only by their quality but their action. 'Tis evident that the more the persons are, the greater will be the variety of the plot. If then the parts are managed so regularly that the beauty of the whole be kept entire, and that the variety become not a perplexed and confused mass of accidents, you will find it infinitely pleasing to be led in a labyrinth of design, where you see some of your way before you, yet discern not the end till you arrive at it. And that all this is practicable, I can produce for examples many of our English plays: as *The Maid's Tragedy*, *The Alchemist*, *The Silent Woman*:[2] I was going to have named *The Fox*, but that the unity of design seems not exactly observed in it; for there appear[3] two actions in the play; the first naturally ending with the fourth act; the second forced from it in the fifth: which yet is the less to be condemned in him, because the disguise of Volpone, though it suited not with his character as a crafty or covetous person, agreed well enough with that of a voluptuary; and by it the poet gained the end he aimed at,[4] the punishment of vice, and the reward of virtue, which[5] that disguise produced. So that to judge equally of it,

[1] 'can reasonably hope to reach,' *1684, 1693*.

[2] *The Maid's Tragedy* (1619) was by Beaumont and Fletcher, the rest by Ben Jonson.

[3] So corrected in *1684, 1693*; in *1668*, 'appears.' The first four acts of *Volpone: or The Fox* (1607) are largely concerned with Volpone's trick to seduce Celia, Corvino's wife; in the fifth act his attempt to trick the suitors of their wealth is exposed and he is sentenced. But Volpone's lust and his greed for ever greater wealth are twin ambitions, explicit from the first scene, and rarely separated at any point in the play; and his disguise of senile infirmity is made to serve both equally.

[4] 'the end at which he aimed,' *1684, 1693*.

[5] 'both which,' *1684, 1693*.

it was an excellent fifth act, but not so naturally proceeding
from the former.

'But to leave this, and pass to the latter part of Lisideius his
discourse, which concerns relations, I must acknowledge with
him that the French have reason when they hide[1] that part of
the action which would occasion too much tumult upon the stage,
and choose[2] rather to have it made known by narration to the
audience. Farther, I think it very convenient, for the reasons he
has given, that all incredible actions were removed; but whether
custom has so insinuated itself into our countrymen, or nature
has so formed them to fierceness, I know not; but they will
scarcely suffer combats and other objects of horror to be taken
from them. And indeed, the indecency of tumults is all which
can be objected against fighting: for why may not our imagination as well suffer itself to be deluded with the probability of it,
as with any other thing in the play? For my part, I can with
as great ease persuade myself that the blows which are struck
are given[3] in good earnest, as I can that they who strike them are
kings or princes, or those persons which they represent. For
objects of incredibility, I would be satisfied from Lisideius,
whether we have any so removed from all appearance of truth
as are those of Corneille's *Andromède*, a play which has been
frequented the most of any he has writ. If the Perseus, or the
son of an heathen god, the Pegasus, and the Monster, were not
capable to choke a strong belief, let him blame any representation of ours hereafter. Those indeed were objects of delight; yet
the reason is the same as to the probability: for he makes it not
a ballette[4] or masque, but a play, which is to resemble truth. But
for death, that it ought not to be represented, I have, besides the
arguments alleged by Lisideius, the authority of Ben Jonson,
who has forborne it in his tragedies; for both the death of Sejanus
and Catiline are related; though in the latter I cannot but observe
one irregularity of that great poet: he has removed the scene in
the same act from Rome to Catiline's army, and from thence
again to Rome; and besides, has allowed a very inconsiderable
time, after Catiline's speech, for the striking of the battle, and the

---

[1] 'reason to hide,' *1684, 1693*.   [2] 'and to choose,' *1684, 1693*.
[3] 'the blows are given,' *1684, 1693*.
[4] A French borrowing, and the first recorded use in English. The
ballet had its origins in the court of the young Louis XIV, himself a dancer,
in the 1650's.

return of Petreius, who is to relate the event of it to the Senate: which I should not animadvert on him, who was otherwise a painful observer of τὸ πρέπον, or the decorum of the stage, if he had not used extreme severity in his judgment on the incomparable Shakespeare for the same fault.[1] To conclude on this subject of relations, if we are to be blamed for showing too much of the action, the French are as faulty for discovering too little of it: a mean betwixt both should be observed by every judicious writer, so as the audience may neither be left unsatisfied by not seeing what is beautiful, or shocked by beholding what is either incredible or undecent.

'I hope I have already proved in this discourse that, though we are not altogether so punctual as the French in observing the laws of comedy, yet our errors are so few, and little, and those things wherein we excel them so considerable, that we ought of right to be preferred before them. But what will Lisideius say, if they themselves acknowledge they are too strictly tied up[2] by those laws for breaking which he has blamed the English? I will allege Corneille's words, as I find them in the end of his 'Discourse of the Three Unities': *Il est facile aux spéculatifs d'estre sévères,&c.* ' 'Tis easy for speculative persons to judge severely; but if they would produce to public view ten or twelve pieces of this nature, they would perhaps give more latitude to the rules than I have done, when by experience they had known how much we are bound up[3] and constrained by them, and how many beauties of the stage they banished from it.'[4] To illustrate a

---

[1] Cf. Ben Jonson, *Every Man in His Humour* (1616), Prologue, ll. 8-16:

> To make a child, now swaddled, to proceed
> Man, and then shoot up, in one beard and weed,
> Past threescore years: or, with three rusty swords,
> And help of some few foot-and-half-foot words,
> Fight over York and Lancaster's long jars:
> And in the tiring-house bring wounds to scars.
> He rather prays you will be pleased to see
> One such, to-day, as other plays should be.
> Where neither Chorus wafts you o'er the seas;
> Nor creaking throne comes down, the boys to please. . . .

[2] 'bounded,' *1684, 1693.*   [3] 'limited,' *1684, 1693.*

[4] 'Il est facile aux spéculatifs d'être sévères; mais s'ils voulaient donner dix ou douze poèmes de cette nature au public, ils élargiraient peut-être les règles encore plus que je ne fais, sitôt qu'ils auraient reconnu par l'expérience quelle contrainte apporte leur exactitude, et combien de belles choses elle bannit de notre théâtre.'

little what he has said, by their servile observations of the unities
of time and place, and integrity of scenes, they have brought on
themselves that dearth of plot, and narrowness of imagination,
which may be observed in all their plays. How many beautiful
accidents might naturally happen in two or three days, which cannot arrive with any probability in the compass of twenty-four
hours? There is time to be allowed also for maturity of design
which, amongst great and prudent persons such as are often represented in tragedy, cannot, with any likelihood of truth, be brought
to pass at so short a warning. Farther, by tying themselves
strictly to the unity of place and unbroken scenes, they are forced
many times to omit some beauties which cannot be shown where
the act began; but might, if the scene were interrupted, and the
stage cleared for the persons to enter in another place; and therefore the French poets are often forced upon absurdities: for if
the act begins in a chamber, all the persons in the play must
have some business or other to come thither, or else they are not
to be shown that act, and sometimes their characters are very
unfitting to appear there. As, suppose it were the King's bed-
chamber, yet the meanest man in the tragedy must come and
dispatch his business there, rather than in the lobby or courtyard
(which is fitter for him), for fear the stage should be cleared and
the scenes broken. Many times they fall by it into a greater inconvenience; for they keep their scenes unbroken, and yet change
the place; as in one of their newest plays,[1] where the act begins
in the street. There a gentleman is to meet his friend; he sees
him with his man, coming out from his father's house; they talk
together, and the first goes out: the second, who is a lover, has
made an appointment with his mistress; she appears at the
window, and then we are to imagine the scene lies under it.
This gentleman is called away, and leaves his servant with his
mistress; presently her father is heard from within; the young
lady is afraid the servingman should be discovered, and thrusts
him in through a door[2] which is supposed to be her closet.
After this, the father enters to the daughter, and now the scene
is in a house; for he is seeking from one room to another for this

---

[1] Thomas Corneille, *L'amour à la mode* (1651), Act III. But the servant
here is Cliton, whom Dryden has apparently confused with the Philipin of
Quinault's *L'amant indiscret* (II.iv).

[2] 'into a place of safety,' *1684, 1693*.

poor Philipin, or French Diego, who is heard from within, drol-
ling and breaking many a miserable conceit upon his sad[1] condition. In this ridiculous manner the play goes on,[2] the stage being
never empty all the while: so that the street, the window, the two
houses, and the closet, are made to walk about, and the persons
to stand still. Now what, I beseech you, is more easy than to
write a regular French play, or more difficult than write an
irregular English one, like those of Fletcher or of Shakespeare?

'If they content themselves, as Corneille did, with some flat
design which, like an ill riddle, is found out ere it be half proposed; such plots we can make every way regular, as easily as
they; but whene'er they endeavour to rise to any quick turns
and counterturns of plot, as some of them have attempted since
Corneille's plays have been less in vogue,[3] you see they write as
irregularly as we, though they cover it more speciously. Hence
the reason is perspicuous why no French plays, when translated,
have, or ever can succeed upon the English stage. For if you consider the plots, our own are fuller of variety; if the writing, ours
are more quick and fuller of spirit; and therefore 'tis a strange
mistake in those who decry the way of writing plays in verse, as
if the English therein imitated the French. We have borrowed
nothing from them; our plots are weaved in English looms:[4] we
endeavour therein to follow the variety and greatness of characters which are derived to us from Shakespeare and Fletcher;
the copiousness and well-knitting of the intrigues we have from
Jonson; and for the verse itself we have English precedents of
elder date than any of Corneille's plays: (not to name our old
comedies before Shakespeare, which were all writ in verse of
six feet, or alexandrines,[5] such as the French now use.) I can
show in Shakespeare many scenes of rhyme together, and the
like in Ben Jonson's tragedies: in *Catiline* and *Sejanus* sometimes

---

[1] 'on the subject of his sad,' *1684, 1693*.   [2] 'goes forward,' *1684, 1693*.
[3] Corneille's successful career as a dramatist had ended in 1653, with the
Pertharite, when Quinault, and later Racine, replaced him as public favourites.
[4] An empty boast, considering how many Restoration plays, including
several of Dryden's, derive their plots from French plays. His *Sir Martin
Mar-All* (1668), performed in August 1667, perhaps only a few weeks before
the appearance of the Essay, was rewritten from a bare translation by the
Duke of Newcastle of Molière's *L'étourdi*.
[5] George Peele, Robert Greene, and others had used pentameters in
comedy before Shakespeare. But some early Elizabethan comedies, e.g.
Gammer·Gurton's Needle (1575), were in hexameters.

thirty or forty lines, I mean besides the Chorus, or the monologues, which, by the way, showed Ben no enemy to this way of writing, especially if you look upon[1] his *Sad Shepherd*, which goes sometimes upon rhyme, sometimes upon blank verse, like an horse who eases himself upon trot and amble.[2] You find him likewise commending Fletcher's pastoral of *The Faithful Shepherdess*, which is for the most part rhyme, though not refined to that purity to which it hath since been brought. And these examples are enough to clear us from a servile imitation of the French.

'But to return from whence[3] I have digressed, I dare boldly affirm these two things of the English drama: first, that we have many plays of ours as regular as any of theirs, and which, besides, have more variety of plot and characters; and secondly, that in most of the irregular plays of Shakespeare or Fletcher (for Ben Jonson's are for the most part regular) there is a more masculine fancy and greater spirit in the writing than there is in any of the French. I could produce, even in Shakespeare's and Fletcher's works, some plays which are almost exactly formed; as *The Merry Wives of Windsor*, and *The Scornful Lady*;[4] but because (generally speaking) Shakespeare, who writ first, did not perfectly observe the laws of comedy, and Fletcher, who came nearer to perfection, yet through carelessness made many faults, I will take the pattern of a perfect play from Ben Jonson, who was a careful and learned observer of the dramatic laws, and from all his comedies I shall select *The Silent Woman*; of which I will make a short examen,[5] according to those rules which the French observe.'

As Neander was beginning to examine *The Silent Woman*,

[1] 'read,' *1684, 1693*.

[2] This sentence, much the loosest in its syntax in the whole Essay, seems peculiarly suited to the author-figure Neander, whose long interventions seem less studied than those of his adversaries.

[3] 'return whence,' *1684, 1693*.

[4] In Shakespeare's *The Merry Wives of Windsor* (1602), the action takes two days, in 'Windsor and the neighbourhood'; Beaumont and Fletcher's *The Scornful Lady* (1616), another prose comedy, occupies less than two days in London.

[5] The first recorded use of the word in English is by Philemon Holland in his translation of Suetonius, *The History of Twelve Caesars* (1606), 'To the Readers,' where he refers to 'the Examen and Review annexed to the end of all,' i.e. the errata list. This is probably a direct borrowing from the Latin, and hardly suggests naturalization: Dryden evidently takes the word afresh from the French of Corneille's *Théâtre* (1660).

Eugenius, looking earnestly upon him:[1] 'I beseech you, Neander,' said he, 'gratify the company and me in particular so far as, before you speak of the play, to give us a character of the author; and tell us frankly your opinion whether you do not think all writers, both French and English, ought to give place to him.'

'I fear,' replied Neander, 'that in obeying your commands I shall draw a little envy[2] upon myself. Besides, in performing them, it will be first necessary to speak somewhat of Shakespeare and Fletcher, his rivals in poesy; and one of them, in my opinion, at least his equal, perhaps his superior.

'To begin, then, with Shakespeare:[3] he was the man who of all modern, and perhaps ancient poets, had the largest and most comprehensive soul. All the images of nature were still present to him, and he drew them not laboriously, but luckily; when he describes any thing, you more than see it, you feel it too. Those who accuse him to have wanted learning[4] give him the greater commendation: he was naturally learned; he needed not the spectacles of books to read nature; he looked inwards, and found her there. I cannot say he is every where alike; were he so, I should do him injury to compare him with the greatest of mankind. He is many times flat, insipid; his comic wit degenerating into clenches, his serious swelling into bombast. But he is always great when some great occasion is presented to him; no man can say he ever had a fit subject for his wit, and did not then raise himself as high above the rest of poets,

> quantum lenta solent inter viburna cupressi.[5]

---

[1] 'earnestly regarding him,' *1684, 1693*.   [2] 'some envy,' *1684, 1693*.

[3] Johnson, in his Life of Dryden, calls the passage 'a perpetual model of ecomiastic criticism: exact without minuteness, and lofty without exaggeration.' Cf. vol. II, p. 284, below.

[4] E.g. Ben Jonson, whose plays contain veiled aspersions against Shakespeare's want of learning and decorum (p. 63, above). Cf. *Bartholomew Fair* (1631), Induction, ll. 127-32, and his commendatory verses 'To the Memory of my Beloved, the Author' in the First Folio of Shakespeare (1623), ll. 31-3:

> And though thou hadst small Latin, and less Greek,
> From thence [i.e. the Elizabethan dramatists] to honour thee, I would not seek
> For names; but call forth thundering Aeschylus. . . .

Dryden's encomium follows Jonson's closely throughout in its reverence for Shakespeare's genius and contempt for his lack of art.

[5] Virgil, *Eclogues*, I.25: 'as cypresses often do among bending osiers.'

The consideration of this made Mr Hales of Eton[1] say that there was no subject of which any poet ever writ, but he would produce it much better treated of[2] in Shakespeare; and however others are now generally preferred before him, yet the age wherein he lived, which had contemporaries with him Fletcher and Jonson, never equalled them to him in their esteem. And in the last King's court, when Ben's reputation was at highest,[3] Sir John Suckling, and with him the greater part of the courtiers, set our Shakespeare far above him.

'Beaumont and Fletcher, of whom I am next to speak, had, with the advantage of Shakespeare's wit, which was their precedent, great natural gifts improved by study; Beaumont especially being so accurate a judge of plays that Ben Jonson, while he lived, submitted all his writing to his censure, and, 'tis thought, used his judgment in correcting, if not contriving, all his plots. What value he had for him, appears by the verses he writ to him;[4] and therefore I need speak no farther of it. The first play which brought Fletcher and him in esteem was their *Philaster*:[5] for before that, they had written two or three very unsuccessfully, as the like is reported of Ben Jonson before he writ *Every Man in his Humour*.[6] Their plots were generally more regular than Shakespeare's, especially those which were made before Beaumont's death; and they understood and imitated the conversation of gentlemen much better; whose wild debaucheries, and quickness of wit in repartees, no poet can ever paint[7]

---

[1] John Hales (1584-1656), a Fellow of Eton College, whose *Golden Remains* were published posthumously in 1659.

[2] 'better done,' *1684, 1693*.

[3] I.e. in the reign of Charles I (1625-49). Cf. p. 54n., above.

[4] Epigram lv (in the 1616 folio of Jonson's *Works*):

> How I do love thee, Beaumont, and thy Muse,
> That unto me dost such religion use! . . .

But Jonson's unpublished comment on Beaumont in the *Conversations with William Drummond* (1833) that his friend and adviser 'loved too much himself and his own verses' disturbs Dryden's picture of untroubled friendship.

[5] First performed between 1608 and 1610 with great success, and published in 1620, *Philaster* marked the turning-point in the careers of the two collaborators after the relative failure of *The Woman Hater* (acted 1606?), *The Knight of the Burning Pestle* (acted 1607-10), and *Cupid's Revenge* (acted 1607-12).

[6] Jonson probably completed Nashe's *Isle of Dogs* in 1597 as a dramatic hack in Henslowe's pay, and was imprisoned for it. The performance of *Every Man in His Humour* in September 1598 established his reputation.

[7] 'before them could paint,' *1684, 1693*.

as they have done. This humour of which[1] Ben Jonson derived from particular persons, they made it not their business to describe: they represented all the passions very lively, but above all love. I am apt to believe the English language in them arrived to its highest perfection: what words have since been taken in, are rather superfluous than necessary.[2] Their plays are now the most pleasant and frequent entertainments of the stage;[3] two of theirs being acted through the year for one of Shakespeare's or Jonson's: the reason is because there is a certain gaiety in their comedies, and pathos in their more serious plays, which suits generally with all men's humours. Shakespeare's language is likewise a little obsolete, and Ben Jonson's wit comes short of theirs.

'As for Jonson, to whose character I am now arrived, if we look upon him while he was himself (for his last plays were but his dotages), I think him the most learned and judicious writer which any theatre ever had. He was a most severe judge of himself as well as others. One cannot say he wanted wit, but rather that he was frugal of it. In his works you find little to retrench or alter. Wit, and language, and humour also in some measure, we had before him; but something of art was wanting to the drama till he came. He managed his strength to more advantage than any who preceded him. You seldom find him making love in any of his scenes, or endeavouring to move the passions; his genius was too sullen and saturnine to do it gracefully, especially when he knew he came after those who had performed both to such an height. Humour was his proper sphere; and in that he delighted most to represent mechanic people. He was deeply conversant in the Ancients, both Greek and Latin, and he borrowed boldly from them: there is scarce a poet or historian among the Roman authors of those times whom he has not translated in *Sejanus* and *Catiline*. But he has done his robberies so openly that one may see he fears not to be taxed by any law. He invades authors like a monarch, and what would be theft in other poets is only victory in him. With the spoils of these writers he so represents old Rome to us, in its rites, ceremonies, and customs, that if one of their poets had written either

---

[1] 'Humour, which,' *1684, 1693*.   [2] 'than ornamental,' *1684, 1693*.
[3] Dryden's admiration for Beaumont and Fletcher is that of a young professional dramatist studious of public taste. Cf. p. 54n., above.

of his tragedies, we had seen less of it than in him. If there was
any fault in his language, 'twas that he weaved it too closely and
laboriously in his serious plays:[1] perhaps, too, he did a little too
much romanize our tongue, leaving the words which he translated
almost as much Latin as he found them: wherein, though he
learnedly followed the idiom of their language,[2] he did not
enough comply with ours. If I would compare him with
Shakespeare, I must acknowledge him the more correct poet,
but Shakespeare the greater wit. Shakespeare was the Homer,
or father of our dramatic poets; Jonson was the Virgil,
the pattern of elaborate writing; I admire him, but I love
Shakespeare. To conclude of him, as he has given us the most
correct plays, so in the precepts which he has laid down in his
Discoveries,[3] we have as many and profitable rules for perfecting
the stage as any wherewith the French can furnish us.

'Having thus spoken of the author, I proceed to the examination of his comedy, *The Silent Woman*.

Examen[4] of the Silent Woman.

'To begin first with the length of the action, it is so far from
exceeding the compass of a natural day that it takes not up an
artificial one. 'Tis all included in the limits of three hours and an
half, which is no more than is required for the presentment on
the stage.[5] A beauty perhaps not much observed; if it had, we
should not have looked on the Spanish translation of *Five Hours*[6]
with so much wonder. The scene of it is laid in London; the
latitude of place is almost as little as you can imagine: for it lies

---

[1] 'in his comedies especially,' *1684, 1693*.
[2] 'followed their language,' *1684, 1693*.
[3] The final sections of *Timber: or Discoveries*, first published posthumously in the 1640 folio of Jonson's *Works*, consist of rather fitful directions
for the writing of plays: but only patriotism could pretend that they equal
Corneille's Discours and Examens in scope and depth.
[4] Cf. p. 66n., above.
[5] The claim has little foundation in the text of the play. All that is certain
about the time-scheme is that it is confined to a single day. I.i. begins with
Clerimont dressing to go out, and the plot hinges upon the discovery, before
his marriage-night, that Morose's 'bride' is a boy; but there is nothing in
the play to contradict the view that the action may have represented twelve
hours or more.
[6] Sir Samuel Tuke, *Adventures of Five Hours* (1663); cf. p. 57n., above.

all within the compass of two houses, and after the first act in one.[1] The continuity of scenes is observed more than in any of our plays, excepting his own *Fox* and *Alchemist*. They are not broken above twice or thrice at most in the whole comedy;[2] and in the two best of Corneille's plays, the *Cid* and *Cinna*, they are interrupted once apiece.[3] The action of the play is entirely one; the end or aim of which is the settling Morose's estate on Dauphine. The intrigue of it is the greatest and most noble of any pure unmixed comedy in any language; you see in it many persons of various characters and humours, and all delightful: as first, Morose, or an old man, to whom all noise but his own talking is offensive. Some who would be thought critics say this humour of his is forced: but to remove that objection, we may consider him first to be naturally of a delicate hearing, as many are to whom all sharp sounds are unpleasant; and secondly, we may attribute much of it to the peevishness of his age, or the wayward authority of an old man in his own house, where he may make himself obeyed; and this the poet seems to allude to[4] in his name *Morose*.[5] Besides this, I am assured from divers persons that Ben Jonson was actually acquainted with such a man, one altogether as ridiculous as he is here represented. Others say it is not enough to find one man of such an humour; it must be common to more, and the more common the more natural. To prove this, they instance in the best of comical characters, Falstaff: there are many men resembling him; old, fat, merry, cowardly, drunken, amorous, vain, and lying. But to convince these people, I need but tell them that humour is the

---

[1] A more flagrant error than the misrepresentation of the time-scheme, above. There are six scenes of action, in or near three houses: a room in Clerimont's house (I.i.), a room in Morose's (II.i, iii, III.ii, IV.i, V.i), a room in Sir John Daw's (II.ii), a lane near Morose's house (II.iv), a room in Otter's house (III.i), and 'a long open gallery' in Morose's house (IV.ii). Dryden has clearly forgotten about the scenes in Daw's and Otter's houses altogether, and it is a clear inference that he had no copy of the play to hand. Cf. *Herford & Simpson*, X.1.

[2] The grossest error of all: there is not a single instance of *liaison des scènes* between any of the ten scenes that comprise it, i.e. there are nine breaks. The third act of *Volpone*, on the other hand, and the third act of *The Alchemist*, both illustrate the principle.

[3] 'interrupted once,' *1684, 1693*.

[4] 'to this the poet seems to allude,' *1684, 1693*.

[5] Dryden's naturalistic explanation of Morose's 'humour' seems uncomprehending and naïve. But his historical sense corrects the error almost at once with two admirable definitions of the Elizabethan theory of humours.

ridiculous extravagance of conversation, wherein one man differs
from all others.[1] If then it be common, or communicated, to
many, how differs it from other men's? or what indeed causes it
to be ridiculous so much as the singularity of it? As for Falstaff,
he is not properly one humour, but a miscellany of humours or
images, drawn from so many several men: that wherein he is
singular is his wit, or those things he says *præter expectatum*,
unexpected by the audience; his quick evasions when you imagine
him surprised, which, as they are extremely diverting of themselves, so receive a great addition from his person; for the very
sight of such an unwieldy, old, debauched fellow is a comedy
alone. And here, having a place so proper for it, I cannot but
enlarge somewhat upon this subject of humour into which I am
fallen. The Ancients had little of it in their comedies; for the
τὸ γελοῖον[2] of the Old Comedy, of which Aristophanes was
chief, was not so much to imitate a man as to make the people
laugh at some odd conceit which had commonly somewhat of
unnatural or obscene in it. Thus, when you see Socrates brought
upon the stage, you are not to imagine him made ridiculous by
the imitation of his actions, but rather by making him perform
something very unlike himself: something so childish and absurd
as, by comparing it with the gravity of the true Socrates,
makes a ridiculous object for the spectators.[3] In their New

[1] This, and the following account of the Jonsonian humour, is no doubt
based on Jonson's own account in the Induction ll. 98-109, to *Every Man
out of His Humour* (1600), with the omission of Jonson's outdated medieval
theory of man's four fluid temperaments:

> In every human body
> The choler, melancholy, phlegm, and blood
> By reason that they flow continually
> In some one part, and are not continent,
> Receive the name of humours. Now, thus far
> It may, by metaphor, apply itself
> Unto the general disposition:
> As when some one peculiar quality
> Doth so possess a man that it doth draw
> All his affects, his spirits, and his powers,
> In their confluctions all to run one way,
> This may be truly said to be a humour.

[2] Aristotle, *Poetics*, ch. V: 'the ridiculous.'

[3] An echo of Ben Jonson, *Timber (Herford & Simpson*, VIII, 644):
'Jests that are true and natural seldom raise laughter with the beast, the
multitude. They love nothing than is right and proper. The farther it runs
from reason or probability with them, the better it is. What could have made
them laugh like to see Socrates presented, that example of all good life.

Comedy,[1] which succeeded, the poets sought indeed to express the ἦθος, as in their tragedies the πάθος[2] of mankind. But this ἦθος contained only the general characters of men and manners; as old men, lovers, serving-men, courtesans, parasites, and such other persons as we see in their comedies; all which they made alike: that is, one old man or father, one lover, one courtesan, so like another as if the first of them had begot the rest of every sort: *ex homine hunc natum dicas*.[3] The same custom they observed likewise in their tragedies. As for the French, though they have the word *humeur* among them,[4] yet they have small use of it in their comedies or farces; they being but ill imitations of the *ridiculum*, or that which stirred up laughter in the Old Comedy. But among the English 'tis otherwise: where by humour is meant some extravagant habit, passion, or affection, particular (as I said before) to some one person, by the oddness of which he is immediately distinguished from the rest of men; which being lively and naturally represented, most frequently begets that malicious pleasure in the audience which is testified by laughter; as all things which are deviations from common customs[5] are ever the aptest to produce it: though, by the way, this laughter is only accidental, as the person represented is fantastic or bizarre; but pleasure is essential to it, as the imitation of what is natural. The description of these humours, drawn from the knowledge and observation of particular persons, was the peculiar genius and talent of Ben Jonson; to whose play I now return.

'Besides Morose, there are at least nine or ten different

honesty, and virtue, hoisted up with a pulley, and there play the philosopher in a basket.' Cf. Aristophanes, *Clouds*, ll. 218f., where Socrates appears suspended in a swing, announcing grandly: 'I tread the air, and look down on the sun.' κρεμάθρα means not 'basket' (as Jonson and Dryden supposed), but more probably a hook and rope, and Aristophanes's satire on the *deus ex machina* of Greek drama ought to have appealed to them both.

[1] The New Comedy of Menander (*c.* 342-291 B.C.), the immediate source of the Latin comedy of Plautus and Terence, replaced the personal and social satire of Aristophanes with a tradition of conventional character-types.

[2] 'character,' 'emotion,' the former (according to Butcher) signifying 'the permanent dispositions of the mind,' the latter 'the more transient emotions, the passing moods of feeling.'

[3] Terence, *Eunuch*, l. 460: 'one the very image of the other.'

[4] Neander is straining the facts in search of an antithesis. 'Humeur' certainly had the same sense of 'temperament' in seventeenth-century French as in Jonson, and Molière's earlier comedies, *Les précieuses ridicules* (1659) and *L'école des femmes* (1662) certainly include characters moved by 'some extravagant habit, passion, or affectation.'

[5] 'from customs,' *1684, 1693*.

characters and humours in *The Silent Woman*,[1] all which persons
have several concernments of their own, yet are all used by the
poet to the conducting of the main design to perfection. I shall
not waste time in commending the writing of this play, but I
will give you my opinion that there is more wit and acuteness of
fancy in it than in any of Ben Jonson's. Besides, that he has here
described the conversation of gentlemen in the persons of True-
Wit[2] and his friends, with more gaiety, air, and freedom, than
in the rest of his comedies. For the contrivance of the plot, 'tis
extreme elaborate, and yet withal easy; for the λύσις,[3] or untying
of it, 'tis so admirable that, when it is done, no one of the audience
would think the poet could have missed it; and yet it was con-
cealed so much before the last scene that any other way would
sooner have entered into your thoughts. But I dare not take
upon me to commend the fabric of it, because it is altogether so
full of art that I must unravel every scene in it to commend it as
I ought. And this excellent contrivance is still the more to be
admired because 'tis comedy, where the persons are only of
common rank, and their business private, not elevated by
passions or high concernments as in serious plays. Here every
one is a proper judge of all he sees; nothing is represented but
that with which he daily converses: so that by consequence all
faults lie open to discovery, and few are pardonable. 'Tis this
which Horace has judiciously observed:

> creditur, ex medio quia res arcessit, habere
> sudoris minimum; sed habet Comedia tanto
> plus oneris, quanto veniæ minus.[4]

But our poet, who was not ignorant of these difficulties, had
prevailed himself[5] of all advantages; as he who designs a large
leap takes his rise from the highest ground. One of these
advantages is that which Corneille has laid down as the greatest
which can arrive to any poem, and which he himself could

---

[1] Apart from Morose, the play calls for sixteen speaking parts.
[2] Cf. p. 150, below.
[3] *1668* has δέσις, corrected *1684*, *1693*. The resolution in Act V is the
revelation to Morose by Dauphine that his uncle's bride, Epicoene, is in fact
a boy.
[4] *Epistles*, II.i.168-70: 'It is thought that comedy, since it draws its
subjects from our daily life, calls for little labour; but it calls for more, in
proportion as less indulgence is shown.'
[5] 'has made use,' *1684*, *1693*.

never compass above thrice[1] in all his plays; viz. the making choice of some signal and long-expected day, whereon the action of the play is to depend. This day was that designed by Dauphine for the settling of his uncle's estate upon him; which to compass, he contrives to marry him. That the marriage had been plotted by him long beforehand is made evident by what he tells True-Wit in the second act, that in one moment he had destroyed what he had been raising many months.[2]

'There is another artifice of the poet which I cannot here omit, because by the frequent practice of it in his comedies he has left it to us almost as a rule: that is, when he has any character or humour wherein he would show a *coup de maistre*, or his highest skill, he recommends it to your observation by a pleasant description of it before the person first appears. Thus, in *Bartholomew Fair* he gives you the pictures of Numps and Cokes, and in this those of Daw, Lafoole, Morose, and the Collegiate Ladies; all which you hear described before you see them. So that before they come upon the stage you have a longing expectation of them, which prepares you to receive them favourably; and when they are there, even from their first appearance you are so far acquainted with them that nothing of their humour is lost to you.

'I will observe yet one thing further of this admirable plot: the business of it rises in every act. The second is greater than the first, the third than the second, and so forward to the fifth. There too you see, till the very last scene, new difficulties arising to obstruct the action of the play; and when the audience is brought into despair that the business can naturally be effected,

[1] A misreading of Corneille which proves Dryden must have used the first edition of Corneille's *Théâtre* (1660) rather than the revised editions of 1663 and 1664. The 1660 text of the 'Discours des trois unités' reads: 'Dans mes deux premiers volumes, vous n'en trouverez de cette nature que celui d'*Horace*. . . . Ce dernier en a trois: celui de *Rodogune*, d'*Andromède*, et de *Don Sanche*'. The word 'trois' refers to the number of plays enacted on a 'long-expected day' which occur in vol. III of the *Théâtre*, the total number (including *Horace*) being four. In *1663* and *1664* the passage was revised by Corneille to read: 'Dans tout ce que j'ai fait ici, vous n'en trouverez de cette nature que quatre: celui d'*Horace*, . . . celui de *Rodogune*, d'*Andromède*, et de *Don Sanche*.' Cf. L. E. Padgett, 'Dryden's Edition of Corneille', *Modern Language Notes*, lxxi (1956).

[2] *Epicoene*, II.iv: 'That which I have plotted for, and been maturing now these four months, you have blasted in a minute.'

then, and not before, the discovery is made. But that the poet might entertain you with more variety all this while, he reserves some new characters to show you, which he opens not till the second and third act. In the second, Morose, Daw, the Barber, and Otter; in the third, the Collegiate Ladies: all which he moves afterwards in by-walks, or under-plots, as diversions to the main design, lest it should grow tedious, though they are still naturally joined with it, and somewhere or other subservient to it. Thus, like a skilful chess-player, by little and little he draws out his men, and makes his pawns of use to his greater persons.

'If this comedy, and some others, of his were translated into French prose (which would now be no wonder to them, since Molière has lately given them plays out of verse which have not displeased them[1]), I believe the controversy would soon be decided betwixt the two nations, even making them the judges. But we need not call our heroes to our aid; be it spoken to the honour of the English, our nation can never want in any age such who are able to dispute the empire of wit with any people in the universe. And though the fury of a civil war, and power for twenty years together abandoned to a barbarous race of men, enemies of all good learning, had buried the Muses under the ruins of monarchy; yet, with the restoration of our happiness, we see revived poesy lifting up its head, and already shaking off the rubbish which lay so heavy on it. We have seen since his Majesty's return many dramatic poems which yield not to those of any foreign nation, and which deserve all laurels but the English. I will set aside flattery and envy: it cannot be denied but we have had some little blemish either in the plot or writing of all those plays which have been made within these seven years[2] (and perhaps there is no nation in the world so quick to discern them, or so difficult to pardon them, as ours): yet if we can persuade ourselves to use the candour of that poet who (though the most

[1] Molière had in fact written in prose from the beginning of his career as a dramatist, e.g. in the one-act Les précieuses ridicules (1659) and L'impromptu de Versailles (1663). Dryden may be thinking of his Dom Juan (1665), his first five-act prose play.

[2] This passage, at least, was evidently written or revised as late as 1667, shortly before the publication of the Essay, and not in Wiltshire in 1665-6. Dryden's praise for English drama between 1660 and 1667 seems extravagant when we recall that it could boast no greater names than Orrery, Howard, and Thomas Killigrew.

severe of critics) has left us this caution by which to moderate our censures:

> ubi plura nitent in carmine, non ego paucis
> offendar maculis;[1]

if, in consideration of their many and great beauties, we can wink at some slight and little imperfections; if we, I say, can be thus equal to ourselves, I ask no favour from the French. And if I do not venture upon any particular judgment of our late plays, 'tis out of the consideration which an ancient writer gives me: *vivorum, ut magna admiratio, ita censura difficilis:*[2] betwixt the extremes of admiration and malice, 'tis hard to judge uprightly of the living. Only I think it may be permitted me to say that as it is no lessening to us to yield to some plays, and those not many, of our own nation in the last age, so can it be no addition to pronounce of our present poets that they have far surpassed all the Ancients, and the modern writers of other countries.'

This, my Lord,[3] was the substance of what was then spoke on that occasion; and Lisideius, I think, was going to reply, when he was prevented thus by Crites:[4] 'I am confident,' said he, 'that the most material things that can be said have been already urged on either side; if they have not, I must beg to Lisideius that he will defer his answer till another time: for I confess I have a joint quarrel to you both, because you have concluded, without any reason given for it, that rhyme is proper for the stage. I will not dispute how ancient it hath been among us to write this way; perhaps our ancestors knew no better till Shakespeare's time. I will grant it was not altogether left by him, and that Fletcher and Ben Jonson used it frequently in their pastorals, and sometimes in other plays. Farther, I will not argue

---

[1] Horace, *Ars poetica*, ll. 351-2: 'When there are many beauties in a poem, it will not be I who find fault with its few blemishes.'

[2] Velleius Paterculus, *Historia romana*, II.36.   [3] 'This,' *1684, 1693*.

[4] Crites's attack on rhyme, as he protests at the end, is cut short by the reflection that, as Sir Robert Howard, he has already published his objections in the preface to *Four New Plays* (1665). This is the frankest moment of identification in the whole Essay, and one well calculated to provoke Howard into an angry reply—the more so because it is used as an excuse for abbreviating Crites's case against rhyme in favour of Neander's defence of it. Some of the language of this speech, the shortest of the six, is nevertheless reminiscent of Howard's preface.

whether we received it originally from our own countrymen, or from the French; for that is an inquiry of as little benefit as theirs who, in the midst of the great plague,[1] were not so solicitous to provide against it as to know whether we had it from the malignity of our own air, or by transportation from Holland. I have therefor only to affirm that it is not allowable in serious plays; for comedies, I find you already concluding with me. To prove this, I might satisfy myself to tell you how much in vain it is for you to strive against the stream of the people's inclination, the greatest part of which are prepossessed so much with those excellent plays of Shakespeare, Fletcher, and Ben Jonson (which have been written out of rhyme) that except you could bring them such as were written better in it, and those too by persons of equal reputation with them, it will be impossible for you to gain your cause with them who will still be judges. This it is to which, in fine, all your reasons must submit. The unanimous consent of an audience is so powerful than even Julius Cæsar (as Macrobius[2] reports of him), when he was perpetual dictator, was not able to balance it on the other side. But when Laberius, a Roman knight, at his request contended in the mime with another poet, he was forced to cry out, *etiam favente me victus es, Laberi.*[3] But I will not on this occasion take the advantage of the greater number, but only urge such reasons against rhyme as I find in the writings of those who have argued for the other way. First, then, I am of opinion that rhyme is unnatural in a play, because dialogue there is presented as the effect of sudden thought. For a play is the imitation of nature; and since no man without premeditation speaks in rhyme, neither ought he to do it on the stage. This hinders not but the fancy may be there elevated to an higher pitch of thought than it is in ordinary discourse; for there is a probability that men of excellent and quick parts may speak noble things *ex tempore*: but those thoughts are never fettered with the numbers or sound of verse without study, and therefore it cannot be but unnatural to present the most free way of speaking in that which is the most constrained. For this

[1] 'the late plague,' *1684, 1693.* In either version the allusion is an obvious anachronism, since the Essay is supposed to be set in June 1665, when the plague had scarcely begun.
[2] *Saturnalia,* II.7.
[3] 'you have been beaten, Laberius, for all my favour.' The winning poet was Publilius Syrus.

reason, says Aristotle,[1] 'tis best to write tragedy in that kind of verse which is the least such, or which is nearest prose: and this amongst the Ancients was the iambic, and with us is blank verse, or the measure of verse kept exactly without rhyme. These numbers therefore are fittest for a play; the others for a paper of verses or a poem; blank verse being as much below them as rhyme is improper for the drama. And if it be objected that neither are blank verses made *ex tempore*, yet, as nearest nature, they are still to be preferred. But there are two particular exceptions which many besides myself have had to verse; by which it will appear yet more plainly how improper it is in plays. And the first of them is grounded on that very reason for which some have commended rhyme: they say the quickness of repartees in argumentative scenes receives an ornament from verse. Now what is more unreasonable than to imagine that a man should not only light upon the wit,[2] but the rhyme too upon the sudden? This nicking[3] of him who spoke before, both in sound and measure, is so great an happiness that you must at least suppose the persons of your play to be born poets, *Arcades omnes, et cantare pares, et respondere parati*,[4] they must have arrived to the degree of *quicquid conabar dicere*:[5] to make verses almost whether they will or no. If they are any thing below this, it will look rather like the design of two than the answer of one: it will appear that your actors hold intelligence together, that they perform their tricks like fortune-tellers, by confederacy. The hand of art will be too visible in it against that maxim of all professions, *ars est celare artem*,[6] that it is the greatest perfection of art to keep itself undiscovered. Nor will it serve you to object that, however you manage it, 'tis still known to be a play; and, consequently, the dialogue of two persons understood to be the labour of one poet. For a play is still an imitation of nature; we know we are to be deceived, and we desire to be so; but no man ever was deceived but with a probability of truth, for who will

[1] *Poetics*, ch. iv: 'The iambic is the most colloquial of metres; this appears in the fact that ordinary speech falls into iambics more readily than into any other kind of verse.'

[2] 'not only imagine the wit,' *1684, 1693*.

[3] I.e. hitting precisely, matching.

[4] Virgil, *Eclogues*, vii, 4-5 ('Arcades ambo, . . .'): 'all Arcadians, ready both to sing and to make reply.'

[5] Perhaps a corruption of Ovid, *Tristia*, IV.10.26.

[6] The familiar tag is of no known authorship.

suffer a gross lie to be fastened on him? Thus we sufficiently understand that the scenes which represent cities and countries to us are not really such, but only painted on boards and canvas: but shall that excuse the ill painture or designment of them? Nay, rather ought they not to be laboured with so much the more diligence and exactness, to help the imagination? since the mind of man does naturally tend to, and seek after truth;[1] and therefore the nearer any thing comes to the imitation of it, the more it pleases.

'Thus, you see, your rhyme is uncapable of expressing the greatest thoughts naturally, and the lowest it cannot with any grace: for what is more unbefitting the majesty of verse than to call a servant, or bid a door be shut, in rhyme? And yet this miserable necessity you are forced upon.[2] But verse, you say, circumscribes a quick and luxuriant fancy, which would extend itself too far on every subject, did not the labour which is required to well turned and polished rhyme set bounds to it. Yet this argument, if granted, would only prove that we may write better in verse, but not more naturally. Neither is it able to evince that: for he who wants judgment to confine his fancy in blank verse, may want it as much in rhyme: and he who has it will avoid errors in both kinds. Latin verse was as great a confinement to the imagination of those poets as rhyme to ours; and yet you find Ovid saying too much on every subject. *Nescivit* (says Seneca) *quod bene cessit relinquere:*[3] of which he gives you one famous instance in his description of the deluge:

> omnia pontus erat, deerant quoque litora ponto.
> Now all was sea, nor had that sea a shore.

Thus Ovid's fancy was not limited by verse, and Virgil needed not verse to have bounded his.

'In our own language we see Ben Jonson confining himself to what ought to be said, even in the liberty of blank verse; and yet Corneille, the most judicious of the French poets, is still

---

[1] 'tend to truth,' *1684, 1693*.
[2] 'you are often forced on this miserable necessity,' *1684, 1693*.
[3] A confusion of two sources: it was Marcus Seneca the rhetorician, in his *Controversiae*, ix.5, who said of Ovid: 'nescit quod bene cessit relinquere' ('he does not know when to leave well enough alone')—but he cited *Metamorphoses*, xiii.503-5. 'omnia pontus erat. . . .' (*ibid.*, i.292) was quoted by the philosopher Lucius Seneca in his *Quaestiones naturales*, iii.27 and singled out for praise.

varying the same sense an hundred ways, and dwelling eternally on the same subject, though confined by rhyme. Some other exceptions I have to verse; but being these[1] I have named are for the most part already public, I conceive it reasonable they should first be answered.'

'It concerns me less than any,' said Neander (seeing he had ended), 'to reply to this discourse; because when I should have proved that verse may be natural in plays, yet I should always be ready to confess that those which I have written in this kind come short of that perfection which is required. Yet since you are pleased I should undertake this province, I will do it, though with all imaginable respect and deference both to that person[2] from whom you have borrowed your strongest arguments, and to whose judgment, when I have said all, I finally submit. But before I proceed to answer your objections, I must first remember you that I exclude all comedy from my defence; and next that I deny not but blank verse may be also used, and content myself only to assert that in serious plays, where the subject and characters are great, and the plot unmixed with mirth, which might allay or divert these concernments which are produced, rhyme is there as natural, and more effectual than blank verse.

'And now having laid down this as a foundation, to begin with Crites, I must crave leave to tell him that some of his arguments against rhyme reach no farther than, from the faults or defects of ill rhyme, to conclude against the use of it in general. May not I conclude against blank verse by the same reason? If the words of some poets who write in it are either ill chosen, or ill placed (which makes not only rhyme, but all kind of verse in any language unnatural) shall I, for their vicious affectation, condemn those excellent lines of Fletcher which are written in that kind? Is there any thing in rhyme more constrained than this line in blank verse?

I heaven invoke, and strong resistance make?[3]

where you see both the clauses are placed unnaturally, that is, contrary to the common way of speaking, and that without the

---

[1] 'but since these,' *1684, 1693*.

[2] The text here, which all the early editions have in common, may well be corrupt. Nichol Smith suggests 'both to you and to that person'; but 'both' might refer back to 'respect and deference.' Nor is it obvious to whom 'that person' refers: it may be Aristotle.

[3] Probably an illustration invented for the occasion.

excuse of a rhyme to cause it: yet you would think me very ridiculous if I should accuse the stubbornness of blank verse for this, and not rather the stiffness of the poet. Therefore, Crites, you must either prove that words, though well chosen and duly placed, yet render not rhyme natural in itself; or that, however natural and easy the rhyme may be, yet it is not proper for a play. If you insist on the former part, I would ask you what other conditions are required to make rhyme natural in itself, besides an election of apt words, and a right disposing[1] of them? For the due choice of your words expresses your sense naturally, and the due placing them adapts the rhyme to it. If you object that one verse may be made for the sake of another, though both the words and rhyme be apt, I answer it cannot possibly so fall out; for either there is a dependence of sense betwixt the first line and the second, or there is none: if there be that connection, then in the natural position of the words the latter line must of necessity flow from the former; if there be no dependence, yet still the due ordering of words makes the last line as natural in itself as the other: so that the necessity of a rhyme never forces any but bad or lazy writers to say what they would not otherwise. 'Tis true, there is both care and art required to write in verse. A good poet never concludes upon[2] the first line till he has sought out such a rhyme as may fit the sense, already prepared to heighten the second: many times the close of the sense falls into the middle of the next verse, or farther off, and he may often prevail himself of the same advantages in English which Virgil had in Latin: he may break off in the hemistich, and begin another line. Indeed, the not observing these two last things makes plays which are writ in verse so tedious: for though, most commonly, the sense is to be confined to the couplet, yet nothing that does *perpetuo tenore fluere*,[3] run in the same channel, can please always. 'Tis like the murmuring of a stream which, not varying in the fall, causes at first attention, at last drowsiness. Variety of cadences is the best rule, the greatest help to the actors, and refreshment to the audience.

'If then verse may be made natural in itself, how becomes it improper to[4] a play? You say the stage is the representation of nature, and no man in ordinary conversation speaks in rhyme.

¹ 'disposition,' *1684, 1693*.   ² 'establishes,' *1684, 1693*.
³ Cicero, *De oratore*, vi.21.   ⁴ 'unnatural in,' *1684, 1693*.

But you foresaw when you said this that it might be answered: neither does any man speak in blank verse, or in measure without rhyme. Therefore you concluded that which is nearest nature is still to be preferred. But you took no notice that rhyme might be made as natural as blank verse by the well placing of the words, &c. All the difference between them, when they are both correct, is the sound in one, which the other wants; and if so, the sweetness of it, and all the advantage resulting from it, which are handled in the preface to *The Rival Ladies*,[1] will yet stand good. As for that place of Aristotle, where he says plays should be writ in that kind of verse which is nearest prose, it makes little for you, blank verse being properly but measured prose. Now measure alone, in any modern language, does not constitute verse; those of the Ancients in Greek and Latin consisted in quantity of words, and a determinate number of feet. But when, by the inundation of the Goths and Vandals into Italy, new languages were brought in,[2] and barbarously mingled with the Latin (of which the Italian, Spanish, French, and ours, made out of them and the Teutonic, are dialects), a new way of poesy was practised; new, I say, in those countries, for in all probability it was that of the conquerors in their own nations.[3] This new way consisted in measure, or number of feet, and rhyme; the sweetness of rhyme, and observation of accent, supplying the place of quantity in words, which could neither exactly be observed by those barbarians, who knew not the rules of it, neither was it suitable to their tongues, as it had been to the Greek and Latin. No man is tied in modern poesy to observe any farther rule in the feet of his verse, but that they be dissyllables; whether spondee, trochee, or iambic, it matters not; only he is obliged to rhyme. Neither do the Spanish, French, Italian, or Germans acknowledge at all, or very rarely, any such kind of poesy as blank verse amongst them.[4] Therefore, at most

---

[1] Cf. pp. 8-9, above.   [2] 'introduced,' *1684, 1693*.

[3] *1684, 1693* add: 'at least we are able to prove that the eastern people have used it from all antiquity. *Vid.* Dan. his *Defence of Rhyme.*' Cf. Samuel Daniel, *Defence* (1603): 'Georgienez, *De Turcarum moribus*, hath an example of the Turkish rhymes just of the measure of our verse of eleven syllables, in feminine rhyme: never begotten, I am persuaded, by any example in Europe, but born no doubt in Scythia, and brought over Caucasus and Mount Taurus.'

[4] This claim is substantially if not precisely true, though (as Ker suggests) the *versi sciolti* of Italian tragedies and Tasso's *Aminta* are left out of account.

'tis but a poetic prose, a *sermo pedestris*; and as such, most fit for comedies, where I acknowledge rhyme to be improper. Farther, as to that quotation of Aristotle, our couplet verses may be rendered as near prose as blank verse itself, by using those advantages I lately named, as breaks in a[1] hemistich, or running the sense into another line, thereby making art and order appear as loose and free as nature: or not tying ourselves to couplets strictly, we may use the benefit of the Pindaric way practised in *The Siege of Rhodes*;[2] where the numbers vary, and the rhyme is disposed carelessly, and far from often chiming. Neither is that other advantage of the Ancients to be despised, of changing the kind of verse when they please with the change of the scene, or some new entrance; for they confine not themselves always to iambics, but extend their liberty to all lyric numbers, and sometimes even to hexameter. But I need not go so far to prove that rhyme, as it succeeds to all other offices of Greek and Latin verse, so especially to this of plays, since the custom of all nations[3] at this day confirms it: all the French,[4] Italian, and Spanish tragedies[5] are generally writ in it; and sure the universal consent of the most civilized parts of the world ought in this, as it doth in other customs, to[6] include the rest.

'But perhaps you may tell me I have proposed such a way to make rhyme natural, and consequently proper to plays, as is unpracticable, and that I shall scarce find six or eight lines together in any play, where the words are so placed and chosen as is required to make it natural. I answer, no poet need constrain himself at all times to it. It is enough he makes it his general rule; for I deny not but sometimes there may be a greatness in placing the words otherwise; and sometimes they may sound better, sometimes also the variety itself is excuse enough. But if, for the most part, the words be placed as they are in the negligence of prose, it is sufficient to denominate the way practicable; for we esteem that to be such, which in the trial oftener succeeds

---

[1] 'an,' *1684, 1693*.

[2] Davenant's opera and heroic play, performed in 1656 and published, expanded into ten acts, in 1663. The fashion for 'Pindaric' verses of unequal length was also popularized by Cowley's Pindaric Odes, published in his *Poems* (1656).

[3] 'of nations,' *1684, 1693*.   [4] 'the French,' *1684, 1693*.

[5] This is generally true—though the Spaniards employed assonance freely in place of rhyme.

[6] The careless omission of 'to' in *1668* is rectified in *1684, 1693*.

than misses. And thus far you may find the practice made good
in many plays: where you do not, remember still that if you
cannot find six natural rhymes together, it will be as hard for
you to produce as many lines in blank verse, even among the
greatest of our poets, against which I cannot make some reasonable exception.

'And this, Sir, calls to my remembrance the beginning of your
discourse, where you told us we should never find the audience
favourable to this kind of writing till we could produce as good
plays in rhyme as Ben Jonson, Fletcher, and Shakespeare had
writ out of it. But it is to raise envy to the living, to compare
them with the dead. They are honoured, and almost adored by
us, as they deserve; neither do I know any so presumptuous of
themselves as to contend with them. Yet give me leave to say
thus much, without injury to their ashes, that not only we shall
never equal them, but they could never equal themselves, were
they to rise and write again. We acknowledge them our fathers
in wit; but they have ruined their estates themselves before
they came to their children's hands. There is scarce an humour, a
character, or any kind of plot, which they have not blown upon:[1]
all comes sullied or wasted to us: and were they to entertain this
age, they could not make[2] so plenteous treatments out of such
decayed fortunes. This therefore will be a good argument to us
either not to write at all, or to attempt some other way. There is
no bays to be expected in their walks: *tentanda via est, qua me
quoque possum tollere humo.*[3]

'This way of writing in verse they have only left free to us;
our age is arrived to a perfection in it which they never knew;
and which, if we may guess by what of theirs we have seen in
verse (as *The Faithful Shepherdess*, and *Sad Shepherd*[4]) 'tis probable they never could have reached. For the genius of every age
is different;[5] and though ours excel in this, I deny not but that

---

[1] 'used,' *1684, 1693*.   [2] 'could not now make,' *1684, 1693*.

[3] Virgil, *Georgics*, III.8-9 (for *possum* read *possim*): 'I must try a way
whereby I, too, may rise from the earth.'

[4] Ben Jonson's *The Sad Shepherd*, a late, unfinished pastoral play, is
partly in rhyme, like John Fletcher's first play *The Faithful Shepherdess*
(acted 1608-9).

[5] A remark which suggests Dryden's casual, but significant, contribution
to the growth of an historical sense in criticism. Francis Bacon had called for
the study of literary history—or rather, of the complete intellectual history
of man, 'a just story of learning', in his *The Advancement of Learning* (1605).

to imitate nature in that perfection which they did in prose, is a greater commendation than to write in verse exactly. As for what you have added, that the people are not generally inclined to like this way; if it were true, it would be no wonder that betwixt the shaking off an old habit, and the introducing of a new, there should be difficulty. Do we not see them stick to Hopkins' and Sternhold's psalms, and forsake those of David, I mean Sandys his translation of them?[1] If by the people you understand the multitude, the οἱ πολλοί, 'tis no matter what they think; they are sometimes in the right, sometimes in the wrong; their judgment is a mere lottery. *Est ubi rectè putat, est ubi peccat.*[2] Horace says it of the vulgar, judging poesy. But if you mean the mixed audience of the populace and the noblesse, I dare confidently affirm that a great part of the latter sort are already favourable to verse; and that no serious plays written since the King's return have been more kindly received by them than *The Siege of Rhodes*, the *Mustapha*,[3] *The Indian Queen*, and *Indian Emperor*.

'But I come now to the inference of your first argument. You said[4] the dialogue of plays is presented as the effect of sudden thought, but no man speaks suddenly, or *ex tempore*, in rhyme; and you inferred from thence that rhyme, which you acknowledge to be proper to epic poesy, cannot equally be proper to dramatic, unless we could suppose all men born so much more than poets that verses should be made in them, not by them.

'It has been formerly urged by you, and confessed by me, that since no man spoke any kind of verse *ex tempore*, that which was nearest nature was to be preferred. I answer you, therefore, by distinguishing betwixt what is nearest to the nature of comedy,

II (cf. his expansion of this passage in *De augmentis scientiarum* (1623), II.iv). But Bacon did not have a high enough opinion of poetry to make him a serious pioneer of literary history—'it is not good to stay too long in the theatre'—and Dryden's claim to be considered the father of English literary history, unsystematic though his historical interests were, is stronger.

[1] The metrical version of the Psalms by Thomas Sternhold (1500-49) and John Hopkins (d. 1570) was first published in 1549 and enjoyed great popularity till the nineteenth century. *A Paraphrase upon the Psalms* (1636) by George Sandys (1578-1644), though vastly superior, never equalled it in favour.

[2] Horace, *Epistles*, II.i.63 (*interdum vulgus rectum videt, est ubi peccat*): 'It is where the common people think they are right that they are wrong.'

[3] One of the heroic plays of Roger Boyle, Earl of Orrery (cf. p. 1, above). It was produced in 1665.

[4] 'said that,' *1684, 1693.*

which is the imitation of common persons and ordinary speaking, and what is nearest the nature of a serious play: this last is indeed the representation of nature, but 'tis nature wrought up to an higher pitch. The plot, the characters, the wit, the passions, the descriptions, are all exalted above the level of common converse, as high as the imagination of the poet can carry them with proportion to verisimility. Tragedy, we know, is wont to image to us the minds and fortunes of noble persons, and to portray these exactly; heroic rhyme is nearest nature, as being the noblest kind of modern verse.

> indignatur enim privatis et prope socco
> dignis carminibus narrari cæna Thyestæ,[1]

(says Horace). And in another place,

> effutire leves indigna tragœdia versus.[2]

Blank verse is acknowledged to be too low for a poem, nay more, for a paper of verses; but if too low for an ordinary sonnet, how much more for tragedy, which is by Aristotle, in the dispute betwixt the epic poesy and the dramatic, for many reasons he there alleges, ranked above it?

'But setting this defence aside, your argument is almost as strong against the use of rhyme in poems as in plays; for the epic way is every where interlaced with dialogue, or discoursive scenes; and therefore you must either grant rhyme to be improper there, which is contrary to your assertion, or admit it into plays by the same title which you have given it to poems. For though tragedy be justly preferred above the other, yet there is a great affinity between them, as may easily be discovered in that definition of a play which Lisideius gave us. The genus of them is the same, a just and lively image of human nature, in its actions, passions, and traverses of fortune: so is the end, namely for the delight and benefit of mankind. The characters and persons are still the same, viz. the greatest of both sorts; only the manner of acquainting us with those actions, passions, and fortunes, is different. Tragedy performs it *viva voce*, or by action, in dialogue; wherein it excels the epic poem, which does it chiefly by narration, and therefore is not so lively an image of

---

[1] Horace, *Ars poetica*, ll. 90-1: 'For Thyestes' supper scorns to be treated in the language of common life, language unworthy of the tragic style.'
[2] *Ibid.*, l. 231: 'Tragedy thinks it unworthy to chatter silly verses.'

human nature. However, the agreement betwixt them is such that, if rhyme be proper for one, it must be for the other. Verse, 'tis true, is not the effect of sudden thought; but this hinders not that sudden thought may be represented in verse, since those thoughts are such as must be higher than nature can raise them without premeditation, especially to a continuance of them, even out of verse; and consequently you cannot imagine them to have been sudden either in the poet or in the actors. A play, as I have said, to be like nature, is to be set above it; as statues which are placed on high are made greater than the life, that they may descend to the sight in their just proportion.

'Perhaps I have insisted too long upon this objection; but the clearing of it will make my stay shorter on the rest. You tell us, Crites, that rhyme appears most unnatural in repartees, or short replies: when he who answers, it being presumed he knew not what the other would say, yet makes up that part of the verse which was left incomplete, and supplies both the sound and measure of it. This, you say, looks rather like the confederacy of two than the answer of one.

'This, I confess, is an objection which is in every one's[1] mouth, who loves not rhyme: but suppose, I beseech you, the repartee were made only in blank verse, might not part of the same argument be turned against you? For the measure is as often supplied there as it is in rhyme; the latter half of the hemistich as commonly made up, or a second line subjoined as a reply to the former; which any one leaf in Jonson's plays will sufficiently clear to you. You will often find in the Greek tragedians, and in Seneca, that when a scene grows up into the warmth of repartees (which is the close fighting of it) the latter part of the trimeter is supplied by him who answers; and yet it was never observed as a fault in them by any of the ancient or modern critics. The case is the same in our verse as it was in theirs; rhyme to us being in lieu of quantity to them. But if no latitude is to be allowed a poet, you take from him not only his licence of *quidlibet audendi*,[2] but you tie him up in a straiter compass than you would a philosopher. This is indeed *Musas colere severiores*.[3] You would have him follow nature, but he must follow her on foot: you have dismounted him from his

---

[1] 'man's,' *1684, 1693*. [2] Horace, *Ars poetica*, l. 10: 'daring anything.'
[3] Martial, *Epigrams*, IX. xi. 17: 'to cultivate the stricter muses.'

Pegasus. But you tell us, this supplying the last half of a verse, or adjoining a whole second to the former, looks more like the design of two than the answer of one. Supposing we acknowledge it: how comes this confederacy to be more displeasing to you than in a dance which is well contrived? You see there the united design of many persons to make up one figure: after they have separated themselves in many petty divisions, they rejoin one by one into a gross: the confederacy is plain amongst them, for chance could never produce any thing so beautiful; and yet there is nothing in it that shocks your sight. I acknowledge the hand of art appears in repartee, as of necessity it must in all kinds of verse. But there is also the quick and poignant brevity of it (which is an high imitation of nature in those sudden gusts of passion) to mingle with it; and this, joined with the cadency and sweetness of the rhyme, leaves nothing in the soul of the hearer to desire. 'Tis an art which appears; but it appears only like the shadowings of painture, which being to cause the rounding of it, cannot be absent; but while that is considered, they are lost: so while we attend to the other beauties of the matter, the care and labour of the rhyme is carried from us, or at least drowned in its own sweetness, as bees are sometimes buried in their honey. When a poet has found the repartee, the last perfection he can add to it is to put it into verse. However good the thought may be, however apt the words in which 'tis couched, yet he finds himself at a little unrest, while rhyme is wanting: he cannot leave it till that comes naturally, and then is at ease, and sits down contented.

'From replies, which are the most elevated thoughts of verse, you pass to the most mean ones, those which[1] are common with the lowest of household conversation. In these, you say, the majesty of verse suffers. You instance in the calling of a servant, or commanding a door to be shut, in rhyme. This, Crites, is a good observation of yours, but no argument: for it proves no more but that such thoughts should be waived, as often as may be, by the address of the poet. But suppose they are necessary in the places where he uses them, yet there is no need to put them into rhyme. He may place them in the beginning of a verse, and break it off, as unfit, when so debased, for any other use; or granting the worst, that they require more room than

---

[1] 'to those which are most mean, and which,' *1684, 1693*.

the hemistich will allow, yet still there is a choice to be made of the best words, and least vulgar (provided they be apt) to express such thoughts. Many have blamed rhyme in general for this fault, when the poet with a little care might have redressed it. But they do it with no more justice than if English poesy should be made ridiculous for the sake of the Water Poet's rhymes.[1] Our language is noble, full, and significant; and I know not why he who is master of it may not clothe ordinary things in it as decently as the Latin, if he use the same diligence in his choice of words. *Delectus verborum origo est eloquentiae.*[2] It was the saying of Julius Cæsar, one so curious in his, that none of them can be changed but for a worse. One would think *unlock the door* was a thing as vulgar as could be spoken; and yet Seneca could make it sound high and lofty in his Latin:

> reserate clusos regii postes laris.
> Set wide the palace gates.[3]

'But I turn from this exception, both because it happens not above twice or thrice in any play that those vulgar thoughts are used; and then too, were there no other apology to be made, yet the necessity of them (which is alike in all kind of writing) may excuse them.[4] Besides that the great eagerness and precipitation with which they are spoken makes us rather mind the substance than the dress; that for which they are spoken, rather than what is spoke. For they are always the effect of some hasty concernment, and something of consequence depends upon them.

'Thus, Crites, I have endeavoured to anwer your objections; it remains only that I should vindicate an argument for verse, which you have gone about to overthrow. It had formerly been said that the easiness of blank verse renders the poet too luxuriant, but that the labour of rhyme bounds and circumscribes an overfruitful fancy; the sense[5] there being commonly confined to the couplet, and the words so ordered that the rhyme naturally follows them, not they the rhyme. To this you answered that

---

[1] John Taylor (1580-1653), a waterman on the Thames whose doggerel verses, published between 1612 and 1654, enjoyed immense popularity.
[2] Cicero, *Brutus*, 72: 'the source of eloquence is choice in words.'
[3] *Hippolytus*, l. 860. The translation was added in *1684-93*, as a corrective, perhaps, to Howard's blunder; cf. 'Defence of *An Essay*,' below.
[4] *1684-93* add a sentence at this point: 'For if they are little and mean in rhyme, they are of consequence such in blank verse.'
[5] 'scene,' *1684, 1693*—an evident misprint.

it was no argument to the question in hand; for the dispute was not which way a man may write best, but which is most proper for the subject on which he writes.

'First, give me leave, Sir, to remember you that the argument against which you raised this objection was only secondary: it was built on this hypothesis, that to write in verse was proper for serious plays. Which supposition being granted (as it was briefly made out in that discourse, by showing how verse might be made natural), it asserted that this way of writing was an help to the poet's judgment, by putting bounds to a wild, overflowing fancy. I think, therefore, it will not be hard for me to make good what it was to prove.[1] But you add that, were this let pass, yet he who wants judgment in the liberty of his fancy, may as well show the defect of it when he is confined to verse: for he who has judgment will avoid errors, and he who has it not will commit them in all kinds of writing.

"This argument, as you have taken it from a most acute person,[2] so I confess it carries much weight in it. But by using the word *judgment* here indefinitely, you seem to have put a fallacy upon us. I grant, he who has judgment, that is, so profound, so strong, so infallible[3] a judgment, that he needs no helps to keep it always poised and upright, will commit no faults either in rhyme or out of it. And on the other extreme, he who has a judgment so weak and crazed that no helps can correct or amend it, shall write scurvily out of rhyme, and worse in it. But the first of these judgments is no where to be found, and the latter is not fit to write at all. To speak therefore of judgment as it is in the best poets: they who have the greatest proportion of it want other helps than from it within. As for example, you would be loth to say that he who was[4] endued with a sound judgment had[5] no need of history, geography, or moral philosophy, to write correctly. Judgment is indeed the master-workman in a play; but he requires many subordinate hands, many tools to his assistance. And verse I affirm to be one of these: 'tis a rule and line by which he keeps his building compact and even, which otherwise lawless imagination would raise either irregularly or loosely. At least, if the poet commits errors with this help, he

---

[1] 'prove on that supposition,' *1684, 1693.
[2] I.e. Sir Robert Howard.
[3] 'or rather so infallible,' *1684, 1693.*
[4] 'is,' *1684, 1693.*
[5] 'has,' *1684, 1693.*

would make greater and more without it: 'tis (in short) a slow and painful, but the surest kind of working. Ovid, whom you accuse for luxuriancy in verse, had perhaps been farther guilty of it, had he writ in prose. And for your instance of Ben Jonson who, you say, writ exactly without the help of rhyme; you are to remember, 'tis only an aid to luxuriant fancy, which his was not: as he did not want imagination, so none ever said he had much to spare. Neither was verse then refined so much to be an help to that age as it is to ours. Thus, then, the second thoughts being usually the best, as receiving the maturest digestion from judgment, and the last and most mature product of those thoughts being artful and laboured verse, it may well be inferred that verse is a great help to a luxuriant fancy; and this is what that argument which you opposed was to evince.'

Neander was pursuing this discourse so eagerly that Eugenius had called to him twice or thrice, ere he took notice that the barge stood still, and that they were at the foot of Somerset Stairs,[1] where they had appointed it to land. The company were all sorry to separate so soon, though a great part of the evening was already spent; and stood a while looking back on the water, which the moon-beams played upon,[2] and made it appear like floating quick-silver; at last they went up through a crowd of French people, who were merrily dancing in the open air, and nothing concerned for the noise of guns which had alarmed the town that afternoon. Walking thence together to the Piazze,[3] they parted there; Eugenius and Lisideius to some pleasant appointment they had made, and Crites and Neander to their several lodgings.

FINIS

---

[1] A landing-place to the west of the former Somerset House, abolished in the late eighteenth century when the palace was rebuilt.

[2] 'upon which the moon-beams played,' *1684, 1693*.

[3] Places of resort then occupying the northern and eastern sides of Covent Garden. Cf. *Spectator*, nos. 14 and 67.

AN ACCOUNT OF THE ENSUING POEM,
IN A LETTER TO THE HONOURABLE
SIR ROBERT HOWARD

Prefixed to *Annus Mirabilis, the Year of Wonders, 1666: an Historical Poem, Containing the Progress and Various Successes of our Naval War with Holland, and Describing the Fire of London* (1667).

AN HISTORICAL POEM—THE QUATRAIN—NAUTICAL TERMS—WIT—DEBT TO OVID AND VIRGIL

Text: 8°, 1667. The second authorized edition (1688)—there was a pirated edition in 1668—includes a few corrections which may be Dryden's, but many degenerations as well.

The poem was published in January 1667 (Pepys, *Diary*, 2 February 1667), soon after Dryden's return from his eighteen-month stay in Wiltshire during the Plague and Fire of London. It must have been sent to press very soon after it was written, since the Great Fire which it describes burned from 2nd to 6th September 1666, and we may safely assume it was written after the greater part at least of the essay *Of Dramatic Poesy* had been drafted, though the Essay did not appear till some seven months after the poem. This explains the warmth of Dryden's references here to his brother-in-law Howard, who seems to have received the manuscript of the poem from Wiltshire, corrected it and helped to see it through the press. The two men did not quarrel until the appearance of the Essay in the autumn of 1667.

Annus Mirabilis celebrates, by a tactful selection of the facts, the naval victories of the second Dutch War (1664-7) and the Great Fire, but omits mention of the Plague, since Dryden's purpose is to compose a poetic defence of the restored monarchy and to rebut charges made in anonymous pamphlets that the Fire might be God's judgment against Charles II. The handling of the war is represented as uniformly expert and heroic, though its commercial objects are frankly stated, and King and people are shown united by their common experience of victory and disaster.

The preface, which follows a superb prose address 'To the Metropolis of Great Britain' in praise of London, is dated 10 November

1666. Apart from its explanation of Dryden's purposes in the poem
and his denial of any epic pretensions, its main interest lies in the
renewed attempt to define 'wit' in more detailed and more comprehensive terms than in the preface to *The Rival Ladies*. The concern
of much of the new preface is inward, almost psychological, and
strictly poetic—in contrast with the Essay he had just drafted, where
the target is the drama and where the undertones of the literary
manifesto are never far away.

Sir,

I AM so many ways obliged to you, and so little able to return
your favours, that, like those who owe too much, I can only live
by getting farther into your debt. You have not only been careful
of my fortune, which was the effect of your nobleness, but you
have been solicitous of my reputation, which is that of your
kindness. It is not long since I gave you the trouble of perusing
a play[1] for me, and now, instead of an acknowledgment, I have
given you a greater in the correction of a poem. But since you
are to bear this persecution, I will at least give you the encouragement of a martyr, you could never suffer in a nobler cause. For
I have chosen the most heroic subject which any poet could
desire: I have taken upon me to describe the motives, the beginning, progress, and successes, of a most just and necessary war;
in it the care, management, and prudence of our King; the
conduct and valour of a royal admiral, and of two incomparable
generals;[2] the invincible courage of our captains and seamen,
and three glorious victories, the result of all. After this I have
in the Fire the most deplorable, but withal the greatest argument
that can be imagined: the destruction being so swift, so sudden,
so vast and miserable, as nothing can parallel in story. The
former part of this poem, relating to the war, is but a due expia-
tion for my not serving my King and country in it. All gentlemen
are almost obliged to it; and I know no reason we should give
that advantage to the commonalty of England, to be foremost
in brave actions, which the noblesse of France would never
suffer in their peasants. I should not have written this but to a
person who has been ever forward to appear in all employments

---

[1] Probably the tragi-comedy *Secret Love* (1668), which it is likely Dryden
wrote in Wiltshire. It was performed in March 1667, if not before.
[2] The Duke of York (later James II), Prince Rupert, and the Duke of
Albemarle. The generals are named in stanza 191 of the poem.

whither his honour and generosity have called him. The latter part of my poem, which describes the Fire, I owe first to the piety and fatherly affection of our Monarch to his suffering subjects; and, in the second place, to the courage, loyalty, and magnanimity of the City; both which were so conspicuous that I have wanted words to celebrate them as they deserve. I have called my poem *historical*, not *epic*, though both the actions and actors are as much heroic as any poem can contain. But since the action is not properly one, nor that accomplished in the last successes, I have judged it too bold a title for a few stanzas, which are little more in number than a single Iliad, or the longest of the Æneids. For this reason (I mean not of length, but broken action, tied too severely to the laws of history), I am apt to agree with those who rank Lucan rather among historians in verse than epic poets;[1] in whose room, if I am not deceived, Silius Italicus,[2] though a worse writer, may more justly be admitted. I have chosen to write my poem in quatrains,[3] or stanzas of four in alternate rhyme, because I have ever judged them more noble, and of greater dignity, both for the sound and number, than any other verse in use amongst us; in which I am sure I have your approbation. The learned languages have certainly a great advantage of us, in not being tied to the slavery of any rhyme; and were less constrained in the quantity of every syllable, which they might vary with spondees or dactyls, besides so many other helps of grammatical figures, for the lengthening or abbreviation of them, than the modern are in the close of that one syllable which often confines, and more often corrupts, the sense of all the rest. But in this necessity of our rhymes, I have always found the couplet verse most easy (though not so proper for this occasion), for there the work is sooner at an end, every two lines concluding the labour of the poet; but in quatrains he is to carry it farther on, and not only so, but to bear along in his

---

[1] E.g. Petronius, *Satyricon*, 118; Quintilian, *Institutio oratoria*, X.i.90; and Davenant, preface to *Gondibert* (1650): 'Lucan, who chose to write the greatest actions that ever were allowed to be true, . . . did not observe that such an enterprise rather became an historian than a poet (*Spingarn*, II.3).

[2] A Roman consul and epic poet (*c*. A.D. 26–*c*. 101), whose *Punica* glorifies the Scipios after the Virgilian manner.

[3] The form had recently been popularized by Davenant's unfinished epic *Gondibert* (1651), though Surrey and Spenser had used it occasionally, and Sir John Davies at length in *Nosce teipsum* (1599).

head the troublesome sense of four lines together. For those who write correctly in this kind must needs acknowledge that the last line of the stanza is to be considered in the composition of the first. Neither can we give ourselves the liberty of making any part of a verse for the sake of rhyme, or concluding with a word which is not current English, or using the variety of female rhymes, all which our fathers practised; and for the female rhymes, they are still in use amongst other nations: with the Italian in every line, with the Spaniard promiscuously, with the French alternately, as those who have read the *Alaric*, the *Pucelle*,[1] or any of their latter poems, will agree with me. And besides this, they write in alexandrines, or verses of six feet; such as, amongst us, is the old translation of Homer by Chapman:[2] all which, by lengthening of their chain, makes the sphere of their activity the larger.

I have dwelt too long upon the choice of my stanza, which you may remember is much better defended in the preface to *Gondibert*,[3] and therefore I will hasten to acquaint you with my endeavours in the writing. In general I will only say I have never yet seen the description of any naval fight in the proper terms which are used at sea;[4] and if there be any such in another language, as that of Lucan in the third of his *Pharsalia*, yet I could not prevail myself of it in the English; the terms of arts in every tongue bearing more of the idiom of it than any other words. We hear indeed among our poets of the thundering of guns, the smoke, the disorder, and the slaughter; but all these are common notions. And certainly as those who, in a logical dispute, keep in general terms, would hide a fallacy; so those who do it in any poetical description would veil their ignorance:

---

[1] Georges de Scudéry's epic *Alaric* appeared in 1654, Jean Chapelain's *Pucelle* two years later.

[2] In fact Chapman's translation of the *Iliad* (1598-1611) is in lines of seven feet, his *Odyssey* (1615?) in lines of five.

[3] 'I believed it would be more pleasant to the reader in a work of length to give this respite or pause between every stanza . . . than to run him out of breath with continued couplets' (*Spingarn*, II.19).

[4] For a modification of this view after thirty years, cf. the dedication to the *Aeneis*, vol. II, p. 254, below. Johnson, in his Life of Dryden, quotes stanzas 146-8, where the terms 'oakum,' 'calking-iron,' 'mallet,' 'marling,' etc., appear, and comments: 'I suppose there is not one term which every reader does not wish away.'

descriptas servare vices, operumque colores,
cur ego, si nequeo ignoroque, poeta salutor?[1]

For my own part, if I had little knowledge of the sea, yet I have thought it no shame to learn; and if I have made some few mistakes, 'tis only, as you can bear me witness, because I have wanted opportunity to correct them; the whole poem being first written, and now sent you from a place where I have not so much as the converse of any seaman. Yet though the trouble I had in writing it was great, it was more than recompensed by the pleasure; I found myself so warm in celebrating the praises of military men, two such especially as the Prince and General,[2] that it is no wonder if they inspired me with thoughts above my ordinary level. And I am well satisfied that, as they are incomparably the best subject I ever had, excepting only the Royal Family; so also, that this I have written of them is much better than what I have performed on any other. I have been forced to help out other arguments, but this has been bountiful to me; they have been low and barren of praise, and I have exalted them, and made them fruitful; but here—*omnia sponte suâ reddit justissima tellus*.[3] I have had a large, a fair, and a pleasant field, so fertile that, without my cultivating, it has given me two harvests in a summer, and in both oppressed the reaper. All other greatness in subjects is only counterfeit, it will not endure the test of danger; the greatness of arms is only real: other greatness burdens a nation with its weight, this supports it with its strength. And as it is the happiness of the age, so it is the peculiar goodness of the best of kings, that we may praise his subjects without offending him. Doubtless it proceeds from a just confidence of his own virtue, which the lustre of no other can be so great as to darken in him; for the good or the valiant are never safely praised under a bad or a degenerate prince.

But to return from this digression to a farther account of my poem, I must crave leave to tell you that as I have endeavoured to adorn it with noble thoughts, so much more to express those thoughts with elocution. The composition of all poems is, or

[1] Horace, *Ars poetica*, ll. 86-7: 'If in my ignorance I lack the skill to maintain a part, as described, and to use rhetorical figures in my works, why should I be hailed as a poet?'
[2] Prince Rupert and the Duke of Albemarle.
[3] A conflation of Virgil, *Georgics*, II.460 and *Eclogues*, IV.39, and Ovid, *Metamorphoses*, I.416-7 and *Fasti*, IV.370: 'The earth, with perfect justice, renders back everything of its own free will.'

ought to be, of wit, and wit in the poet, or wit writing (if you will give me leave to use a school-distinction) is no other than the faculty of imagination in the writer which, like a nimble spaniel, beats over and ranges through the field of memory, till it springs the quarry it hunted after;[1] or, without metaphor, which searches over all the memory for the species or ideas of those things which it designs to represent. Wit written is that which is well defined, the happy result of thought, or product of imagination. But to proceed from wit, in the general notion of it, to the proper wit of an heroic or historical poem, I judge it chiefly to consist in the delightful imaging of persons, actions, passions, or things. 'Tis not the jerk or sting of an epigram, nor the seeming contradiction of a poor antithesis (the delight of an ill-judging audience in a play of rhyme), nor the jingle of a more poor paronomasia; neither is it so much the morality of a grave sentence affected by Lucan, but more sparingly used by Virgil; but it is some lively and apt description, dressed in such colours of speech that it sets before your eyes the absent object as perfectly and more delightfully than nature. So then, the first happiness of the poet's imagination is properly invention, or finding of the thought; the second is fancy, or the variation, driving,[2] or moulding of that thought, as the judgment represents it proper to the subject; the third is elocution, or the art of clothing and adorning that thought so found and varied, in apt, significant, and sounding words: the quickness of the imagination is seen in the invention, the fertility in the fancy, and the accuracy in the expression.[3] For the two first of these, Ovid is famous amongst

---

[1] Cf. preface to *The Rival Ladies*, p. 8, above.

[2] The 4° of 1688 has 'deriving', which Ker follows. But there is no reason for thinking the 1688 revisions to be Dryden's, and the original reading is not clearly wrong. Cf. p. 29, above.

[3] One of the few passages in Dryden where abstract criticism—in this case, an enquiry into the nature of the creative act of poetry—is elaborated without the intrusion of some practical advice. The definition of 'fancy' as one of the three aspects of 'imagination' is eccentric; though it was common enough, long before Coleridge's celebrated distinction in *Biographia Literaria* (1817), chh. iv, xiii, for English critics to write as if fancy were, in one way or another, an inferior form of the imagination. The real curiosity of the passage lies in the fact that Dryden has chosen to define the creative act in terms of 'imagination' rather than in terms of 'wit,' thus leaving the door ajar to a new kind of criticism which would concern itself with the mind of the poet rather than with rhetorical forms. Cf. 'Parallel,' vol. II, p. 194, below.

The passage has been discussed by T. S. Eliot, *The Use of Poetry and the Use of Criticism* (1933), pp. 55-8.

the poets; for the latter, Virgil. Ovid images more often the movements and affections of the mind, either combating between two contrary passions, or extremely discomposed by one. His words therefore are the least part of his care; for he pictures nature in disorder, with which the study and choice of words is inconsistent. This is the proper wit of dialogue or discourse, and consequently of the drama, where all that is said is to be supposed the effect of sudden thought; which, though it excludes not the quickness of wit in repartees, yet admits not a too curious election of words, too frequent allusions, or use of tropes or, in fine, anything that shows remoteness of thought or labour in the writer. On the other side, Virgil speaks not so often to us in the person of another, like Ovid, but in his own; he relates almost all things as from himself, and thereby gains more liberty than the other to express his thoughts with all the graces of elocution, to write more figuratively, and to confess as well the labour as the force of his imagination. Though he describes his Dido well and naturally in the violence of her passions, yet he must yield in that to the Myrrha, the Biblis, the Althæa, of Ovid; for, as great an admirer of him as I am, I must acknowledge that if I see not more of their souls than I see of Dido's, at least I have a greater concernment for them: and that convinces me that Ovid has touched those tender strokes more delicately than Virgil could. But when action or persons are to be described, when any such image is to be set before us, how bold, how masterly, are the strokes of Virgil! We see the objects he presents us with in their native figures, in their proper motions; but so we see them, as our own eyes could never have beheld them so beautiful in themselves. We see the soul of the poet, like that universal one of which he speaks, informing and moving through all his pictures,

> totamque infusa per artus
> mens agitat molem, et magno se corpore miscet;[1]

we behold him embellishing his images, as he makes Venus breathing beauty upon her son Æneas:

> lumenque juventæ
> purpureum, et lætos oculis afflarat honores:

[1] *Aeneid*, VI.726-7: 'and mind, pervading all, sways the mass and mingles with its mighty bulk.'

> quale manus addunt ebori decus, aut ubi flavo
> argentum, Pariusve lapis circumdatur auro.[1]

See his Tempest, his Funeral Sports, his Combat of Turnus and Æneas; and in his *Georgics*, which I esteem the divinest part of all his writings, the Plague, the Country, the Battle of Bulls, the Labour of the Bees, and those many other excellent images of nature, most of which are neither great in themselves, nor have any natural ornament to bear them up: but the words wherewith he describes them are so excellent that it might be well applied to him which was said by Ovid, *materiam superabat opus*:[2] the very sound of his words have often somewhat that is connatural to the subject; and while we read him, we sit, as in a play, beholding the scenes of what he represents. To perform this, he made frequent use of tropes, which you know change the nature of a known word by applying it to some other signification; and this is it which Horace means in his *Epistle to the Pisos*:

> dixeris egregie, notum si callida verbum
> reddiderit junctura novum.[3]

But I am sensible I have presumed too far to entertain you with a rude discourse of that art which you both know so well, and put into practice with so much happiness. Yet before I leave Virgil, I must own the vanity to tell you, and by you the world, that he has been my master in this poem. I have followed him everywhere, I know not with what success, but I am sure with diligence enough; my images are many of them copied from him, and the rest are imitations of him.[4] My expressions also are as near as the idioms of the two languages would admit of in translation. And this, Sir, I have done with that boldness, for which I will stand accomptable to any of our little critics who, perhaps, are not better acquainted with him than I am. Upon your first perusal of this poem, you have taken notice of some words which I have innovated (if it be too bold for me to say *refined*) upon his Latin; which, as I offer not to introduce into

---

[1] *Aeneid*, I.590-3: 'and the ruddy light of youth, and his eyes glowed brightly; like the beauty which the hand gives to ivory, or when silver or Parian marble is set in gold.'

[2] *Metamorphoses*, II.5: 'the workmanship surpasses the material.'

[3] *Ars poetica*, ll. 47-8: 'You will write excellently if a skilful setting gives new force to a well-known word.'

[4] For a list of parallels, cf. *Kinsley*, IV.1827-8.

English prose, so I hope they are neither improper, nor altogether unelegant in verse; and in this Horace will again defend
me:

> et nova, fictaque nuper, habebunt verba fidem, si
> Græco fonte cadant, parce detorta.[1]

The inference is exceeding plain; for if a Roman poet might
have liberty to coin a word, supposing only that it was derived
from the Greek, was put into a Latin termination, and that he
used this liberty but seldom, and with modesty: how much more
justly may I challenge that privilege to do it with the same pre-
requisites, from the best and most judicious of Latin writers? In
some places, where either the fancy or the words were his, or
any other's, I have noted it in the margin, that I might not seem
a plagiary; in others I have neglected it, to avoid as well
tediousness, as the affectation of doing it too often. Such descriptions or images, well wrought, which I promise not for mine,
are, as I have said, the adequate delight of heroic poesy; for they
beget admiration, which is its proper object; as the images of
the burlesque, which is contrary to this, by the same reason
beget laughter: for the one shows nature beautified, as in the
picture of a fair woman, which we all admire; the other shows
her deformed, as in that of a lazar, or of a fool with distorted
face and antic gestures, at which we cannot forbear to laugh,
because it is a deviation from nature. But though the same
images serve equally for the epic poesy, and for the historic
and panegyric, which are branches of it, yet a several sort of
sculpture is to be used in them: if some of them are to be like
those of Juvenal, *stantes in curribus Aemiliani*,[2] heroes drawn in
their triumphal chariots, and in their full proportion; others
are to be like that of Virgil, *spirantia mollius æra*:[3] there is somewhat more of softness and tenderness to be shown in them. You
will soon find I write not this without concern. Some, who have
seen a paper of verses which I wrote last year to her Highness
the Duchess, have accused them of that only thing I could

---

[1] *Ars poetica*, ll. 52-3: 'New words, and newly coined, will be accepted
if they flow from a Greek source with only slight distortion.'

[2] *Satires*, VIII.3 (*stantis in curribus Aemilianos*): 'Aemiliani standing in
their chariots.'

[3] *Aeneid*, VI.847: 'give softer lines to breathing statues of bronze.'

defend in them. They have said I did *humi serpere*,[1] that I
wanted not only height of fancy, but dignity of words to set it
off. I might well answer with that of Horace, *nunc non erat his
locus*,[2] I knew I addressed them to a lady, and accordingly I
affected the softness of expression, and the smoothness of
measure, rather than the height of thought; and in what I did
endeavour, it is no vanity to say I have succeeded. I detest
arrogance, but there is some difference betwixt that and a just
defence. But I will not farther bribe your candour, or the reader's.
I leave them to speak for me and, if they can, to make out that
character, not pretending to a greater, which I have given
them.[3]

And now, Sir, 'tis time I should relieve you from the tedious
length of this account. You have better and more profitable
employment for your hours, and I wrong the public to detain
you longer. In conclusion, I must leave my poem to you with all
its faults, which I hope to find fewer in the printing by your
emendations. I know you are not of the number of those of
whom the younger Pliny speaks: *nec sunt parum multi qui carpere
amicos suos judicium vocant*;[4] I am rather too secure of you on that
side. Your candour in pardoning my errors may make you more
remiss in correcting them; if you will not withal consider that
they come into the world with your approbation, and through
your hands. I beg from you the greatest favour you can confer
upon an absent person, since I repose upon your management
what is dearest to me, my fame and reputation; and therefore
I hope it will stir you up to make my poem fairer by many of
your blots; if not, you know the story of the gamester who married the rich man's daughter, and when her father denied the
portion, christened all the children by his surname, that if, in
conclusion, they must beg, they should do so by one name as
well as by the other. But since the reproach of my faults will light
on you, 'tis but reason I should do you that justice to the readers,
to let them know that if there be anything tolerable in this poem,

[1] Horace, *Ars poetica*, l. 28: 'crawl on the earth.'

[2] *Ars poetica*, l. 19: 'This was not the place for such things.'

[3] There follows in *1667* the text of Dryden's 'Verses to the Duchess,'
printed here for the first time. Evidently the poem had been circulated in
manuscript and so suffered the criticisms which Dryden answers here.

[4] *Epistles*, VII.28: 'There are many who think they show judgment by
criticizing their friends.'

they owe the argument to your choice, the writing to your encouragement, the correction to your judgment, and the care of it to your friendship, to which he must ever acknowledge himself to owe all things, who is,

SIR,

The most obedient, and most
faithful of your servants,

JOHN DRYDEN.

From Charlton in Wiltshire,
    Novem. 10, 1666.

PREFACE, PROLOGUES
to *Secret Love: or The Maiden Queen* (1668)

POET AS CRITIC—DEFENCE OF THE TRAGI-COMEDY—
UNITIES—RESTORATION AUDIENCES

Text: 4°, 1668.

This tragi-comedy was probably written in 1665-6, during Dryden's stay in Wiltshire, and was first performed in March 1667. The quarto appeared in January 1668 (cf. Pepys, *Diary*, 18 January 1668), and the preface was probably written late in 1667, some months after the two prologues with which, for once, Dryden provided his play. Their repeated assertion that the play is 'regular' is disingenuous; but the preface is interesting for Dryden's attempt to justify his own rôle as a poet-critic.

PREFACE

IT has been the ordinary practice of the French poets to dedicate their works of this nature to their King, especially when they have had the least encouragement to it by his approbation of them on the stage. But I confess I want the confidence to follow their example, though perhaps I have as specious pretences to it for this piece as any they can boast of: it having been owned in so particular a manner by His Majesty, that he has graced it with the title of his play, and thereby reduced it from the severity (that I may not say malice) of its enemies. But, though a character so high and undeserved has not raised in me the presumption to offer such a trifle to his more serious view, yet I will own the vanity to say that after this glory which it received from a sovereign prince, I could not send it to seek protection from any subject. Be this poem, then, sacred to him without the tedious form of a Dedication, and without presuming to interrupt those hours which he is daily giving to the peace and settlement of his people.

For what else concerns this play, I would tell the reader that it is regular,[1] according to the strictest of dramatic laws, but that it is a commendation which many of our poets now despise, and a beauty which our common audiences do not easily discern. Neither, indeed, do I value myself upon it because, with all that symmetry of parts, it may want an air and spirit (which consists in the writing) to set it off. 'Tis a question variously disputed whether an author may be allowed as a competent judge of his own works. As to the fabric and contrivance of them, certainly he may, for that is properly the employment of the judgment; which, as a master-builder may determine, and that without deception, whether the work be according to the exactness of the model; still granting him to have a perfect idea of that pattern by which he works, and that he keeps himself always constant to the course of his judgment, without admitting self-love, which is the false surveyor of his fancy, to intermeddle in it. These qualifications granted (being such as all sound poets are presupposed to have within them), I think all writers, of what kind soever, may infallibly judge of the frame and contexture of their works. But for the ornament of writing, which is greater, more various and bizarre in poesy than in any other kind, as it is properly the child of fancy, so it can receive no measure, or at least but a very imperfect one, of its own excellencies or failures from the judgment. Self-love (which enters but rarely into the offices of the judgment) here predominates. And fancy (if I may so speak), judging of itself, can be no more certain or demonstrative of its own effects than two crooked lines can be the adequate measure of each other. What I have said on this subject may, perhaps, give me some credit with my readers in my opinion of this play, which I have ever valued above the rest of my follies of this kind: yet not thereby in the least dissenting from their judgment who have concluded the writing of this to be so much inferior to my *Indian Emperor*. But the argument of that was much more noble, not having the allay of comedy to depress it: yet if this be more perfect, either in its

---

[1] I.e. in observing the unities of time, place, and action; cf. the first Prologue, l. 4, below. In fact *Secret Love* fails to observe the third unity, as most Renaissance critics understood it, being a tragi-comedy. And the chronology of Dryden's criticism hardly helps us to explain why, in the present case, he should be so anxious to assert his classicism against all the facts: the prologues and preface must have been written before the 'Defence of *An Essay of Dramatic Poesy*' (probably composed in the summer of 1668), i.e. before his quarrel with Howard developed.

kind, or in the general notion of a play, 'tis as much as I desire to have granted for the vindication of my opinion and, what as nearly touches me, the sentence of a royal judge.

Many have imagined the character of Philocles to be faulty; some for not discovering the Queen's love, others for his joining in her restraint. But though I am not of their number who obstinately defend what they have once said, I may with modesty take up those answers which have been made for me by my friends; namely that Philocles, who was but a gentleman of ordinary birth, had no reason to guess so soon at the Queen's passion, she being a person so much above him, and by the suffrages of all her people already destined to Lysimantes; besides, that he was prepossessed (as the Queen sometimes hints it to him) with another inclination which rendered him less clear-sighted in it, since no man at the same time can distinctly view two different objects. And if this, with any shew of reason, may be defended, I leave my masters the critics to determine whether it be not much more conducing to the beauty of my plot that Philocles should be long kept ignorant of the Queen's love, than that with one leap he should have entered into the knowledge of it, and thereby freed himself, to the disgust of the audience, from that pleasing labyrinth of errors which was prepared for him. As for that other objection of his joining in the Queen's imprisonment, it is indisputably that which every man, if he examines himself, would have done on the like occasion. If they answer that it takes from the height of his character to do it, I would enquire of my over-wise censors: who told them I intended him a perfect character, or indeed what necessity was there he should be so, the variety of images being one great beauty of a play? It was as much as I designed to show one great and absolute pattern of honour in my poem, which I did in the person of the Queen: all the defects of the other parts being set to show, the more to recommend that one character of virtue to the audience. But neither was the fault of Philocles so great if the circumstances be considered which, as moral philosophy assures us, make the essential differences of good and bad; he himself best explaining his own intentions in his last act, which was the restoration of his Queen; and even before that, in the honesty of his expressions when he was unavoidably led by the impulsion of his love to do it.

That which, with more reason, was objected as an indecorum, is the management of the last scene in the play, where Celadon and Florimell[1] are treating too lightly of their marriage in the presence of the Queen, who likewise seems to stand idle while the great action of the drama is still depending. This I cannot otherwise defend than by telling you I so designed it on purpose to make my play go off more smartly; that scene being in the opinion of the best judges the most divertising of the whole comedy. But though the artifice succeeded, I am willing to acknowledge it as a fault, since it pleased His Majesty, the best judge, to think so. I have only to add that the play is founded on a story in the *Cyrus*,[2] which he calls 'the Queen of Corinth';[3] in whose character, as it has been affirmed to me, he represents that of the most famous Christina, Queen of Sweden.[4]

This is what I thought convenient to write by way of preface to *The Maiden Queen*; in the reading of which I fear you will not meet with the satisfaction which you have had in seeing it on the stage; the chief parts of it, both serious and comic, being performed to that height of excellence, that nothing but a command which I could not handsomely disobey could have given me the courage to have made it public.

PROLOGUE

I

He who writ this, not without pains and thought,
From French and English theatres has brought
Th' exactest rules by which a play is wrought.

---

[1] According to Pepys (*Diary*, 2 March 1667), the comic rôle of Florimell was brilliantly played by Nell Gwyn, so that 'I never hope ever to see the like again.'

[2] *Artamène: ou le grand Cyrus* (1649-53), the French heroic romance, was in fact by Madeleine de Scudéry, though it was published under the name of her brother Georges. An English version appeared in 1653-4.

[3] The story of Cleobuline, Queen of Corinth, appears in *Artamène*, VII.ii.

[4] Christina (1626-89), whose story resembles that of Dryden's Maiden Queen in that she married her favourite, the Count de la Gardie, to her cousin, whose brother succeeded her at her abdication in 1654.

II

The unities of action, place, and time;
The scenes unbroken; and a mingled chime   5
Of Jonson's humour with Corneille's rhyme.

III

But while dead colours[1] he with care did lay,
He fears his wit or plot he did not weigh,
Which are the living beauties of a play.

IV

Plays are like towns, which howe'er fortifi'd   10
By engineers, have still some weaker side
By the o'erseen defendant unespy'd.

V

And with that art you make approaches now;
Such skilful fury in assaults you show
That every poet without shame may bow.   15

VI

Ours therefore humbly would attend your doom
If, soldier-like, he may have terms to come
With flying colours, and with beat of drum.

*The Prologue goes out, and stays while a tune is played, after which
he returns again.*

SECOND PROLOGUE

I had forgot one half I do protest,
And now am sent again to speak the rest.   20
He bows to every great and noble wit,
But to the little Hectors of the pit
Our poet's sturdy, and will not submit.
He'll be beforehand with 'em, and not stay
To see each peevish critic stab his play: 25

---

[1] I.e. the first layer of colour in an oil-painting.

Each puny censor who, his skill to boast,
Is cheaply witty on the poet's cost.
No critic's verdict should, of right, stand good,
They are accepted all as men of blood:
And the same law should shield him from their fury   30
Which has excluded butchers from a jury.
You'd all be Wits—
But writing's tedious, and that way may fail;
The most compendious method is to rail:
Which you so like, you think yourselves ill us'd   35
When in smart prologues you are not abus'd.
A civil prologue is approv'd by no man;
You hate it as you do a civil woman.
Your fancy's pall'd, and liberally you pay
To have it quicken'd ere you see a play;   40
Just as old sinners, worn from their delight,
Give money to be whipped to appetite.
But what a pox keep I so much ado
To save our poet? He is one of you:
A brother judgment, and as I hear say,   45
A cursed critic as e'er damned a play.
Good salvage gentlemen, your own kind spare,
He is, like you, a very wolf, or bear;
Yet think not he'll your ancient rights invade,
Or stop the course of your free damning trade: 50
For he (he vows) at no friend's play can sit
But he must needs find fault to shew his wit:
Then, for his sake, ne'er stint your own delight;
Throw boldly, for he sets[1] to all that write.
With such he ventures on an even lay,   55
For they bring ready money into play.
Those who write not, and yet all writers nick,[2]
Are bankrupt gamesters, for they damn on tick.

---

[1] I.e. stakes, as in a card-game.   [2] I.e. win at cards.

A DEFENCE OF *AN ESSAY OF DRAMATIC POESY*, BEING AN ANSWER TO THE PREFACE OF *THE GREAT FAVOURITE, OR THE DUKE OF LERMA*

Prefixed to *The Indian Emperor* (1668)

AN ATTACK ON HOWARD—A DEFENCE OF RHYME—THE THREE UNITIES

Text: The 'Defence' was first published in the second edition of *The Indian Emperor* (1668), and suppressed in all later editions of the play.

This essay represents the final stage in the Dryden-Howard controversy on rhyming plays—a controversy that had begun in 1664, in Dryden's preface to *The Rival Ladies*, and continued in Howard's preface to *Four Plays* (1665) and Dryden's *Of Dramatic Poesy*, which appeared in August 1667. The portrait of Crites there no doubt stung Howard to a reply in defence of blank verse, in the preface to his tragedy *The Great Favourite*, published in the summer of 1668. Dryden's final retort, published a few weeks later in the second edition of his tragedy *The Indian Emperor* (1668), is among the most personal and contemptuous of his critical essays. It is hastily and carelessly worded, spiteful, and logically evasive; but the pressure of debate forces Dryden into a more explicitly anti-naturalistic position than he had formerly held: 'There may be too great a likeness,' he now argues, between drama and real conversation. Thrown on the defensive by his brother-in-law's attack, Dryden in the 'Defence' alternates between malicious ridicule of Howard and moments of exasperated self-revelation: 'For I confess,' he bluntly declares, 'my chief endeavours are to delight the age in which I live.'

THE former edition of the *Indian Emperor* being full of faults which had escaped the printer, I have been willing to over-look this second with more care: and though I could not allow myself so much time as was necessary, yet by that little I have done, the press is freed from some gross errors which it had to answer for before. As for the more material faults of writing, which are properly mine, though I see many of them, I want leisure to amend them. 'Tis enough for those who make one poem the business of their lives to leave that correct: yet, excepting Virgil, I never met with any which was so in any language.

But while I was thus employed about this impression, there came to my hands a new printed play called *The Great Favourite, or the Duke of Lerma*; the author of which, a noble and most ingenious person, has done me the favour to make some observations and animadversions upon my *Dramatic Essay*. I must confess he might have better consulted his reputation than by matching himself with so weak an adversary. But if his honour be diminished in the choice of his antagonist, it is sufficiently recompensed in the election of his cause: which being the weaker, in all appearance, as combating the received opinions of the best ancient and modern authors, will add to his glory if he overcome, and to the opinion of his generosity, if he be vanquished, since he engages at so great odds; and, so like a cavalier, undertakes the protection of the weaker party. I have only to fear, on my own behalf, that so good a cause as mine may not suffer by my ill management, or weak defence; yet I cannot in honour but take the glove when 'tis offered me; though I am only a champion by succession, and no more able to defend the right of Aristotle and Horace than an infant Dimock[1] to maintain the title of a king.

For my own concernment in the controversy, it is so small that I can easily be contented to be driven from a few notions of dramatic poesy; especially by one who has the reputation of understanding all things:[2] and I might justly make that excuse for my yielding to him which the philosopher made to the Emperor: why should I offer to contend with him who is master of more than twenty legions of arts and sciences?[3] But I am

[1] The Dymokes of Scrivelsby in Lincolnshire have held the hereditary title of the Sovereign's Champion since the fourteenth century.

[2] A thrust at Howard's reputation as a know-all. Cf. p. 19n., above.

[3] This remark by the philosopher Favorinus of the Emperor Hadrian occurs in the history of Aelius Spartianus (*fl.* A.D. 240), and is quoted by John Barclay in his *Icon animorum* (1614) and by Francis Bacon in his twenty-sixth apophthegm (1625), and repeated by Dryden in his attack upon Rochester, in the preface to *All for Love*, p. 227, below.

forced to fight, and therefore it will be no shame to be overcome.

Yet I am so much his servant as not to meddle with anything which does not concern me in his preface: therefore I leave the good sense and other excellencies of the first twenty lines to be considered by the critics.[1] As for the play of *The Duke of Lerma*, having so much altered and beautified it as he has done, it can justly belong to none but him. Indeed they must be extreme ignorant, as well as envious, who would rob him of that honour; for you see him putting in his claim to it, even in the first two lines:

> Repulse upon repulse, like waves thrown back,
> That slide to hang upon obdurate rocks.[2]

After this, let detraction do its worst; for if this be not his, it deserves to be. For my part, I declare for distributive justice; and from this, and what follows, he certainly deserves *those advantages which he acknowledges to have received from the opinion of sober men.*[3]

In the next place, I must beg leave to observe his great address in courting the reader to his party. For intending to assault all poets, both ancient and modern, he discovers not his whole design at once, but seems only to aim at me, and attacks me on my weakest side, my defence of verse.

To begin with me, he gives me the compellation of *The Author of a Dramatic Essay*; which is a little discourse in dialogue, for the most part borrowed from the observations of others;[4] therefore, that I may not be wanting to him in civility, I return his compliment by calling him *The Author of the Duke of Lerma*.

But (that I may pass over his salute) he takes notice of my great pains to prove rhyme as natural in a serious play, and more

---

[1] The first paragraph of Howard's preface is exceptionally fatuous: the play, he explains, is to be published not because of 'the importunity of friends; for, I confess, I was myself willing, at the first desire of Mr Herringman, to print it.'

[2] The opening lines of the play, from Lerma's soliloquy, all of which is over-written in the same manner.

[3] Another reference to the first paragraph of Howard's preface: 'the others, perhaps the best bred performers, by continuing their displeasure towards me, since I most gratefully acknowledge to have received some advantage in the opinion of the sober part of the world by the loss of theirs.'

[4] An over-modest disclaimer—though parts of the Essay are deeply indebted to Corneille's 'Discours des trois unités.'

effectual than blank verse. Thus indeed I did state the question; but he tells me, *I pursue that which I call natural in a wrong application; for 'tis not the question whether rhyme, or not rhyme, be best, or most natural for a serious subject, but what is nearest the nature of that it represents.*[1]

If I have formerly mistaken the question, I must confess my ignorance so far as to say I continue still in my mistake. But he ought to have proved that I mistook it; for 'tis yet but *gratis dictum*; I still shall think I have gained my point if I can prove that rhyme is best or most natural for a serious subject. As for the question as he states it, whether rhyme be nearest the nature of what it represents, I wonder he should think me so ridiculous as to dispute whether prose or verse[2] be nearest to ordinary conversation.

It still remains for him to prove his inference: that, since verse is granted to be more remote than prose from ordinary conversation, therefore no serious plays ought to be writ in verse; and when he clearly makes that good, I will acknowledge his victory as absolute as he can desire it.

The question now is which of us two has mistaken it; and if it appear I have not, the world will suspect *what gentleman that was, who was allowed to speak twice in Parliament because he had not yet spoken to the question*; and perhaps conclude it to be the same who, as 'tis reported, maintained a contradiction *in terminis*, in the face of three hundred persons.[3]

But to return to verse, whether it be natural or not in plays is a problem which is not demonstrable of either side: 'tis enough for me that he acknowledges he had rather read good verse than prose: for if all the enemies of verse will confess as much, I shall not need to prove that it is natural. I am satisfied if it cause delight; for delight is the chief, if not the only end of poesy; instruction can be admitted but in the second place, for poesy

[1] Howard, preface, *op. cit*, on the three unities: 'and that is called nearest to nature; for that is concluded most natural which is most probable, and nearest to that which it presents.'

[2] Dryden's argument suffers in clarity from his failure to distinguish 'verse' from 'rhyme.' But his clear enumeration, in the Prince analogy, p. 115, below, of the three categories involved—prose, blank verse, and rhyming verse—make one suspect him guilty of equivocation rather than of confusion of mind.

[3] At the Restoration, Howard had been elected Member for Stockbridge in Hampshire, and remained in Parliament till his death in 1698.

only instructs as it delights. 'Tis true that to imitate well is a poet's work;[1] but to affect the soul, and excite the passions, and, above all, to move admiration (which is the delight of serious plays), a bare imitation will not serve. The converse, therefore, which a poet is to imitate, must be heightened with all the arts and ornaments of poesy; and must be such as, strictly considered, could never be supposed spoken by any without premeditation.

As for what he urges, that *a play will still be supposed to be a composition of several persons speaking* ex tempore; *and that good verses are the hardest things which can be imagined to be spoken*: I must crave leave to dissent from his opinion, as to the former part of it. For, if I am not deceived, a play is supposed to be the work of the poet, imitating or representing the conversation of several persons: and this I think to be as clear, as he thinks the contrary.

But I will be bolder, and do not doubt to make it good, though a paradox, that one great reason why prose is not to be used in serious plays is because it is too near the nature of converse: there may be too great a likeness; as the most skilful painters affirm that there may be too near a resemblance in a picture: to take every lineament and feature is not to make an excellent piece, but to take so much only as will make a beautiful resemblance of the whole: and, with an ingenious flattery of nature, to heighten the beauties of some parts, and hide the deformities of the rest. For so says Horace,

> ut pictura poesis erit, etc. . .
> hæc amat obscurum, vult hæc sub luce videri,
> judicis argutum quæ non formidat acumen.
> . . . et quæ
> desperat tractata nitescere posse, relinquit.[2]

In *Bartholomew Fair*, or the lowest kind of comedy, that degree of heightening is used which is proper to set off that subject: 'tis true the author was not there to go out of prose, as he does in his higher arguments of comedy, *The Fox* and

[1] Cf. Aristotle, *Poetics*, ch. i.
[2] *Ars poetica*, ll. 361-4, 149-50: 'As with a painting, so with a poem: . . . one likes the shade, another prefers to be seen in the light, fearing none of the critic's keen judgment.
'And [the poet] omits those points he cannot hope to excel in by any treatment.'

Alchemist; yet he does so raise his matter in that prose as to render it delightful; which he could never have performed, had he only said or done those very things that are daily spoken or practised in the fair: for then the fair itself would be as full of pleasure to an ingenious person as the play, which we manifestly see it is not. But he hath made an excellent lazar of it; the copy is of price, though the original be vile. You see in *Catiline* and *Sejanus*, where the argument is great, he sometimes ascends to verse,[1] which shews he thought it not unnatural in serious plays; and had his genius been as proper for rhyme as it was for humour, or had the age in which he lived attained to as much knowledge in verse as ours, 'tis probable he would have adorned those subjects with that kind of writing.

Thus prose, though the rightful prince, yet is by common consent deposed as too weak for the government of serious plays: and he failing, there now start up two competitors; one the nearer in blood, which is blank verse; the other more fit for the ends of government, which is rhyme. Blank verse is, indeed, the nearer prose, but he is blemished with the weakness of his predecessor. Rhyme (for I will deal clearly) has somewhat of the usurper in him, but he is brave, and generous, and his dominion pleasing. For this reason of delight, the Ancients (whom I will still believe as wise as those who so confidently correct them) wrote all their tragedies in verse, though they knew it most remote from conversation.

But I perceive I am falling into the danger of another rebuke from my opponent; for when I plead that the Ancients used verse, I prove not that they would have admitted rhyme, had it then been written. All I can say is only this, that it seems to have succeeded verse[2] by the general consent of poets in all modern languages; for almost all their serious plays are written in it; which, though it be no demonstration that therefore they ought to be so, yet at least the practice first, and then the continuation

---

[1] I.e. rhyme. The occasional use made of rhyme by Shakespeare, Jonson, and others rather suggests that the Elizabethans thought it better suited to scenes of high comedy than to tragic or farcical scenes—apart from its use in the final couplet of any kind of scene, to terminate the action.

[2] I.e. blank verse—an unparalleled usage, to be explained only by careless composition or a corrupt text. But Dryden's argument is very confused in general: his claim, for instance, that all modern authors of 'serious plays' have written in rhyme makes nonsense of his praise of Shakespeare.

of it, shews that it attained the end, which was to please; and if
that cannot be compassed here, I will be the first who shall lay
it down. For I confess my chief endeavours are to delight the
age in which I live. If the humour of this be for low comedy,
small accidents, and raillery, I will force my genius to obey it,
though with more reputation I could write in verse. I know I
am not so fitted by nature to write comedy:[1] I want that gaiety
of humour which is required to it. My conversation is slow and
dull; my humour saturnine and reserved: in short, I am none
of those who endeavour to break jests in company, or make
repartees. So that those who decry my comedies do me no
injury, except it be in point of profit: reputation in them is the
last thing to which I shall pretend. I beg pardon for entertaining
the reader with so ill a subject; but before I quit that argument,
which was the cause of this digression, I cannot but take notice
how I am corrected for my quotation of Seneca in my defence
of plays in verse. My words are these: 'Our language is noble,
full, and significant; and I know not why he who is master of
it may not clothe ordinary things in it as decently as the Latin,
if he use the same diligence in his choice of words. One would
think *unlock a door* was a thing as vulgar as could be spoken;
yet Seneca could make it sound high and lofty in his Latin:

> reserate clusos regii postes laris.'[2]

But he says of me, 'That being filled with the precedents of
the Ancients, who writ their plays in verse, I commend the thing,
declaring our language to be full, noble, and significant, and
charging all defects upon the *ill placing of words*, which I prove
by quoting Seneca loftily expressing such an ordinary thing as
shutting a door.'

Here he manifestly mistakes; for I spoke not of the placing,
but of the choice of words; for which I quoted that aphorism of
Julius Caesar, *delectus verborum est origo eloquentiae*;[3] but *delectus
verborum* is no more Latin for the *placing of words*, than *reserate*
is Latin for *shut the door*, as he interprets it, which I ignorantly
construed *unlock* or *open* it.

---

[1] The first of Dryden's plays to be acted, *The Wild Gallant* (1669), performed in February 1663, was a prose comedy. But, apart from *Sir Martin
Mar-All* (1668), an adaptation from Molière, he scarcely attempted the form
again.

[2] Cf. p. 90n., above.   [3] Cf. p. 90 and n., above.

He supposes I was highly affected with the sound of those words; and I suppose I may more justly imagine it of him; for if he had not been extremely satisfied with the sound, he would have minded the sense a little better.

But these are now to be no faults; for ten days after his book is published, and that his mistakes are grown so famous that they are come back to him, he sends his *Errata*[1] to be printed, and annexed to his play; and desires that instead of *shutting* you would read *opening*; which, it seems, was the printer's fault. I wonder at his modesty, that he did not rather say it was Seneca's or mine; and that, in some authors, *reserare* was to *shut* as well as to *open*, as the word *barach*, say the learned, is both to *bless* and *curse*[2].

Well, since it was the printer, he was a naughty man to commit the same mistake twice in six lines: I warrant you *delectus verborum*, for *placing of words*, was his mistake too, though the author forgot to tell him of it: if it were my book I assure you I should. For those rascals ought to be the proxies of every gentleman author, and to be chastised for him when he is not pleased to own an error. Yet since he has given the *Errata*, I wish he would have enlarged them only a few sheets more, and then he would have spared me the labour of an answer: for this cursed printer is so given to mistakes that there is scarce a sentence in the preface without some false grammar or hard sense in it; which will all be charged upon the poet, because he is so good-natured as to lay but three errors to the printer's account, and to take the rest upon himself, who is better able

---

[1] Only one surviving copy of *The Great Favourite* (1668) is known to contain Howard's Errata leaf, bound in as a later addition: the copy in the Pepys Library, Magdalene College, Cambridge (no. 1,604). It reads as follows:

'ERRATA

'Though there may be many errors in the play itself, yet I will neither give myself nor the reader any trouble in the correcting; but [in?] the Epistle to the Reader, containing matter of argument, I would not have my sense, which, possibly, may not be very strong, rendered weaker by mistakes in printing.

'Page 4, l. 20, for *like*, r. *likes*; l. ult., for *shutting*, r. *opening*; p. 5, l. 5, for *so*, r. *as*, to make the sense entire, as I intended it; which was, *That the shutting of a door should be as loftily exprest by the author there mentioned, as he fancied the opening a door was by Seneca.* P. 6, l. 24, for *than*, r. *then*; p. ult., l. 12, the word *fancy* is by a comma made the end of a sentence, which should have begun the next.'

[2] According to context, in the Hebrew language: cf. Genesis 9.26 ('bless'), and Numbers 22.12 ('curse').

to support them. But he needs not apprehend that I should strictly examine those little faults, except I am called upon to do it: I shall return therefore to that quotation of Seneca, and answer not to what he writes, but to what he means. I never intended it as an argument, but only as an illustration of what I had said before concerning the election of words; and all he can charge me with is only this, that if Seneca could make an ordinary thing sound well in Latin by the choice of words, the same with the like care might be performed in English: if it cannot, I have committed an error on the right hand, by commending too much the copiousness and well sounding of our language, which I hope my countrymen will pardon me. At least the words which follow in my *Dramatic Essay* will plead somewhat in my behalf; for I say there that this objection happens but seldom in a play; and then too either the meanness of the expression may be avoided, or shut out from the verse by breaking it in the midst.

But I have said too much in the defence of verse; for after all 'tis a very indifferent thing to me whether it obtain or not. I am content hereafter to be ordered by his rule, that is, to write it sometimes because it pleases me, and so much the rather, because he has declared that it pleases him. But he has taken his last farewell of the Muses, and he has done it civilly, by honouring them with the name of *his long acquaintances*, which is a compliment they have scarce deserved from him. For my own part, I bear a share in the public loss, and how emulous soever I may be of his fame and reputation, I cannot but give this testimony of his style, that it is extreme poetical, even in oratory; his thoughts elevated, sometimes above common apprehension; his notions politic and grave, and tending to the instruction of princes, and reformation of states; that they are abundantly interlaced with variety of fancies, tropes, and figures, which the critics have enviously branded with the name of obscurity and false grammar.

Well, he is now fettered in business of more unpleasant nature: the Muses have lost him, but the Commonwealth gains by it; the corruption of a poet is the generation of a statesman.[1]

---

[1] Howard, in fact, never rose in politics above the secretaryship to the Commissioners of the Treasury. The same ironic formula was employed by Dryden a quarter of a century later, in the preface to *Examen poeticum*

He will not venture again into the civil wars of censure, ubi . . . nullos habitura triumphos:[1] if he had not told us he had left the Muses, we might have half suspected it by that word *ubi*, which does not any way belong to them in that place: the rest of the verse is indeed Lucan's, but that *ubi*, I will answer for it, is his own. Yet he has another reason for this disgust of poesy; for he says immediately after, that *the manner of plays which are now in most esteem is beyond his power to perform*: to perform the manner of a thing, I confess, is new English to me. *However, he condemns not the satisfaction of others, but rather their unnecessary understanding, who, like Sancho Pança's doctor, prescribe too strictly to our appetites; for*, says he, *in the difference of tragedy and comedy, and of farce itself, there can be no determination but by the taste, nor in the manner of their composure.*

We shall see him now as great a critic as he was a poet, and the reason why he excelled so much in poetry will be evident, for it will appear to have proceeded from the exactness of his judgment. *In the difference of tragedy, comedy, and farce itself, there can be no determination but by the taste.* I will not quarrel with the obscurity of his phrase, though I justly might; but beg his pardon if I do not rightly understand him. If he means that there is no essential difference betwixt comedy, tragedy, and farce, but what is only made by the people's taste, which distinguishes one of them from the other, that is so manifest an error that I need not lose time to contradict it. Were there neither judge, taste, nor opinion in the world, yet they would differ in their natures; for the action, character, and language of tragedy would still be great and high; that of comedy lower and more familiar; admiration would be the delight of one, and satire of the other.

I have but briefly touched upon these things because, whatever his words are, I can scarce imagine that *he, who is always concerned for the true honour of reason, and would have no spurious issue fathered upon her*, should mean anything so

(1693), vol. II, p. 157, below: 'The corruption of a poet is the generation of a critic.' The antithesis is Aristotelian, and common in medieval and Renaissance literature. Cf. Thomas Middleton, *The Roaring Girl* (1611), III: 'the corruption of a citizen is the generation of a sergeant'; and Sir Thomas Browne, *Vulgar Errors* (1646), III.ix: 'that axiom in philosophy that the generation of one thing is the corruption of another.' Cf. vol. II, pp. 212, 282, below.,

[1] Lucan, *Pharsalia*, I.12.

absurd as to affirm *that there is no difference betwixt comedy and tragedy but what is made by the taste only*; unless he would have us understand the comedies of my Lord L.[1], where the first act should be pottages, the second fricasses, &c., and the fifth a *chère entière* of women.

I rather guess he means that betwixt one comedy or tragedy and another there is no other difference but what is made by the liking or disliking of the audience. This is indeed a less error than the former, but yet it is a great one. The liking or disliking of the people gives the play the denomination of good or bad, but does not really make or constitute it such. To please the people ought to be the poet's aim, because plays are made for their delight; but it does not follow that they are always pleased with good plays, or that the plays which please them are always good. The humour of the people is now for comedy, therefore in hope to please them, I write comedies rather than serious plays: and so far their taste prescribes to me: but it does not follow from that reason that comedy is to be preferred before tragedy in its own nature; for that which is so in its own nature cannot be otherwise, as a man cannot but be a rational creature: but the opinion of the people may alter, and in another age, or perhaps in this, serious plays may be set up above comedies.

This I think a sufficient answer; if it be not, he has provided me of an excuse; it seems, in his wisdom, he foresaw my weakness, and has found out this expedient for me, *that it is not necessary for poets to study strict reason, since they are so used to a greater latitude than is allowed by that severe inquisition, that they must infringe their own jurisdiction to profess themselves obliged to argue well.*

I am obliged to him for discovering to me this back door; but I am not yet resolved on my retreat: for I am of opinion that they cannot be good poets who are not accustomed to argue well. False reasonings and colours of speech are the certain marks of one who does not understand the stage; for moral truth is the mistress of the poet as much as of the philosopher: poesy must resemble natural truth, but it must *be* ethical. Indeed the poet dresses truth, and adorns nature, but does not alter them:

[1] Ker suggests John Maitland (1616-82), second Earl and first Duke of Lauderdale, who restored the power of the Crown in Scotland after the Restoration. His reputation for profligacy was remarkable even in the court of Charles II.

ficta voluptatis causâ sint proxima veris.[1]

Therefore that is not the best poesy which resembles notions of things that are not to things that are: though the fancy may be great and the words flowing, yet the soul is but half satisfied when there is not truth in the foundation. This is that which makes Virgil be preferred before the rest of poets. In variety of fancy, and sweetness of expression, you see Ovid far above him; for Virgil rejected many of those things which Ovid wrote. *A great wit's great work is to refuse*, as my worthy friend Sir John Berkenhead[2] has ingeniously expressed it: you rarely meet with anything in Virgil but truth, which therefore leaves the strongest impression of pleasure in the soul. This I thought myself obliged to say in behalf of poesy; and to declare, though it be against myself, that when poets do not argue well, the defect is in the workmen, not in the art.

And now I come to the boldest part of his discourse, wherein he attacks not me, but all the Ancients and Moderns; and undermines, as he thinks, the very foundations on which dramatic poesy is built.[3] I could wish he would have declined that envy which must of necessity follow such an undertaking, and contented himself with triumphing over me in my opinions of verse, which I will never hereafter dispute with him; but he must pardon me if I have that veneration for Aristotle, Horace, Ben Jonson, and Corneille, that I dare not serve him in such a cause, and against such heroes, but rather fight under their protection, as Homer reports of little Teucer, who shot the Trojans from under the large buckler of Ajax Telamon:

Στῆ δ' ἄρ' ὑπ' Αἴαντος σάκεϊ Τελαμωνιάδαω, &c.[4]
He stood beneath his brother's ample shield;
And, cover'd there, shot death through all the field.

[1] Horace, *Ars poetica*, l. 338: 'Let fiction made for delight be near to the truth.'

[2] A Fellow of All Souls College, Oxford, and editor of a Royalist weekly in the early years of the Civil War. Berkenhead (1616-79) was an early member of the Royal Society, and Dryden probably met him there. The line is from his complimentary poem 'In Memory of Mr William Cartwright', published in a posthumous collection of Cartwright's plays and poems (1651).

[3] 'To show therefore upon what ill grounds they dictate laws for dramatic poesy, I shall endeavour to make it evident that there's no such thing as what they all pretend. . . .' (Howard).

[4] *Iliad*, viii.267.

The words of my noble adversary are these:

But if we examine the general rules laid down for plays by strict reason, we shall find the errors equally gross; for the great foundation which is laid to build upon is nothing as it is generally stated, as[1] will appear upon the examination of the particulars.

These particulars in due time shall be examined. In the meanwhile, let us consider what this great foundation is, which he says is nothing, as it is generally stated. I never heard of any other foundation of dramatic poesy than the imitation of nature; neither was there ever pretended any other by the Ancients or Moderns, or me, who endeavour to follow them in that rule. This I have plainly said in my definition[2] of a play: that it is a just and lively image of human nature, &c. Thus the foundation, as it is generally stated, will stand sure, if this definition of a play be true; if it be not, he ought to have made his exception against it, by proving that a play is not an imitation of nature, but somewhat else which he is pleased to think it.

But 'tis very plain that he has mistaken the foundation for that which is built upon it, though not immediately; for the direct and immediate consequence is this: if nature be to be imitated, then there is a rule for imitating nature rightly; otherwise there may be an end, and no means conducing to it. Hitherto I have proceeded by demonstration; but as our divines, when they have proved a Deity because there is order, and have inferred that this Deity ought to be worshipped, differ afterwards in the manner of the worship; so having laid down that nature is to be imitated, and that proposition proving the next, that then there are means which conduce to the imitating of nature, I dare proceed no further positively; but have only laid down some opinions of the Ancients and Moderns, and of my own, as means which they used, and which I thought probable for the attaining of that end. Those means are the same which my antagonist calls the foundations, how properly the world may judge; and to prove that this is his meaning, he clears it immediately to you by enumerating those rules or propositions against which he makes his particular exceptions as namely,

---

[1] 'which,' Howard.

[2] Cf. p. 25, above, where a definition of a play is offered by Lisideius (Sedley). Dryden here seems ready to acknowledge it as his own; though in the next paragraph but one he emphasizes the 'sceptical' character of his dialogue.

those of time and place, in these words: *First, we are told the plot should not be so ridiculously contrived as to crowd two several countries into one stage; secondly, to cramp the accidents of many years or days into the representation of two hours and a half; and, lastly, a conclusion drawn, that the only remaining dispute is concerning time, whether it should be contained in twelve or twenty-four hours; and the place to be limited to that spot of ground where the play is supposed to begin: and this is called nearest nature;*[1] *for that is concluded most natural which is most probable, and nearest to that which it presents.*

Thus he has only made a small mistake of the means conducing to the end for the end itself, and of the superstructure for the foundation; but he proceeds: *to shew therefore upon what ill grounds they dictate laws for dramatic poesy,* &c. He is here pleased to charge me with being magisterial, as he has done in many other places of his preface. Therefore, in vindication of myself, I must crave leave to say that my whole discourse was sceptical, according to that way of reasoning which was used by Socrates, Plato, and all the Academics of old, which Tully and the best of the Ancients followed, and which is imitated by the modest inquisitions of the Royal Society.[2] That it is so, not only the name will shew, which is *An Essay*,[3] but the frame and composition of the work. You see it is a dialogue sustained by persons of several opinions, all of them left doubtful, to be determined by the readers in general; and more particularly deferred to the accurate judgment of my Lord Buckhurst, to whom I made a dedication of my book. These are my words in my epistle, speaking of the persons whom I introduced in my dialogue: ' 'Tis true they differed in their opinions, as 'tis probable they would; neither do I take upon me to reconcile, but to

---

[1] 'nearest to nature,' Howard.

[2] I.e. in the conversations held by the Society since its foundation in 1660. Dryden, as an early member, had some experience of them, though he was soon dropped through failure to attend. The implications of this passage are considerable: the Royal Society (though it did not publish dialogues) evidently saw itself as a successor to the Socratic tradition; and Dryden is apparently insensitive to the cardinal difference between a Platonic and a Ciceronian dialogue. His own Essay, in its long and ponderous speeches, is decidedly in the Latin tradition. Cf. p. x, above.

[3] I.e. an attempt. The modern sense was introduced by Bacon in his title *Essays* (1597), in imitation of Montaigne's *Essais* (1580). Dryden is taking dialectical advantage of the current ambiguity of the term. Cf. Glossary, vol. II, below.

relate them, leaving your Lordship to decide it in favour of that part which you shall judge most reasonable.'[1] And after that, in my advertisement to the reader, I said this: 'The drift of the ensuing discourse is chiefly to vindicate the honour of our English writers from the censure of those who unjustly prefer the French before them. This I intimate, lest any should think me so exceeding vain as to teach others an art which they understand much better than myself.'[2] But this is more than necessary to clear my modesty in that point: and I am very confident that there is scarce any man who has lost so much time as to read that trifle, but will be my compurgator as to that arrogance whereof I am accused. The truth is, if I had been naturally guilty of so much vanity as to dictate my opinions, yet I do not find that the character of a positive or self-conceited person is of such advantage to any in this age that I should labour to be publicly admitted of that order.

But I am not now to defend my own cause, when that of all the Ancients and Moderns is in question: for this gentleman who accuses me of arrogance has taken a course not to be taxed with the other extreme of modesty. Those propositions which are laid down in my discourse, as helps to the better imitation of nature, are not mine (as I have said), nor were ever pretended so to be, but derived from the authority of Aristotle and Horace, and from the rules and examples of Ben Jonson and Corneille. These are the men with whom properly he contends, and against *whom he will endeavour to make it evident, that there is no such thing as what they all pretend.*

His argument against the unities of place and time is this: *that 'tis as impossible for one stage to present two rooms or houses[3] truly, as two countries or kingdoms; and as impossible that five hours or twenty-four hours should be two hours,[4] as that a thousand hours or years should be less than what they are, or the greatest part of time to be comprehended in the less: for all of them[5] being impossible, they are none of them nearest the truth or nature of what they present; for impossibilities are all equal, and admit of no degree.[6]*

This argument is so scattered into parts that it can scarce be

---

[1] Cf. p. 16, above.   [2] Cf. p. 17, above.
[3] 'two houses or two rooms,' Howard.   [4] 'two hours and a half,' Howard.
[5] 'for all,' Howard.   [6] 'admit no degree,' Howard.

united into a syllogism; yet, in obedience to him, *I will abbreviate*,[1] and comprehend as much of it as I can in few words, that my answer to it may be more perspicuous. I conceive his meaning to be what follows, as to the unity of place: (if I mistake, I beg his pardon, professing it is not out of any design to play the *argumentative poet*). If one stage cannot properly present two rooms or houses, much less two countries or kingdoms, then there can be no unity of place: but one stage cannot properly perform this; therefore there can be no unity of place.

I plainly deny his minor proposition; the force of which, if I mistake not, depends on this, that the stage being one place cannot be two. This indeed is as great a secret as that we are all mortal; but to requite it with another, I must crave leave to tell him that though the stage cannot be two places, yet it may properly represent them successively, or at several times. His argument is indeed no more than a mere fallacy, which will evidently appear when we distinguish place, as it relates to plays, into real and imaginary. The real place is that theatre, or piece of ground, on which the play is acted. The imaginary, that house, town, or country where the action of the *drama* is supposed to be; or, more plainly, where the scene of the play is laid. Let us now apply this to that Herculean argument, *which if strictly and duly weighed, is to make it evident that there is no such thing as what they all pretend.* 'Tis impossible, he says, for one stage to present two rooms or houses: I answer, 'tis neither impossible, nor improper, for one real place to represent two or more imaginary places, so it be done successively, which in other words is no more than this: that the imagination of the audience, aided by the words of the poet, and painted scenes, may suppose the stage to be sometimes one place, sometimes another, now a garden, or wood, and immediately a camp: which I appeal to every man's imagination, if it be not true. Neither the Ancients nor Moderns, as much fools as he is pleased to think them, ever asserted that they could make one place two; but they might hope, by the good leave of this author, that the change of a scene might lead the imagination to suppose the place altered: so that he cannot fasten those absurdities upon this scene of a play, or imaginary place of action, that it is one place and yet two.

[1] Perhaps a mannerism of Howard's.

And this being so clearly proved, that 'tis past any shew of reasonable denial, it will not be hard to destroy that other part of his argument which depends upon it, namely, that 'tis as impossible for a stage to represent two rooms or houses, as two countries or kingdoms: for his reason is already overthrown, which was because both were alike impossible. This is manifestly otherwise; for 'tis proved that a stage may properly represent two rooms or houses; for the imagination being judge of what is represented, will in reason be less shocked with the appearance of two rooms in the same house, or two houses in the same city, than with two distant cities in the same country, or two remote countries in the same universe. Imagination in a man, or reasonable creature, is supposed to participate of reason, and when that governs, as it does in the belief of fiction, reason is not destroyed, but misled, or blinded: that can prescribe to the reason, during the time of the representation, somewhat like a weak belief of what it sees and hears; and reason suffers itself to be so hoodwinked, that it may better enjoy the pleasures of the fiction: but it is never so wholly made a captive as to be drawn headlong into a persuasion of those things which are most remote from probability: 'tis in that case a free-born subject, not a slave; it will contribute willingly its assent, as far as it sees convenient, but will not be forced. Now there is a greater vicinity in nature betwixt two rooms than betwixt two houses; betwixt two houses than betwixt two cities; and so of the rest: reason therefore can sooner be led by imagination to step from one room into another than to walk to two distant houses, and yet rather to go thither than to fly like a witch through the air, and be hurried from one region to another. Fancy and reason go hand in hand; the first cannot leave the last behind: and though fancy, when it sees the wide gulf, would venture over, as the nimbler, yet it is withheld by reason, which will refuse to take the leap when the distance over it appears too large. If Ben Jonson himself will remove the scene from Rome into Tuscany in the same act, and from thence return to Rome in the scene which immediately follows, reason will consider there is no proportionable allowance of time to perform the journey, and therefore will choose to stay at home. So, then, the less change of place there is, the less time is taken up in transporting the persons of the drama, with analogy to reason; and in that analogy, or resemblance of fiction to truth, consists the excellency of the play.

For what else concerns the unity of place, I have already given my opinion of it in my *Essay*, that there is a latitude to be allowed to it, as several places in the same town or city, or places adjacent to each other in the same country; which may all be comprehended under the larger denomination of one place; yet with this restriction, that the nearer and fewer those imaginary places are, the greater resemblance they will have to truth; and reason, which cannot make them one, will be more easily led to suppose them so.

What has been said of the unity of place, may easily be applied to that of time: I grant it to be impossible that the greater part of time should be comprehended in the less, that twenty-four hours should be crowded into three: but there is no necessity of that supposition; for as *place*, so *time* relating to a play is either imaginary or real: the real is comprehended in those three hours, more or less, in the space of which the play is represented; the imaginary is that which is supposed to be taken up in the representation, as twenty-four hours more or less. Now no man ever could suppose that twenty-four real hours could be included in the space of three; but where is the absurdity of affirming that the feigned business of twenty-four imagined hours may not more naturally be represented in the compass of three real hours, than the like feigned business of twenty-four years in the same proportion of real time? For the proportions are always real, and much nearer, by his permission, of twenty-four to three, than of four thousand to it.

I am almost fearful of illustrating anything by similitude, lest he should confute it for an argument; yet I think the comparison of a glass will discover very aptly the fallacy of his argument, both concerning time and place. The strength of his reason depends on this, that the less cannot comprehend the greater. I have already answered that we need not suppose it does; I say not that the less can comprehend the greater, but only that it may represent it; as in a glass or mirror of half-a-yard diameter, a whole room and many persons in it may be seen at once: not that it can comprehend that room or those persons, but that it represents them to the sight.

But the author of the *Duke of Lerma* is to be excused for his declaring against the unity of time; for, if I be not much mistaken, he is an interested person; the time of that play taking up so many years as the favour of the Duke of Lerma continued; nay, the second and third act including all the time of his prosperity, which was a great part of the reign of Philip the Third: for in the beginning of the second act he was not yet a favourite, and before the end of the third was in disgrace. I say not this with the least design of limiting the stage too servilely to twenty-four hours, however he be pleased to tax me with dogmatizing on that point. In my dialogue, as I before hinted, several persons maintained their several opinions: one of them, indeed, who supported the cause of the French poesy, said how strict they were in that particular; but he who answered in behalf of our nation was willing to give more latitude to the rule, and cites the words of Corneille himself, complaining against the severity of it, and observing, what beauties it banished from the stage, *pag.* 44 of my *Essay*.[1] In few words, my own opinion is this (and I willingly submit it to my adversary, when he will please impartially to consider it) that the imaginary time of every play ought to be contrived into as narrow a compass as the nature of the plot, the quality of the persons, and variety of accidents will allow. In comedy, I would not exceed twenty-four or thirty hours; for the plot, accidents, and persons of comedy are small, and may be naturally turned in a little compass: but in tragedy the design is weighty, and the persons great; therefore there will naturally be required a greater space of time in which to move them. And this, though Ben Jonson has not told us, yet 'tis manifestly his opinion: for you see that to his comedies he allows generally but twenty-four hours; to his two tragedies, *Sejanus* and *Catiline*, a much larger time, though he draws both of them into as narrow a compass as he can. For he shews you only the latter end of Sejanus his favour, and the conspiracy of Catiline already ripe, and just breaking out into action.

But as it is an error, on the one side, to make too great a disproportion betwixt the imaginary time of the play, and the real time of its representation; so, on the other side, 'tis an oversight to compress the accidents of a play into a narrower compass than that in which they could naturally be produced. Of this last error the French are seldom guilty, because the thinness of their plots

[1] Cf. p. 63, above.

prevents them from it; but few Englishmen, except Ben Jonson, have ever made a plot with variety of design in it included in twenty-four hours which was altogether natural. For this reason, I prefer the *Silent Woman* before all other plays, I think justly, as I do its author in judgment above all other poets. Yet, of the two, I think that error the most pardonable, which in too strait a compass crowds together many accidents, since it produces more variety and, consequently more pleasure to the audience; and because the nearness of proportion betwixt the imaginary and real time does speciously cover the compression of the accidents.

Thus I have endeavoured to answer the meaning of his argument; for as he drew it, I humbly conceive that it was none: as will appear by his proposition, and the proof of it. His proposition was this:

If strictly and duly weighed, 'tis as impossible for one stage to present two rooms or houses, as two countries or kingdoms, &c. And his proof this: *For all being impossible, they are none of them nearest the truth or nature of what they present.*

Here you see, instead of proof or reason, there is only *petitio principii*. For, in plain words, his sense is this: two things are as impossible as one another, because they are both equally impossible; but he takes those two things to be granted as impossible which he ought to have proved such before he had proceeded to prove them equally impossible; he should have made out first that it was impossible for one stage to represent two houses, and then have gone forward to prove that it was as equally impossible for a stage to present two houses as two countries.

After all this, the very absurdity to which he would reduce me is none at all: for he only drives at this, that if his argument be true, I must then acknowledge that there are degrees in impossibilities, which I easily grant him without dispute: and, if I mistake not, Aristotle and the School are of my opinion. For there are some things which are absolutely impossible, and others which are only so *ex parte*; as 'tis absolutely impossible for a thing *to be* and *not be* at the same time: but for a stone to move naturally upward, is only impossible *ex parte materiæ*; but it is not impossible for the First Mover to alter the nature of it.

His last assault, like that of a Frenchman, is most feeble; for whereas I have observed that none have been violent against verse, but such only as have not attempted it, or have succeeded ill in their attempt, he will needs, according to his usual custom, improve my observation to an argument that he might have the glory to confute it. But I lay my observation at his feet, as I do my pen, which I have often employed willingly in his deserved commendations, and now most unwillingly against his judgment. For his person and parts, I honour them as much as any man living, and have had so many particular obligations to him that I should be very ungrateful if I did not acknowledge them to the world. But I gave not the first occasion of this difference in opinions. In my epistle dedicatory before my *Rival Ladies*, I had said somewhat in behalf of verse which he was pleased to answer in his preface to his plays: that occasioned my reply in my *Essay*; and that reply begot this rejoinder of his, in his preface to the *Duke of Lerma*. But as I was the last who took up arms, I will be the first to lay them down. For what I have here written, I submit it wholly to him; and if I do not hereafter answer what may be objected against this paper,[1] I hope the world will not impute it to any other reason than only the due respect which I have so for so noble an opponent.

[1] Dryden kept his promise, and even withdrew the 'Defence' from later editions of the *Indian Emperor*. The only known reply was an anonymous pamphlet in defence of Howard, *A Letter from a Gentleman, Occasioned by a Civilized Epistle of Mr Dryden's* (1668). The text is signed 'R.F.'—probably Richard Flecknoe (c. 1620-78?), the insignificant poet whom Dryden mocked after his death in the satire *Mac Flecknoe* (1682). Pepys found it 'mighty silly' (*Diary*, 20 September 1668). Cf. Preface to *Tyrannic Love*, p. 142n., below, and *Macdonald*, no. 159.

PREFACE

to *The Wild Gallant: a Comedy* (1669)

FIRST FAILURE—COMEDY

Text: 4°, 1669.

Dryden's first play, unsuccessfully performed in February 1663, was a prose comedy, and its failure set him against the form for ever after, though many of his tragi-comedies contain comic scenes in prose. The play was revised for a revival in 1667, but Dryden's shame over its failure remained, and it is difficult to see why he allowed the play to be published six years after its first performance.

IT would be a great imprudence in me to say much of a comedy which has had but indifferent success in the action. I made the Town my judges; and the greater part condemned it. After which I do not think it my concernment to defend it with the ordinary zeal of a poet for his decried poem. Though Corneille is more resolute in his preface before *Pertharite*,[1] which was condemned more universally than this: for he avows boldly that, in spite of censure, his play was well and regularly written; which is more than I dare say for mine. Yet it was received at Court, and was more than once the divertisement of His Majesty, by his own command.[2] But I have more modesty than to ascribe that to my merit which was his particular act of grace. It was the first attempt I made in dramatic poetry; and, I find since, a very bold one to begin with comedy, which is the most difficult

---

[1] First performed, unsuccessfully, in 1652. In the Examen of the play in his *Théâtre* (1660), Corneille wrote: 'Le succès de cette tragédie a été si malheureux, que pour m'épargner le chagrin de m'en souvenir, je n'en dirai presque rien ... Les sentiments en sont assez vifs et nobles, les vers assez bien tournés, et ... la façon dont le sujet s'explique dans la première scène ne manque pas d'artifice.'

[2] But, according to Pepys's account of the Court performance of 23 February 1663, 'The King did not seem pleased at all.'

part of it. The plot was not originally my own:[1] but so altered
by me (whether for the better or worse, I know not) that, whoever
the author was, he could not have challenged a scene of it. I
doubt not but you will see in it the uncorrectness of a young
writer: which is yet but a small excuse for him who is so little
amended since. The best apology I can make for it, and the
truest, is only this: that you have since that time received with
applause as bad, and as uncorrect, plays from other men.

[1] The chief source of the play, probably Spanish, has never been identified.
Lope de Vega's *El galán escarmentado* ('The Gallant Chastised'), written
c. 1600, is one of his many lost plays, but Dryden may have seen it in manuscript.

PREFACE, PROLOGUE

to *The Tempest: or The Enchanted Island* (1670)

DAVENANT'S GENIUS—AND SHAKESPEARE'S

Text: 4°, 1670.

This adaptation by Dryden and Davenant of Shakespeare's *Tempest* was first performed in November 1667 before Charles II and his Court. (Cf. Pepys, *Diary*, 7 November 1667). It was later turned into an opera (1674), though whether by Dryden or Shadwell remains uncertain. The play was not published until two years after its first performance, for the preface, which is largely a tribute by Dryden to the genius of his late collaborator, is dated December 1669, some twenty months after Davenant's death.

PREFACE TO *THE ENCHANTED ISLAND*

THE writing of prefaces to plays was probably invented by some very ambitious poet who never thought he had done enough: perhaps by some ape of the French eloquence, which uses to make a business of a letter of gallantry, an examen of a farce;[1] and, in short, a great pomp and ostentation of words on every trifle. This is certainly the talent of that nation, and ought not

---

[1] Dryden thus disingenuously covers his tracks in respect of his debt to Corneille's Discours and Examens, which he had freely owned in the essay *Of Dramatic Poesy*; as usual, he is writing on the principle that the memory of the public is a short one. In point of fact Corneille was not the first dramatist of either nation to provide his plays with critical—as against merely complimentary—prefaces. Five of Ben Jonson's plays are so provided: *Sejanus* (1605) ('To the Readers'), *Volpone* (1607) ('To the Sisters, the two Universities'), *Catiline* (1611) ('To the Reader in Ordinary'), *The Alchemist* (1612) ('To the Reader'), and *The New Inn* (1631) ('The Dedication to the Reader'); they seem to have grown out of the custom of printing a letter of dedication to a noble patron. In France, Jean Mairet (1610-86), whose reputation Corneille supplanted early with *Le Cid* in 1636, had published his tragedy *La Silvanire* (1631) with a 'Préface en forme de discours poétique,' an analysis of the kinds of poetry and of the drama.

to be invaded by any other. They do that out of gaiety which would be an imposition upon us.

We may satisfy ourselves with surmounting them in the scene,[1] and safely leave them those trappings of writing and flourishes of the pen with which they adorn the borders of their plays, and which are indeed no more than good landskips to a very indifferent picture. I must proceed no farther in this argument, lest I run myself beyond my excuse for writing this. Give me leave therefore to tell you, Reader, that I do it not to set a value on any thing I have written in this play, but out of gratitude to the memory of Sir William Davenant, who did me the honour to join me with him in the alteration of it.

It was originally Shakespeare's: a poet for whom he had particularly a high veneration, and whom he first taught me to admire. The play itself had formerly been acted with success in the Blackfriars;[2] and our excellent Fletcher had so great a value for it that he thought fit to make use of the same design, not much varied, a second time.[3] Those who have seen his *Sea-Voyage* may easily discern that it was a copy of Shakespeare's *Tempest*: the storm, the desert island, and the woman who had never seen a man, are all sufficient testimonies of it. But Fletcher was not the only poet who made use of Shakespeare's plot: Sir John Suckling, a professed admirer of our author, has followed his footsteps in his *Goblins*, his Reginella[4] being an open imitation of Shakespeare's Miranda; and his spirits, though counterfeit, yet are copied from Ariel. But Sir William Davenant, as he was a man of quick and piercing imagination, soon found that somewhat might be added to the design of Shakespeare of which neither Fletcher nor Suckling had ever thought: and therefore to put the last hand to it, he

---

[1] I.e. surpassing them upon the stage. Cf. Neander's claims for the superiority of the English drama over the French, pp. 56-77, above.

[2] A very early source of the tradition that Shakespeare's *Tempest* was performed in the indoor Blackfriars Theatre, probably between 1611 and 1613; and in view of the elaborate stage-effects called for, it seems likely enough.

[3] *The Sea Voyage* (1622), probably by John Fletcher and Massinger, where Shakespeare's Prospero is turned into Rosellia, an Amazonian Queen. The Dryden-Davenant adaptation is far less violent and less vulgar, and it is hard to believe Dryden can have thought Fletcher's play 'not much varied' from Shakespeare's.

[4] 'Regmella' in 1670, an evident misprint. *The Goblins* (1646) had recently been revived, in January 1667.

designed the counterpart to Shakespeare's plot, namely that of a man who had never seen a woman,[1] that by this means those two characters of innocence and love might the more illustrate and commend each other. This excellent contrivance he was pleased to communicate to me, and to desire my assistance in it. I confess that from the very first moment it so pleased me that I never writ anything with more delight. I must likewise do him that justice to acknowledge that my writing received daily his amendments, and that is the reason why it is not so faulty as the rest, which I have done without the help or correction of so judicious a friend. The comical parts of the sailors were also his invention and for the most part his writing, as you will easily discover by the style. In the time I writ with him, I had the opportunity to observe somewhat more nearly of him than I had formerly done when I had only a bare acquaintance with him: I found him then of so quick a fancy that nothing was proposed to him on which he could not suddenly produce a thought extremely pleasant and surprising; and those first thoughts of his, contrary to the old Latin proverb,[2] were not always the least happy. And as his fancy was quick, so likewise were the products of it remote and new. He borrowed not of any other; and his imaginations were such as could not easily enter into any other man. His corrections were sober and judicious: and he corrected his own writings much more severely than those of another man, bestowing twice the time and labour in polishing which he used in invention. It had perhaps been easy enough for me to have arrogated more to myself than was my due in the writing of this play, and to have passed by his name with silence in the publication of it, with the same ingratitude which others have used to him, whose writings he hath not only corrected, as he has done this, but has had a greater inspection over them, and sometimes added whole scenes together, which may as easily be distinguished from the rest as true gold from counterfeit by the weight. But besides the unworthiness of the action which deterred me from it (there being nothing so base as to rob the dead of his reputation) I am satisfied I could never have received so much honour

---

[1] The character of Hippolito.
[2] Cicero, *Philippic*, xii.2.5: 'Posteriores cogitationes sapientiores solent esse' ('Second thoughts are usually best').

in being thought the author of any poem, how excellent soever,
as I shall be from the joining my imperfections with the merit
and name of Shakespeare and Sir William Davenant.

    Decemb. 1,
    1669.   JOHN DRYDEN

PROLOGUE TO *THE TEMPEST: OR THE ENCHANTED ISLAND*

As when a tree's cut down, the secret root
Lives under ground, and thence new branches shoot,
So, from old Shakespeare's honoured dust, this day
Springs up and buds a new reviving play.
Shakespeare who (taught by none) did first impart   5
To Fletcher wit, to labouring Jonson art.
He monarch-like gave those his subjects law,
And is that nature which they paint and draw.
Fletcher reached that which on his heights did grow,
Whilst Jonson crept and gathered all below.   10
This did his love, and this his mirth digest:
One imitates him most, the other best.
If they have since outwrit all other men,
'Tis with the drops which fell from Shakespeare's pen.
The storm which vanished on the neighbouring shore   15
Was taught by Shakespeare's *Tempest* first to roar.
That innocence and beauty which did smile
In Fletcher, grew on this Enchanted Isle.
But Shakespeare's magic could not copied be,
Within that circle[1] none durst walk but he.   20
I must confess 'twas bold, nor would you now
That liberty to vulgar wits allow
Which works by magic supernatural things:
But Shakespeare's power is sacred as a King's.
Those legends from old priesthood were received   25

---

[1] A very early attribution of the character of Prospero to Shakespeare,
which much modern scholarship has laboured to deny, in spite of Shakespeare's Epilogue. Cf. *Tempest*, V.i.58f., where the shipwrecked men,
according to the stage-direction, 'all enter the circle which Prospero has
made, and there stand charmed.'

And he then writ as people then believed.
But if for Shakespeare we your grace implore,
We for our theatre shall want it more:
Who by our dearth of youths are forced t'employ
One of our women to present a boy.[1]   30
And that's a transformation, you will say,
Exceeding all the magic in the play.
Let none expect in the last act to find
Her sex transformed from man to womankind.
Whate'er she was before the play began,   35
All you shall see of her is perfect man.
Or if your fancy will be farther led
To find her woman, it must be abed.

[1] Probably the character of Hippolito, 'one that never saw woman.'

PREFACE, PROLOGUE

to *Tyrannic Love, or the Royal Martyr: a Tragedy* (1670)

MORALITY IN DRAMA—A DEFENCE OF THE TRAGEDY— CRITICS *v.* POETS

Text: 4°, 1670. The second edition of 1672, 'reviewed by the author,' adds a last paragraph to the preface.

This tragedy, first performed in June 1669 with great success, though avowedly written in haste, was probably published with its defensive preface towards the end of that year. It represents one of Dryden's earlier attempts at heroic tragedy, and tirades of the tyrant Maximin anticipate in their extravagance those of Almanzor in *The Conquest of Granada*. Dryden lived to apologize for both, in the dedication to *The Spanish Friar* (p. 276, below). Maximin, the pagan emperor, falls in love with the Christian princess Catherine of Alexandria and seeks to divorce his wife Berenice. Catherine refuses his appeals and dies in torture as a martyr, and the tyrant is killed by one of his officers. The part of Catherine was incongruously taken by Nell Gwyn.

I WAS moved to write this play by many reasons: amongst others, the commands of some persons of honour,[1] for whom I have a most particular respect, were daily sounding in my ears that it would be of good example to undertake a poem of this nature. Neither was my own inclination wanting to second their desires. I considered that pleasure was not the only end of poesy; and that even the instructions of morality were not so wholly the business of the poet as that the precepts and examples of piety were to be omitted. For to leave the employment altogether to the clergy were to forget that religion was first taught in verse (which the laziness or dullness of succeeding priesthood turned afterwards into prose). And it were also to

---

[1] The subject of St Catherine may have been chosen as a compliment to Charles II's queen, Catherine of Braganza.

grant (which I never shall) that representations of this kind may not as well be conducing to holiness as to good manners. Yet far be it from me to compare the use of dramatic poesy with that of divinity: I only maintain, against the enemies of the stage, that patterns of piety, decently represented and equally removed from the extremes of superstition and profaneness, may be of excellent use to second the precepts of our religion. By the harmony of words we elevate the mind to a sense of devotion, as our solemn music, which is inarticulate poesy, does in churches; and by the lively images of piety, adorned by action, through the senses allure the soul; which while it is charmed in a silent joy of what it sees and hears, is struck at the same time with a secret veneration of things celestial, and is wound up insensibly into the practice of that which it admires. Now if, instead of this, we sometimes see on our theatres the examples of vice rewarded, or at least unpunished; yet it ought not to be an argument against the art, any more than the extravagances and impieties of the pulpit in the late times of rebellion can be against the office and dignity of the clergy.

But many times it happens that poets are wrongfully accused; as it is in my own case in this very play, where I am charged by some ignorant or malicious persons with no less crimes than profaneness and irreligion. The part of Maximin,[1] against which these holy critics so much declaim, was designed by me to set off the character of S. Catherine. And those who have read the Roman history[2] may easily remember that Maximin was not only a bloody tyrant, *vastus corpore, animo ferus*,[3] as Herodian describes him, but also a persecutor of the Church, against which he raised the sixth persecution. So that whatsoever he speaks or acts in this tragedy is no more than a record of his life and manners, a picture, as near as I could

[1] Daja Maximinus (Emperor, A.D. 310-313), one of the last pagan emperors, who condemned St Catherine to imprisonment, the wheel, and finally beheading.

[2] Herodian, *Roman History*, vii. Dryden, as he confesses below, has confused the later tormentor of St Catherine with the first barbarian emperor Maximinus Thrax (Emperor, A.D. 235-238), to whom the following details relate.

[3] Herodian, *op. cit.*: 'vast in body, fierce in mind.' The Greek-Latin edition of Daniel Pareus contains a Latin analysis of each book, and the heading to Book VII describes the earlier Maximinus Thrax as 'vasto corpore et crudeli animo praeditus'—Dryden's probable source. Cf. *Summers*, II.519-20.

take it, from the original. If with much pains and some success I have drawn a deformed piece, there is as much of art, and as near an imitation of nature, in a lazar as in a Venus. Maximin was an heathen, and what he speaks against religion is in contempt of that which he professed. He defies the Gods of Rome, which is no more than S. Catherine might with decency have done. If it be urged that a person of such principles who scoffs at any religion ought not to be presented on the stage; why then are the lives and sayings of so many wicked and profane persons recorded in the Holy Scriptures? I know it will be answered that a due use may be made of them; that they are remembered with a brand of infamy fixed upon them; and set as sea-marks for those who behold them to avoid. And what other use have I made of Maximin? Have I proposed him as a pattern to be imitated, whom even for his impiety to his false gods I have so severely punished? Nay, as if I had foreseen this objection, I purposely removed the scene of the play, which ought to have been at Alexandria in Egypt (where S. Catherine suffered) and laid it under the walls of Aquileia in Italy, where Maximin was slain, that the punishment of his crime might immediately succeed its execution.

This, Reader, is what I owed to my just defence, and the due reverence of that religion which I profess, to which all men who desire to be esteemed good or honest are obliged: I have neither leisure nor occasion to write more largely on this subject, because I am already justified by the sentence of the best and most discerning Prince in the world, by the suffrage of all unbiassed judges, and above all by the witness of my own conscience, which abhors the thought of such a crime; to which I ask leave to add my outward conversation, which shall never be justly taxed with the note of atheism or profaneness.

In what else concerns the play, I shall be brief: for the faults of the writing and contrivance, I leave them to the mercy of the reader. For I am as little apt to defend my own errors as to find those of other poets. Only I observe that the great censors of wit and poetry either produce nothing of their own, or what is more ridiculous than any thing they reprehend. Much of ill nature, and a very little judgment, go far in the finding the mistakes of writers.

I pretend not that anything of mine can be correct: this poem, especially, which was contrived and written in seven weeks, though afterwards hindered by many accidents from a speedy representation, which would have been its best excuse. Yet the scenes are everywhere unbroken, and the unities of place and time more exactly kept than perhaps is requisite in a tragedy; or at least than I have since preserved them in the *Conquest of Granada*. I have not everywhere observed the equality of numbers in my verse: partly by reason of my haste; but more especially because I would not have my sense a slave to syllables.

'Tis easy to discover that I have been very bold in my alteration of the story, which of itself was too barren for a play; and that I have taken from the Church two martyrs, in the persons of Porphyrius and the Empress, who suffered for the Christian faith under the tyranny of Maximin.

I have seen a French play called the *Martyrdom of S. Catherine*;[1] but those who have read it will soon clear me from stealing out of so dull an author. I have only borrowed a mistake from him, of one Maximin for another: for finding him in the French poet called the son of a Thracian herdsman and an Alane woman,[2] I too easily believed him to have been the same Maximin mentioned in Herodian. Till afterwards consulting Eusebius and Metaphrastes,[3] I found the Frenchman had betrayed me into an error (when it was too late to alter it) by mistaking that first Maximin for a second, the contemporary of Constantine the Great, and one of the usurpers of the Eastern Empire.

But neither was the other name of my play more fortunate: for as some who had heard of a tragedy of S. Catherine imagined I had taken my plot from thence; so others, who had heard of another play called *L'amour tyrannique*,[4] with the same ignorance accused me to have borrowed my design from it, because I have accidentally given my play the same title, not having to this day seen it; and knowing only by report that such a comedy is extant in French under the name of Monsieur Scudéry.

[1] *Sainte Catherine* (1650), one of the unsuccessful tragedies of the Abbé d'Aubignac (1604-76), sometimes attributed to Desfontaines. It has, indeed, nothing in common with *Tyrannic Love* but the subject.

[2] *Sainte Catherine, op. cit.,* V.v.

[3] Eusebius (d. A.D. 339), bk viii; Symeon Metaphrastes (*fl.* A.D. 960-970), *Menologion.*

[4] A tragedy of Georges de Scudéry published in 1639. Like d'Aubignac's, it reveals no debt on the part of Dryden.

As for what I have said of astral or aerial spirits,[1] it is no invention of mine, but taken from those who have written on that subject. Whether there are such beings or not, it concerns not me; 'tis sufficient for my purpose that many have believed the affirmative; and that these heroic representations, which are of the same nature with the epic, are not limited but with the extremest bounds of what is credible.

For[2] the little critics who pleased themselves with thinking they have found a flaw in that line of the Prologue (*And he who servilely creeps after sense Is safe,*[3] etc.), as if I patronized my own nonsense, I may reasonably suppose they have never read Horace; *serpit humi tutus*[4] etc., are his words: he who creeps after plain, dull, common sense is safe from committing absurdities, but can never reach any height or excellence of wit; and sure I could not mean that any excellence were to be found in nonsense. With the same ignorance or malice, they would accuse me for using *empty arms*,[5] when I writ of a ghost or shadow, which has only the appearance of body or limbs, and is empty or void of flesh and blood; and *vacuis amplectitur ulnis*[6] was an expression of Ovid's on the same subject. Some fool[7] before them had charged me in the *Indian Emperor* with nonsense in these words: *And follow fate which does too fast*

---

[1] *Tyrannic Love*, IV, where Nigrinus the conjuror unsuccessfully tries to induce in Catherine love for Maximin by invoking spirits out of the air. Dryden's attitude to magic remained uncommitted. In his dedication 'To the Marquis of Halifax' prefixed to his libretto *King Arthur* (1691), which he had written in 1684 for Purcell's music, he recommended the supernatural elements on the sole grounds that they pleased his 'first and best patroness the Duchess of Monmouth': 'the parts of the airy and earthy spirits, and that fairy kind of writing, which depends only upon the force of imagination, were the grounds of her liking the poem, and afterwards of her recommending it to the Queen,' i.e. to Mary II.

[2] This paragraph was added in the second and revised edition of 1672.

[3] Prologue, ll. 14-15, below.   [4] *Ars poetica*, l. 28.

[5] *Tyrannic Love*, III (Berenice's last speech):

I'll come all soul and spirit to your love.
With silent steps I'll follow you all day,
Or else before you in the sunbeams play.
I'll lead you thence to melancholy groves,
And there repeat the scenes of our past loves.
At night, I will within your curtains peep,
With empty arms embrace you while you sleep.

[6] Dryden again misquotes to suit his purpose. Ovid, *Metamorphoses*, VIII.818 has 'geminis amplectitur ulnis' ('she wrapped her thin arms around him'). 'Vacuis' occurs two lines later ('in vacuis . . . venis').

[7] Probably Richard Flecknoe (c. 1620-78?). Cf. 'Defence of *An Essay*,' p. 130n., above.

pursue,[1] which was borrowed from Virgil in the eleventh of his Aeneids, *eludit gyro interior, sequitur sequentem*.[2] I quote not these to prove that I never writ nonsense, but only to shew that they are so unfortunate as not to have found it.

VALE.

PROLOGUE

Self-love (which never rightly understood)
Makes poets still conclude their plays are good:
And malice in all critics reigns so high
That for small errors they whole plays decry;
So that to see this fondness, and that spite,　　5
You'd think that none but madmen judge or write.
Therefore our poet, as he thinks not fit
T'impose upon you what he writes for wit,
So hopes that leaving you your censures free,
You equal judges of the whole will be:　　　　10
They judge but half who only faults will see.
Poets like lovers should be bold and dare,
They spoil their business with an over-care.
And he who servilely creeps after sense
Is safe, but ne'er will reach an excellence.　　15
Hence 'tis our poet in his conjuring
Allowed his fancy the full scope and swing.
But when a tyrant for his theme he had,
He loosed the reins, and bid his Muse run mad:
And though he stumbles in a full career,　　　20
Yet rashness is a better fault than fear.
He saw his way; but in so swift a pace,
To choose the ground might be to lose the race.
They then who of each trip th'advantage take
Find but those faults which they want wit to make.　25

---

[1] *The Indian Emperor* (1667), IV.iii, from the song of the Indian woman (l. 5). *1667* has 'that does,' the second edition of 1668 'which would.'

[2] *Aeneid*, xi.695: 'She eludes him, wheels inward and pursues the pursuer.'

PREFACE

to *An Evening's Love: or the Mock Astrologer* (1671)

TRAGEDY, COMEDY, FARCE—WIT AND HUMOUR—PLAGIARISM

Text: 4°, 1671. Two editions appeared in this year, both very careless.

The preface, a considered statement of Dryden's view of comedy—its inferiority to tragedy, and superiority to farce—follows a dedicatory epistle 'To his Grace William, Duke of Newcastle' (1592-1676), a supporter of the royalist cause during the Civil War and Protectorate. Newcastle had retired to live the life of a country gentleman after the Restoration. He was himself the author of several comedies, including a translation of Molière's *L'étourdi* (1658), adapted by Dryden as *Sir Martin Mar-All* and published in 1668 under the Duke's name. But his real fame was as a patron of letters: Langbaine later called him 'our English Maecenas,' Aubrey records he entertained Descartes, Gassendi, and Hobbes together at his table when an exile in Paris, Jonson wrote two masques for him, as well as occasional poems, and Davenant was for a time one of his officers. The dedication praises Newcastle as a patron and author of comedy, but the preface suggests that, for Dryden in his fortieth year, comedy took second place to tragedy. *The Conquest of Granada*, the most ambitious of his heroic plays, had recently been performed, and the publication of *An Evening's Love*, a prose comedy which had been played three years before, in June 1668, seemed only an occasion for an apologetic definition of this inferior kind of drama, where 'the persons . . . are of a lower quality, the action is little.'

I HAD thought, Reader, in this preface to have written somewhat concerning the difference betwixt the plays of our age and those of our predecessors on the English stage: to have shewn in what parts of dramatic poesy we were excelled by Ben Jonson, I mean humour and contrivance of comedy; and in what we may justly claim precedence of Shakespeare and Fletcher, namely in heroic plays. But this design I have waived on second considerations; at least deferred it till I publish the *Conquest of Granada*, where the discourse will be more proper. I have also prepared to treat of the improvement of our language since Fletcher's and Jonson's days, and consequently of our refining the courtship, raillery, and conversation of plays: but as I am willing to decline that envy which I should draw on myself from some old opiniatre[1] judges of the stage; so likewise I am pressed in time so much that I have not leisure, at present, to go through with it.

Neither, indeed, do I value a reputation gained from comedy so far as to concern myself about it any more than I needs must in my own defence: for I think it, in its own nature, inferior to all sorts of dramatic writing. Low comedy especially requires, on the writer's part, much of conversation with the vulgar: and much of ill nature in the observation of their follies. But let all men please themselves according to their several tastes: that which is not pleasant to me may be to others who judge better; and, to prevent an accusation from my enemies, I am sometimes ready to imagine that my disgust of low comedy proceeds not so much from my judgment as from my temper; which is the reason why I so seldom write it; and that when I succeed in it (I mean so far as to please the audience), yet I am nothing satisfied with what I have done; but am often vexed to hear the people laugh, and clap, as they perpetually do, where I intended 'em no jest; while they let pass the better things without taking notice of them. Yet even this confirms me in my opinion of slighting popular applause, and of contemning that approbation which those very people give, equally with me, to the zany of a mountebank; or to the appearance of an antic on the theatre, without wit on the poet's part, or any occasion of laughter from the actor besides the ridiculousness of his habit and his grimaces.

But I have descended, before I was aware, from comedy to farce:[2] which consists principally of grimaces. That I admire not any comedy equally with tragedy is, perhaps, from the sullenness of my humour; but that I detest those farces which are now the most frequent entertainments of the stage, I am sure

---

[1] I.e. stubborn—a French borrowing recorded as early as 1591 and used by Milton and Pepys before Dryden. The word reoccurs in the text of *An Evening's Love*: 'If she begins to fly before me, I grow opiniatre as the Devil' (Act II).

[2] One of the earliest recorded uses of the word as a kind of play. Howard had already used it in this sense in his preface to *The Great Favourite* (1668), quoted derisively by Dryden in his 'Defence,' p. 119, above.

I have reason on my side. Comedy consists, though of low persons, yet of natural actions and characters; I mean such humours, adventures, and designs as are to be found and met with in the world. Farce, on the other side, consists of forced humours and unnatural events. Comedy presents us with the imperfections of human nature. Farce entertains us with what is monstrous and chimerical: the one causes laughter in those who can judge of men and manners, by the lively representation of their folly or corruption; the other produces the same effect in those who can judge of neither, and that only by its extravag-. ances. The first works on the judgment and fancy; the latter on the fancy only: there is more of satisfaction in the former kind of laughter, and in the latter more of scorn. But how it happens that an impossible adventure should cause our mirth, I cannot so easily imagine. Something there may be in the oddness of it, because on the stage it is the common effect of things unexpected to surprise us into a delight: and that is to be ascribed to the strange appetite, as I may call it, of the fancy; which, like that of a longing woman, often runs out into the most extravagant desires; and is better satisfied sometimes with loam, or with the rinds of trees, than with the wholesome nourishments of life. In short, there is the same difference betwixt farce and comedy as betwixt an empiric[1] and a true physician: both of them may attain their ends; but what the one performs by hazard, the other does by skill. And as the artist is often unsuccessful while the mountebank succeeds; so farces more commonly take the people than comedies. For to write unnatural things is the most probable way of pleasing them, who understand not nature. And a true poet often misses of applause because he cannot debase himself to write so ill as to please his audience.

After all, it is to be acknowledged that most of those comedies which have been lately written have been allied too much to farce; and this must of necessity fall out till we forbear the translation of French plays: for their poets, wanting judgment to make or to maintain true characters, strive to cover their defects with ridiculous figures and grimaces. While I say this, I accuse myself as well as others: and this very play would rise up in judgment against me, if I would defend all things I have written to be

---

[1] I.e. given to prescribing according to private observation rather than scientific theory—hence, a quack.

natural: but I confess I have given too much to the people in it, and am ashamed for them as well as for myself, that I have pleased them at so cheap a rate. Not that there is anything here which I would not defend to an ill-natured judge (for I despise their censures, who I am sure would write worse on the same subject): but because I love to deal clearly and plainly, and to speak of my own faults with more criticism than I would of another poet's. Yet I think it no vanity to say that this comedy has as much of entertainment in it as many other which have been lately written: and, if I find my own errors in it, I am able at the same time to arraign all my contemporaries for greater. As I pretend not that I can write humour,[1] so none of them can reasonably pretend to have written it as they ought. Jonson was the only man of all ages and nations who has performed it well, and that but in three or four of his comedies: the rest are but a *crambe bis cocta*;[2] the same humours a little varied and written worse. Neither was it more allowable in him than it is in our present poets to represent the follies of particular persons; of which many have accused him. *Parcere personis, dicere de vitiis*[3] is the rule of plays. And Horace tells you that the Old Comedy amongst the Grecians was silenced for the too great liberties of the poets:

> in vitium libertas excidit et vim
> dignam lege regi: lex est accepta, chorusque
> turpiter obticuit, sublato jure nocendi.[4]

Of which he gives you the reason in another place: where, having given the precept,

> neve immunda crepent, ignominiosaque dicta,

he immediately subjoins,

---

[1] Evidently used in a sense more modern than Jonsonian, though its meaning in the following sentence is less clear. Dryden had defined the Elizabethan sense of the word with pedantic thoroughness in *Of Dramatic Poesy* (pp. 71-3, above); but, as this preface repeatedly suggests, the word had already evolved far beyond this point.

[2] Juvenal, *Satires*, VII.154 has 'crambe repetita' ('the mess served up again and again').

[3] 'To spare individuals and speak of vices' (Latin tag).

[4] *Ars poetica*, ll. 282-4: 'Liberty turned to licence, and to an excess that called for legal restraint. A law was passed and, the right of libel gone, the chorus to its shame fell silent.'

offenduntur enim quibus est equus, et pater, et res.[1]

But Ben Jonson is to be admired for many excellencies; and can be taxed with fewer failings than any English poet. I know I have been accused as an enemy of his writings; but without any other reason than that I do not admire him blindly, and without looking into his imperfections. For why should he only be exempted from those frailties from which Homer and Virgil are not free? Or why should there be any *ipse dixit* in our poetry, any more than there is in our philosophy? I admire and applaud him where I ought: those who do more do but value themselves in their admiration of him; and, by telling you they extol Ben Jonson's way, would insinuate to you that they can practise it. For my part, I declare that I want judgment to imitate him; and should think it a great impudence in myself to attempt it. To make men appear pleasantly ridiculous on the stage was, as I have said, his talent; and in this he needed not the acumen of wit, but that of judgment. For the characters and representations of folly are only the effects of observation; and observation is an effect of judgment. Some ingenious men, for whom I have a particular esteem, have thought I have much injured Ben Jonson when I have not allowed his wit to be extraordinary: but they confound the notion of what is witty with what is pleasant.[2] That Ben Jonson's plays were pleasant, he must want reason who denies: but that pleasantness was not properly wit, or the sharpness of conceit, but the natural imitation of folly: which if I confess to be excellent in its kind, but not to be of that kind which they pretend. Yet if we will believe Quintilian in his chapter *De movendo risu*, he gives his opinion of both in these following words: *stulta reprehendere facillimum est; nam per se sunt ridicula: et a derisu non procul abest risus: sed rem urbanum facit aliqua ex nobis adjectio.*[3]

And some perhaps would be apt to say of Jonson as it was said of Demosthenes: *non displicuisse illi jocos, sed non contigisse.*[4]

I will not deny but that I approve most the mixed way of

---

[1] *Ars poetica*, ll. 247-8: 'nor should they give way to foul and scurrilous expressions, for persons of rank, birth, and fortune are offended by them.'

[2] I.e. amusing. For Jonson's wit, cf. p. 69, above.

[3] *Institutio oratoria*, VI.iii.71: 'It is easy to make fun of folly, for folly is ridiculous in itself; but something of our own makes the joke graceful.'

[4] *Ibid.*, VI.iii.2: 'not to have disliked jokes, but to have lacked the power to make them.'

comedy; that which is neither all wit, nor all humour, but the result of both. Neither so little of humour as Fletcher shows, nor so little of love and wit as Jonson; neither all cheat, with which the best plays of the one are filled, nor all adventure, which is the common practice of the other. I would have the characters well chosen, and kept distant from interfering with each other; which is more than Fletcher or Shakespeare did: but I would have more of the *urbana, venusta, salsa, faceta*,[1] and the rest which Quintilian reckons up as the ornaments of wit; and these are extremely wanting in Ben Jonson. As for repartee in particular; as it is the very soul of conversation, so it is the greatest grace of comedy, where it is proper to the characters. There may be much of acuteness in a thing well said; but there is more in a quick reply: *sunt enim longe venustiora omnia in respondendo quam in provocando*.[2] Of one thing I am sure, that no man ever will decry wit but he who despairs of it himself; and who has no other quarrel to it but that which the fox had to the grapes. Yet, as Mr Cowley (who had a greater portion of it than any man I know) tells us in his character of wit, rather than all wit let there be none.[3] I think there's no folly so great in any poet of our age as the superfluity and waste of wit was in some of our predecessors: particularly we may say of Fletcher and of Shakespeare what was said of Ovid, *in omni ejus ingenio, facilius quod rejici, quam quod adjici potest, invenies*.[4] The contrary of which was true in Virgil, and our incomparable Jonson.

Some enemies of repartee have observed to us that there is a great latitude in their characters which are made to speak it: and that it is easier to write wit than humour; because, in the characters of humour, the poet is confined to make the person speak what is only proper to it. Whereas all kind of wit is proper in the character of a witty person. But, by their favour, there are

[1] *Ibid.*, VI.iii.17-20, where Quintilian distinguishes a number of words by which wit is described, the first four being *urbanitas* (of the language of cities and learning), *venustus* (graceful, charming), *salsus* (salty, piquant), and *facetus* (polished, elegant).

[2] Quintilian, VI.iii.13: 'for wit always looks more graceful in reply than in attack.'

[3] 'Ode: Of Wit,' ll. 35-6:
> Jewels at nose, and lips but ill appear;
> Rather than all things, Wit, let none be there.'

[4] Quintilian, VI.iii.5 ('. . . possit, invenient'): 'In all his wit you will find it easier to reject than to add.'

as different characters in wit as in folly. Neither is all kind of wit proper in the mouth of every ingenious person. A witty coward and a witty brave must speak differently. Falstaff and the Liar speak not like Don John in the *Chances*, and Valentine in *Wit without Money*.[1] And Jonson's Truewit in the *Silent Woman* is a character different from all of them. Yet it appears that this one character of wit was more difficult to the author than all his images of humour in the play: for those he could describe and manage from his observations of men; this he has taken, at least a part of it, from books: witness the speeches in the first act, translated *verbatim* out of Ovid *De arte amandi*; to omit what afterwards he borrowed from the sixth satire of Juvenal against women.[2]

However, if I should grant that there were a greater latitude in characters of wit than in those of humour; yet that latitude would be of small advantage to such poets who have too narrow an imagination to write it. And to entertain an audience perpetually with humour is to carry them from the conversation of gentlemen, and treat them with the follies and extravagances of Bedlam.

I find I have launched out farther than I intended in the beginning of this preface. And that, in the heat of writing, I have touched at something which I thought to have avoided. 'Tis time now to draw homeward: and to think rather of defending myself than assaulting others. I have already acknowledged that this play is far from perfect: but I do not think myself obliged to discover the imperfections of it to my adversaries, any more than a guilty person is bound to accuse himself before his judges. 'Tis charged upon me that I make debauched persons (such as, they say, my Astrologer and Gamester are) my protagonists, or the chief persons of the drama; and that I make them happy in the conclusion of my play; against the law of comedy, which is to reward virtue and punish vice. I answer first, that I know no such law to have been constantly observed in comedy, either by the ancient or modern poets. Chærea is made happy in the *Eunuch*, after having deflowered a virgin; and Terence generally does the same through all his plays,

---

[1] Two of Fletcher's comedies.

[2] E.g. *Epicoene*, I.i.105-9 and *Ars amatoria*, III.135-40; *Epicoene*, I.i.114-26 and *Ars*, 217-18, 225-34, etc. Cf. *Herford & Simpson*, X.7f. Jonson's portrait of the Collegiate Ladies owes something to Juvenal.

where you perpetually see not only debauched young men enjoy their mistresses, but even the courtesans themselves rewarded and honoured in the catastrophe. The same may be observed in Plautus almost everywhere. Ben Jonson himself, after whom I may be proud to err, has given me more than once the example of it. That in the *Alchemist* is notorious, where Face, after having contrived and carried on the great cozenage of the play, and continued in it without repentance to the last, is not only forgiven by his master, but enriched by his consent with the spoils of those whom he had cheated. And, which is more, his master himself, a grave man and a widower, is introduced taking his man's counsel, debauching the widow first, in hope to marry her afterward. In the *Silent Woman*, Dauphine (who, with the other two gentlemen, is of the same character with my Celadon in the *Maiden Queen*, and with Wildblood in this) professes himself in love with all the Collegiate Ladies: and they likewise are all of the same character with each other, excepting only Madam Otter, who has something singular: yet this naughty Dauphine is crowned in the end with the possession of his uncle's estate, and with the hopes of enjoying all his mistresses; and his friend Mr Truewit (the best character of a gentleman which Ben Jonson ever made) is not ashamed to pimp for him. As for Beaumont and Fletcher, I need not allege examples out of them; for that were to quote almost all their comedies.

But now it will be objected that I patronize vice by the authority of former poets, and extenuate my own faults by recrimination. I answer that, as I defend myself by their example, so that example I defend by reason, and by the end of all dramatic poesy. In the first place, therefore, give me leave to shew you their mistake who have accused me. They have not distinguished, as they ought, betwixt the rules of tragedy and comedy. In tragedy, where the actions and persons are great, and the crimes horrid, the laws of justice are more strictly to be observed; and examples of punishment to be made to deter mankind from the pursuit of vice. Faults of this kind have been rare amongst the ancient poets: for they have punished in Oedipus, and in his posterity, the sin which he knew not he had committed. Medea is the only example I remember at present who escapes from punishment after murder. Thus tragedy fulfils one great part of

its institution: which is, by example, to instruct. But in comedy
it is not so; for the chief end of it is divertisement and delight:
and that so much, that it is disputed, I think, by Heinsius,
before Horace his *Art of Poetry*, whether instruction be any part
of its employment.[1] At least I am sure it can be but its secondary end: for the business of the poet is to make you laugh:
when he writes humour, he makes folly ridiculous; when wit,
he moves you, if not always to laughter, yet to a pleasure that
is more noble. And if he works a cure on folly, and the small
imperfections in mankind, by exposing them to public view,
that cure is not performed by an immediate operation. For it
works first on the ill nature of the audience; they are moved to
laugh by the representation of deformity; and the shame of that
laughter teaches us to amend what is ridiculous in our manners.
This being, then, established, that the first end of comedy is
delight, and instruction only the second, it may reasonably be
inferred that comedy is not so much obliged to the punishment of
faults which it represents, as tragedy. For the persons in
comedy are of a lower quality, the action is little, and the faults
and vices are but the sallies of youth, and the frailties of human
nature, and not premeditated crimes: such to which all men are
obnoxious, not such as are attempted only by few, and those
abandoned to all sense of virtue: such as move pity and commiseration, not detestation and horror; such, in short, as may
be forgiven, not such as must of necessity be punished. But, lest
any man should think that I write this to make libertinism
amiable, or that I cared not to debase the end and institution of
comedy so I might thereby maintain my own errors, and those
of better poets, I must further declare, both for them and for
myself, that we make not vicious persons happy, but only as
Heaven makes sinners so; that is, by reclaiming them first
from vice. For so 'tis to be supposed they are, when they
resolve to marry; for then enjoying what they desire in one,
they cease to pursue the love of many. So Chærea is made happy
by Terence, in marrying her whom he had deflowered: and so
are Wildblood and the Astrologer in this play.

There is another crime with which I am charged, at which I

---

[1] Dryden's memory is at fault. The 1610 edition of Horace by the Dutch
scholar Daniel Heinsius (1580-1655), in a note to *Ars poetica*, l. 270, claims
that the end of comedy is to teach as well as to delight (*delectare enim ac
docere est comediae*).

am yet much less concerned, because it does not relate to my manners, as the former did, but only to my reputation as a poet: a name of which I assure the reader I am nothing proud; and therefore cannot be very solicitous to defend it. I am taxed with stealing all my plays, and that by some who should be the last men from whom I would steal any part of 'em. There is one answer which I will not make; but it has been made for me by him to whose grace and patronage I owe all things,

et spes et ratio studiorum in Caesare tantum,[1]

and without whose command they should no longer be troubled with any thing of mine, that he only desired that they who accused me of theft would always steal him plays like mine.[2] But though I have reason to be proud of this defence, yet I should waive it, because I have a worse opinion of my own comedies than any of my enemies can have. 'Tis true that, where ever I have liked any story in a romance, novel, or foreign play, I have made no difficulty, nor ever shall, to take the foundation of it, to build it up, and to make it proper for the English stage. And I will be so vain to say it has lost nothing in my hands: but it always cost me so much trouble to heighten it for our theatre (which is incomparably more curious in all the ornaments of dramatic poesy than the French or Spanish), that when I had finished my play, it was like the hulk of Sir Francis Drake, so strangely altered that there scarcely remained any plank of the timber which first built it. To witness this, I need go no farther than this play: it was first Spanish, and called *El astrologo fingido*; then made French by the younger Corneille; and is now translated into English, and in print, under the name of the *Feigned Astrologer*.[3] What I have performed in this will best appear by comparing it with those: you will see that I have rejected some adventures which I judged were not divertising; that I have heightened those which I have chosen, and that I have added others which were neither in the French nor Spanish. And besides, you will easily discover that the walk of

[1] Juvenal, *Satires*, VII.1: 'On Caesar alone all the hopes and prospects of scholars depend.'

[2] No doubt a second compliment to the Duke of Newcastle, himself the author of several comedies, to whom *An Evening's Love* is dedicated.

[3] Calderón's comedy was the source of Thomas Corneille's *Le feint astrologue* (1651), which in turn was anonymously adapted into English as *The Feigned Astrologer* (1668).

the Astrologer is the least considerable in my play: for the design of it turns more on the parts of Wildblood and Jacinta, who are the chief persons in it. I have farther to add that I seldom use the wit and language of any romance or play, which I undertake to alter: because my own invention (as bad as it is) can furnish me with nothing so dull as what is there. Those who have called Virgil, Terence, and Tasso plagiaries (though they much injured them), had yet a better colour for their accusation; for Virgil has evidently translated Theocritus, Hesiod, and Homer, in many places; besides what he has taken from Ennius in his own language. Terence was not only known to translate Menander (which he avows also in his prologues), but was said also to be helped in those translations by Scipio the African and Lælius. And Tasso, the most excellent of modern poets, and whom I reverence next to Virgil, has taken both from Homer many admirable things which were left untouched by Virgil, and from Virgil himself where Homer could not furnish him. Yet the bodies of Virgil's and Tasso's poems were their own; and so are all the ornaments of language and elocution in them. The same (if there were any thing commendable in this play) I could say for it. But I will come nearer to our own countrymen. Most of Shakespeare's plays, I mean the stories of them, are to be found in the *Hecatommithi* or *Hundred Novels* of Cinthio.[1] I have myself read in his Italian that of *Romeo and Juliet*, the *Moor of Venice*, and many others of them. Beaumont and Fletcher had most of theirs from Spanish novels: witness the *Chances*, the *Spanish Curate*, *Rule a Wife and have a Wife*, the *Little French Lawyer*, and so many others of them as compose the greatest part of their volume in folio. Ben Jonson, indeed, has designed his plots himself; but no man has borrowed so much from the Ancients as he has done: and he did well in it, for he has thereby beautified our language.

But these little critics do not well consider what is the work of a poet, and what the graces of a poem. The story is the least part of either: I mean the foundation of it, before it is modelled by the art of him who writes it; who forms it with more care, by exposing only the beautiful parts of it to view, than a skilful

---

[1] Giraldi Cinthio, *Hecatommithi* (1565) was indeed the source of *Othello*, but not of *Romeo and Juliet*. It was also a partial source for *Two Gentlemen of Verona*, *Twelfth Night*, and *Measure for Measure*.

lapidary sets a jewel. On this foundation of the story the characters are raised: and, since no story can afford characters
enough for the variety of the English stage, it follows that it is
to be altered and enlarged with new persons, accidents, and
designs, which will almost make it new. When this is done, the
forming it into acts and scenes, disposing of actions and passions
into their proper places, and beautifying both with descriptions,
similitudes, and propriety of language, is the principal employment of the poet; as being the largest field of fancy, which is the
principal quality required in him: for so much the word
ποιητής implies. Judgment, indeed, is necessary in him; but 'tis
fancy that gives the life-touches, and the secret graces to it;
especially in the serious plays, which depend not much on
observation. For to write humour in comedy (which is the
theft of poets from mankind), little of fancy is required; the
poet observes only what is ridiculous and pleasant folly, and
by judging exactly what is so, he pleases in the representation
of it.

But in general, the employment of a poet is like that of a
curious gunsmith or watchmaker: the iron or silver is not his
own; but they are the least part of that which gives the value:
the price lies wholly in the workmanship. And he who works
dully on a story, without moving laughter in a comedy, or
raising concernments in a serious play, is no more to be
accounted a good poet than a gunsmith of the Minories[1] is to be
compared with the best workman of the town.

But I have said more of this than I intended; and more,
perhaps, than I needed to have done. I shall but laugh at them
hereafter who accuse me with so little reason; and withal
condemn their dullness who, if they could ruin that little reputation I have got, and which I value not, yet would want both
wit and learning to establish their own; or to be remembered
in after ages for any thing but only that which makes them
ridiculous in this.

[1] A street near the Tower of London noted for its armourers. John Stow,
in his *Survey of London* (1603), reports that in 1593 it contained 'divers fair
and large storehouses for armour and habilaments of war, with divers work-
houses serving to the same purpose.'

OF HEROIC PLAYS: AN ESSAY

Prefixed to *The Conquest of Granada by the Spaniards, in Two Parts* (1672)

DAVENANT—MAGIC IN DRAMA—THE HERO—
REFINEMENT OF ENGLISH—POETIC STYLE—
INFERIORITY OF ELIZABETHAN PLAYWRIGHTS

Text: 4°, 1672. The 'Defence of the Epilogue,' below, was dropped from the fourth edition of the play (1687) and not reprinted in Dryden's lifetime.

The Conquest of Granada, Dryden's culminating achievement in the heroic play, was first performed in two successive parts in December 1670 and January 1671, but the quarto probably did not appear until early in 1672. The two critical essays it contains—the ten acts of the play are sandwiched between them—fulfil Dryden's promise made in the preface to *An Evening's Love* (1671) 'to have written somewhat concerning the difference betwixt the plays of our age and those of our predecessors,' a 'discourse . . . more proper' to *The Conquest of Granada*, as he there explained, since it was in the heroic play rather than in comedy that Restoration playwrights surpassed the Elizabethans. The promise, however, is oddly fulfilled: the preface is largely taken up with a defence of the *Conquest* itself, and especially of its posturing hero Almanzor, so that the comparative essay had to be deferred a second time, and then artificially provoked by an Epilogue to the Second Part which boldly asserted the superiority of Restoration plays and called for a 'Defence.'

The preface follows a dedicatory letter 'To his Royal Highness the Duke,' i.e. the Duke of York (later James II), addressed to one whose 'whole life has been a continued series of heroic actions.'

WHETHER heroic verse ought to be admitted into serious plays is not now to be disputed: 'tis already in possession of the stage, and I dare confidently affirm that very few tragedies, in this age, shall be received without it. All the arguments which are formed against it can amount to no more than this, that it is not so near conversation as prose, and therefore not so natural.[1] But it is very clear to all who understand poetry that serious plays ought not to imitate conversation too nearly. If nothing were to be raised above that level, the foundation of poetry would be destroyed. And, if you once admit of a latitude, that thoughts may be exalted and that images and actions may be raised above the life, and described in measure without rhyme, that leads you insensibly from your own principles to mine: you are already so far onward of your way that you have forsaken the imitation of ordinary converse. You are gone beyond it; and to continue where you are, is to lodge in the open fields, betwixt two inns. You have lost that which you call natural, and have not acquired the last perfection of art. But it was only custom which cozened us so long; we thought, because Shakespeare and Fletcher went no farther, that there the pillars of poetry were to be erected; that, because they excellently described passion without rhyme, therefore rhyme was not capable of describing it. But time has now convinced most men of that error. 'Tis indeed so difficult to write verse that the adversaries of it have a good plea against many who undertake that task, without being formed by art or nature for it. Yet, even they who have written worst in it, would have written worse without it. They have cozened many with their sound, who never took the pains to examine their sense. In fine, they have succeeded: though 'tis true they have more dishonoured rhyme by their good success than they could have done by their ill. But I am willing to let fall this argument: 'tis free for every man to write, or not to write, in verse, as he judges it to be, or not to be, his talent; or as he imagines the audience will receive it.

For heroic plays (in which only I have used it without the mixture of prose), the first light we had of them on the English theatre was from the late Sir William Davenant. It being forbidden him in the rebellious times to act tragedies and comedies, because they contained some matter of scandal to those good people who could more easily dispossess their lawful sovereign than endure a wanton jest, he was forced to turn his thoughts another way, and to introduce the examples of moral virtue writ

[1] A summary of Sir Robert Howard's arguments against rhyme in his preface to *The Great Favourite* (1668). But it is clear from Dryden's tone that the debate over rhyme that occupied his critical energies in 1667-8 is now over.

in verse, and performed in recitative music. The original of this music, and of the scenes which adorned his work, he had from the Italian operas;[1] but he heightened his characters (as I may probably imagine) from the example of Corneille and some French poets. In this condition did this part of poetry remain at his Majesty's return; when, growing bolder, as being now owned by a public authority, he reviewed his *Siege of Rhodes*, and caused it be acted as a just drama. But as few men have the happiness to begin and finish any new project, so neither did he live to make his design perfect: there wanted the fulness of a plot, and the variety of characters to form it as it ought; and, perhaps, something might have been added to the beauty of the style. All which he would have performed with more exactness, had he pleased to have given us another work of the same nature. For myself and others, who come after him, we are bound, with all veneration to his memory, to acknowledge what advantage we received from that excellent ground-work which he laid: and, since it is an easy thing to add to what already is invented, we ought all of us, without envy to him, or partiality to ourselves, to yield him the precedence in it.

Having done him this justice, as my guide, I may do myself so much as to give an account of what I have performed after him. I observed then, as I said, what was wanting to the perfection of his *Siege of Rhodes*; which was design, and variety of characters. And in the midst of this consideration, by mere accident, I opened the next book that lay by me, which was an Ariosto in Italian; and the very first two lines of that poem gave me light to all I could desire:

> Le donne, i cavalier, l'arme, gli amori,
> Le cortesie, l'audaci imprese io canto, etc.[2]

For the very next reflection which I made was this, that an heroic play ought to be an imitation, in little, of an heroic poem; and, consequently, that Love and Valour ought to be the subject of it. Both these Sir William Davenant had begun to

---

[1] Davenant's *The Siege of Rhodes* escaped the Puritan ban on plays by being performed as an opera in 1656. It was expanded into two parts and published in 1663.

[2] *Orlando furioso*, I.i:

> 'Of dames, of knights, of arms, of love's delight,
> Of courtesies, of high attempts I speak.'
> (Harington's translation.)

shadow; but it was so, as first discoverers draw their maps,[1] with headlands, and promontories, and some few outlines of somewhat taken at a distance, and which the designer saw not clearly. The common drama obliged him to a plot well formed and pleasant or, as the Ancients called it, one entire and great action.[2] But this he afforded not himself in a story which he neither filled with persons, nor beautified with characters, nor varied with accidents. The laws of an heroic poem did not dispense with those of the other, but raised them to a greater height, and indulged him a farther liberty of fancy, and of drawing all things as far above the ordinary proportion of the stage as that is beyond the common words and actions of human life; and therefore, in the scanting of his images and design, he complied not enough with the greatness and majesty of an heroic poem.

I am sorry I cannot discover my opinion of this kind of writing without dissenting much from his, whose memory I love and honour. But I will do it with the same respect to him as if he were now alive, and overlooking my paper while I write. His judgment of an heroic poem was this: *That it ought to be dressed in a more familiar and easy shape; more fitted to the common actions and passions of human life; and, in short, more like a glass of nature, showing us ourselves in our ordinary habits, and figuring a more practicable virtue to us than was done by the Ancients or Moderns.*[3] Thus he takes the image of an heroic poem from the drama, or stage poetry; and accordingly intended to divide it into five books, representing the same number of acts; and every book into several cantos, imitating the scenes which compose our acts.[4]

But this, I think, is rather a play in narration, as I may call it, than an heroic poem; if at least you will not prefer the opinion of a single man to the practice of the most excellent authors, both of ancient and latter ages. I am no admirer of quotations; but

---

[1] The simile is aptly converted from Davenant's preface to *Gondibert* (1650), where cartographical images abound, e.g. 'Whilst we imitate others, we can no more excel them than he that sails by others' maps can make a new discovery' (*Spingarn*, II.7).

[2] Aristotle, *Poetics*, ch. vii.   [3] A paraphrase of Davenant.

[4] Cf. Davenant, *op. cit.*: 'I did not only observe the symmetry [of drama]—proportioning five books to five acts, and cantos to scenes, the scenes having their number ever governed by occasion—but all the shadowings, happy strokes, and even the drapery, which together make the second beauty, I have, I hope, exactly followed' (*Spingarn*, II.17).

you shall hear, if you please, one of the Ancients delivering his judgment on this question; 'tis Petronius Arbiter, the most elegant, and one of the most judicious authors of the Latin tongue; who, after he had given many admirable rules for the structure and beauties of an epic poem, concludes all in these following words:

Non enim res gestæ versibus comprehendendæ sunt, quod longe melius historici faciunt: sed, per ambages, deorumque ministeria, præcipitandus est liber spiritus, ut potius furentis animi vaticinatio appareat, quam religiosæ orationis, sub testibus, fides.[1]

In which sentence, and in his own essay of a poem which immediately he gives you, it is thought he taxes Lucan, who followed too much the truth of history, crowded sentences together, was too full of points, and too often offered at somewhat which had more of the sting of an epigram than of the dignity and state of an heroic poem. Lucan used not much the help of his heathen deities, there was neither the ministry of the gods, nor the precipitation of the soul, nor the fury of a prophet (of which my author speaks), in his *Pharsalia*: he treats you more like a philosopher than a poet, and instructs you, in verse, with what he had been taught by his uncle Seneca in prose. In one word, he walks soberly afoot, when he might fly. Yet Lucan is not always this religious historian. The oracle of Appius, and the witchcraft of Erictho,[2] will somewhat atone for him, who was, indeed, bound up by an ill-chosen and known argument, to follow truth with great exactness. For my part, I am of opinion that neither Homer, Virgil, Statius, Ariosto, Tasso, nor our English Spenser could have formed their poems half so beautiful without those gods and spirits, and those enthusiastic parts of poetry which compose the most noble parts of all their writings.[3] And I will ask any man

[1] *Satyricon*, 118: 'It is not real events that are to be recorded in verse, which historians can do much better. But the free spirit [of the epic poet] must plunge into allusions, into divine interventions, and strive after mythological references, so that there appears rather the prophecies of an inspired soul than the precision of a statement made by oaths before witnesses.' As Ker points out, the quotation was a favourite among critics of the epic before Dryden, and is cited by Fanshawe in his translation of Camoens's *Lusiad* (1655), as well as by St Evremond, Rapin, and Le Bossu.

[2] *Pharsalia*, V.64f. and VI.507f.

[3] Davenant, in his *Gondibert* preface, had condemned epic machinery, 'those remote regions of Heaven and Hell,' and Dryden here attempts to restore a balance. For his real opinion of 'machines,' cf. the dedication to Juvenal, vol. II, pp. 86f., below.

who loves heroic poetry (for I will not dispute their tastes who do not), if the ghost of Polydorus in Virgil, the Enchanted Wood in Tasso, and the Bower of Bliss in Spenser (which he borrows from that admirable Italian) could have been omitted without taking from their works some of the greatest beauties in them. And if any man object the improbabilities of a spirit appearing or of a palace raised by magic, I boldly answer him that an heroic poet is not tied to a bare representation of what is true, or exceeding probable: but that he may let himself loose to visionary objects, and to the representation of such things as depending not on sense, and therefore not to be comprehended by knowledge, may give him a freer scope for imagination. 'Tis enough that in all ages and religions the greatest part of man-kind have believed the power of magic, and that there are spirits or spectres which have appeared. This, I say, is foundation enough for poetry: and I dare farther affirm that the whole doctrine of separated beings, whether those spirits are incorporeal substances (which Mr Hobbes, with some reason, thinks to imply a contradiction), or that they are a thinner and more aërial sort of bodies (as some of the Fathers have conjectured), may better be explicated by poets than by philosophers or divines.[1] For their speculations on this subject are wholly poetical; they have only their fancy for their guide, and that, being sharper in an excellent poet than it is likely it should in a phlegmatic, heavy gown-man, will see farther in its own empire, and produce more satisfactory notions on those dark and doubtful problems.

Some men think they have raised a great argument against the use of spectres and magic in heroic poetry by saying they are unnatural: but whether they or I believe there are such things is not material; 'tis enough that, for aught we know, they

[1] The orthodox Catholic view, at least since the Lateran Council of 1215, was that angels were incorporeal substances. In Dryden's day this position was under attack from two sides: Hobbes declared it to be nonsensical, while the Cambridge Platonists thought it simply false, and insisted that angels had physical existence—a view adopted by Milton in *Paradise Lost*. Cf. Hobbes, *Leviathan* (1651), III.xxxiv: '*Substance* and *body* signify the same thing; and therefore *substance incorporeal* are words which, when they are joined together, destroy one another, as if a man should say *an incorporeal body*.' For Dryden, characteristically, the question is an open one, to be decided (by poets at least) as a matter of convenience. He makes no attempt to contradict Hobbes as a philosopher; but he refuses to accept Hobbes's view in *The Answer to Davenant's Preface before Gondibert* (1650) that 'beyond the actual works of nature a poet may now go; but beyond the conceived possibility of nature, never' (*Spingarn*, II.62). Cf. p. 253 and n., below.

may be in nature; and whatever is, or may be, is not properly
unnatural. Neither am I much concerned at Mr Cowley's verses
before *Gondibert*[1] (though his authority is almost sacred to me):
'tis true, he has resembled the old epic poetry to a fantastic fairy
land; but he has contradicted himself by his own example. For
he has himself made use of angels and visions in his *Davideis*,
as well as Tasso in his *Godfrey*.

What I have written on this subject will not be thought a
digression by the reader, if he please to remember what I said
in the beginning of this Essay, that I have modelled my heroic
plays by the rules of an heroic poem. And if that be the most
noble, the most pleasant, and the most instructive way of writing
in verse, and withal the highest pattern of human life, as all
poets have agreed, I shall need no other argument to justify my
choice in this imitation. One advantage the drama has above the
other, namely that it represents to view what the poem only does
relate; and *segnius irritant animum demissa per aures, quam quæ
sunt oculis subjecta fidelibus*,[2] as Horace tells us.

To those who object my frequent use of drums and trumpets,
and my representations of battles, I answer, I introduced them
not on the English stage. Shakespeare used them frequently;
and though Jonson shows no battle in his *Catiline*, yet you hear
from behind the scenes the sounding of trumpets, and the shouts
of fighting armies. But I add farther: that these warlike instru-
ments, and even the representations of fighting on the stage, are
no more than necessary to produce the effects of an heroic play;
that is, to raise the imagination of the audience, and to persuade
them, for the time, that what they behold on the theatre is
really performed. The poet is, then, to endeavour an absolute
dominion over the minds of the spectators;[3] for, though our
fancy will contribute to its own deceit, yet a writer ought
to help its operation. And that the Red Bull[4] has formerly
done the same, is no more an argument against our practice
than it would be for a physician to forbear an approved

---

[1]   Methinks heroic poesy till now
                  Like some fantastic fairyland did show. . . .
[2] *Ars poetica*, l. 180: 'What enters through the ears stirs the soul less than
what is submitted to the trusty eyes.'
[3] The same failure to recognize the nature of dramatic illusion that
vitiates much of Dryden's argument in the essay *Of Dramatic Poesy*. Cf.
p. 51 and n., above.
[4] Cf. p. 46n., above.

medicine because a mountebank has used it with success.

Thus I have given a short account of heroic plays. I might now, with the usual eagerness of an author, make a particular defence of this. But the common opinion (how unjust soever) has been so much to my advantage that I have reason to be satisfied, and to suffer with patience all that can be urged against it.

For otherwise, what can be more easy for me than to defend the character of Almanzor, which is one great exception that is made against the play? 'Tis said that Almanzor is no perfect pattern of heroic virtue, that he is a contemner of kings, and that he is made to perform impossibilities.[1]

I must therefore avow, in the first place, from whence I took the character. The first image I had of him was from the Achilles of Homer, the next from Tasso's Rinaldo (who was a copy of the former), and the third from the Artaban of Monsieur Cal-prenède[2] (who has imitated both). The original of these (Achilles) is taken by Homer for his hero; and is described by him as one who in strength and courage surpassed the rest of the Grecian army; but, withal, of so fiery a temper, so impatient of an injury, even from his King and General, that when his mistress was to be forced from him by the command of Agamemnon, he not only disobeyed it, but returned him an answer full of contumely, and in the most opprobrious terms he could imagine. They are Homer's words which follow, and I have cited but some few amongst a multitude:

οἰνοβαρές, κυνὸς ὄμματ' ἔχων, κραδίην δ' ἐλάφοιο:
δημοβόρος βασιλεύς, etc.[3]

[1] This defence of the hero Almanzor resumes an argument begun in the dedication of the play to the Duke of York: 'I have formed a hero, I confess, not absolutely perfect, but of an excessive and overboiling courage. But Homer and Tasso are my precedents. Both the Greek and the Italian poet had well considered that a tame hero who never transgresses the bounds of moral virtue would shine but dimly in an epic poem. The strictness of those rules might well give precepts to the reader, but would administer little of occasion to the writer. But a character of an eccentric virtue is the more exact image of human life, because he [is] not wholly exempted from its frailties. Such a person is Almanzor. . . .'

[2] Gauthier de la Calprenède (1614-63), a Gascon poet of tragedies and historical romances, including *Cléopâtre* (1647-56), in which the character of Artaban soon became a byword for heroic arrogance—'fier comme Artaban.' An English translation by Robert Loveday and others appeared 1652-9.

[3] *Iliad*, I.225,231 (Achilles's speech to Agamemnon): 'You, heavy with wine, with the front of a dog but the heart of a deer . . . a king that devours his people.'

Nay, he proceeded so far in his insolence as to draw out his sword, with intention to kill him:

ἕλκετο δ' ἐκ κολεοῖο μέγα ξίφος.[1]

And, if Minerva had not appeared, and held his hand, he had executed his design; and 'twas all she could do to dissuade him from it: the event was that he left the army, and would fight no more. Agamemnon gives his character thus to Nestor:

ἀλλ' ὅδ' ἀνὴρ ἐθέλει περὶ πάντων ἔμμεναι ἄλλων,
πάντων μὲν κρατέειν ἐθέλει, πάντεσσι δ' ἀνάσσειν[2]

and Horace gives the same description of him in his *Art of Poetry*:

honoratum si fortè reponis Achillem,
impiger, iracundus, inexorabilis, acer,
jura neget sibi nata, nihil non arroget armis.[3]

Tasso's chief character, Rinaldo, was a man of the same temper; for when he had slain Gernando in his heat of passion, he not only refused to be judged by Godfrey, his general, but threatened that if he came to seize him, he would right himself by arms upon him; witness these following lines of Tasso:

Venga egli, o mandi, io terrò fermo il piede:
Giudici fian tra noi la sorte e l'arme;
Fera tragedia vuol che s'appresenti,
Per lor diporto, alle nemiche genti.[4]

You see how little these great authors did esteem the point of honour, so much magnified by the French, and so ridiculously aped by us. They made their heroes men of honour; but so as not to divest them quite of human passions and frailities, they contented themselves to show you what men of great spirits would certainly do when they were provoked, not what they were

---

[1] *Iliad*, I.194: '[While Achilles] was drawing his great sword from his sheath.'

[2] *Iliad*, I.287-8: 'But this man feels he must be above all others; he wants to govern all, to be king and to give all orders himself.'

[3] ll. 120-2: 'If by chance you bring upon the stage the famous Achilles, let him be restless, angry, obdurate and fierce. Let him deny laws were made for him, and claim all for his arms.'

[4] *Gerusalemme liberata*, V.43:
Let Godfrey come or send, I will not hence
Until we know who shall this bargain rue,
That of our tragedy the late-done fact
May be the first, and this the second act.
(Fairfax's translation.)

obliged to do by the strict rules of moral virtue. For my own part
I declare myself for Homer and Tasso, and am more in love with
Achilles and Rinaldo than with Cyrus and Oroondates.[1] I shall
never subject my characters to the French standard, where love
and honour are to be weighed by drams and scruples. Yet where
I have designed the patterns of exact virtues, such as in this play
are the parts of Almahide, of Ozmyn, and Benzayda, I may
safely challenge the best of theirs.

But Almanzor is taxed with changing sides: and what tie has
he on him to the contrary? He is not born their subject whom he
serves, and he is injured by them to a very high degree. He
threatens them, and speaks insolently of soverign power; but
so do Achilles and Rinaldo, who were subjects and soldiers to
Agamemnon and Godfrey of Bulloigne. He talks extravagantly
in his passion; but, if I would take the pains to quote an hundred
passages of Ben Jonson's Cethegus,[2] I could easily shew you
that the rhodomontades of Almanzor are neither so irrational
as his, nor so impossible to be put in execution; for Cethegus
threatens to destroy nature, and to raise a new one out of it; to
kill all the Senate for his part of the action; to look Cato dead;[3]
and a thousand other things as extravagant he says, but performs
not one action in the play.

But none of the former calumnies will stick: and therefore,
'tis at last charged upon me that Almanzor does all things; or
if you will have an absurd accusation, in their nonsense who
make it, that he performs impossibilities. They say that being a
stranger he appeases two fighting factions, when the authority of
their lawful sovereign could not. This is indeed the most improb-
able of all his actions, but 'tis far from being impossible. Their

---

[1] Both types of the romantic, as against the heroic, character. Cyrus is the
hero of Madeleine de Scudéry, *Artamène: ou le Grand Cyrus* (1649-53), which
was translated into English in 1653; Oroondates is the hero of La Calprenède,
Cassandre (1644-50), translated by Sir Charles Cotterell in 1652.

[2] A character in *Catiline* (1611).

[3] In Act III of *Catiline* it is Catiline himself who wishes to 'pluck all into
chaos, with myself' (l. 177). In the same passage he asks:

Who would not fall with all the world about him?

and Cethegus replies:

Not I, that would stand on it, when it falls,
And form new nature out to make another.

It is Catiline, too, who in Act IV, l. 501, tells Cato, 'I'll look thee dead.'

king had made himself contemptible to his people, as the *History of Granada*[1] tells us. And Almanzor, though a stranger, yet was already known to them by his gallantry, in the *juego de toros*,[2] his engagement on the weaker side, and more especially by the character of his person and brave actions, given by Abdalla just before. And, after all, the greatness of the enterprise consisted only in the daring; for he had the King's guards to second him. But we have read both of Cæsar, and many other generals, who have not only calmed a mutiny with a word, but have presented themselves single before an army of their enemies; which upon sight of them has revolted from their own leaders and come over to their trenches. In the rest of Almanzor's actions, you see him for the most part victorious; but the same fortune has constantly attended many heroes who were not imaginary. Yet you see it no inheritance to him. For, in the first part, he is made a prisoner; and, in the last, defeated, and not able to preserve the city from being taken. If the history of the late Duke of Guise[3] be true, he hazarded more and performed not less in Naples than Almanzor is feigned to have done in Granada.

I have been too tedious in this apology; but to make some satisfaction, I will leave the rest of my play exposed to the critics, without defence.

The concernment of it is wholly passed from me, and ought to be in them who have been favourable to it, and are somewhat obliged to defend their own opinions. That there are errors in it, I deny not:

ast opere in tanto fas est obrepere somnum.[4]

But I have already swept the stakes; and with the common good fortune of prosperous gamesters, can be content to sit quietly; to hear my fortune cursed by some, and my faults arraigned by others, and to suffer both without reply.

---

[1] Ginés Perez de Hita, *Guerras civiles* (1595-1619), a romantic history of the capture of Granada and the source of Madeleine de Scudéry's *Almahide* (1660-3), which Dryden also knew.

[2] I.e. bullfight. Cf. *Conquest of Granada*, Part I, I.i.

[3] Duc de Guise, *Mémoires* (1668), translated into English in the following year. The 'Eloge' which accompanies the Duke's memoirs of 1647-8 describes how 'toute la noblesse du royaume de Naples l'a vu avec étonnement lui résister presque seul, et percer l'épée à la main tout ce qui s'opposait aux efforts de son courage.'

[4] Horace, *Ars poetica*, l. 360 (*verum operi longo fas est obrepere somnum*): 'It is only right that sleep should steal over a long poem.'

EPILOGUE TO THE SECOND PART OF
GRANADA

THEY who have best succeeded on the stage,
Have still conform'd their genius to their age,
Thus Jonson did mechanic humour show,
When men were dull, and conversation low.[1]
Then comedy was faultless, but 'twas coarse: 5
Cobb's tankard was a jest, and Otter's horse.[2]
And, as their comedy, their love was mean:
Except, by chance, in some one labour'd scene,
Which must atone for an ill-written play:
They rose, but at their height could seldom stay.   10
Fame then was cheap, and the first comer sped;
And they have kept it since, by being dead.
But, were they now to write, when critics weigh
Each line, and ev'ry word, throughout a play,
None of them, no, not Jonson in his height,   15
Could pass without allowing grains for weight.
Think it not envy that these truths are told,
Our poet's not malicious, though he's bold.
'Tis not to brand 'em that their faults are shown,
But, by their errors, to excuse his own.   20
If love and honour now are higher rais'd,
'Tis not the poet but the age is prais'd.
Wit's now arriv'd to a more high degree;
Our native language more refin'd and free.
Our ladies and our men now speak more wit   25
In conversation than those poets writ.
Then one of these is, consequently, true;
That what this poet writes comes short of you,
And imitates you ill (which most he fears),
Or else his writing is not worse than theirs.   30

[1] For Rochester's attack on this passage, see p. 225n., below.
[2] Cobb is a poor water-carrier in Jonson's *Every Man in His Humour* (1601), Otter a hen-pecked captain in *Epicoene, op. cit.*, whose favourite tankard is called 'Horse' (III.i.21-7).

167

Yet, though you judge (as sure the critics will),
That some before him writ with greater skill,
In this one praise he has their fame surpast,
To please an age more gallant than the last.

audiences knew no better; and therefore were satisfied with what they brought. Those who call theirs the Golden Age of poetry have only this reason for it, that they were then content with acorns before they knew the use of bread; or that ἅλις δρυὸς[1] was become a proverb. They had many who admired them, and few who blamed them. And certainly a severe critic is the greatest help to good wit. He does the office of a friend, while he designs that of an enemy; and his malice keeps a poet within those bounds which the luxuriancy of his fancy would tempt him to overleap.

But it is not their plots which I meant principally to tax: I was speaking of their sense and language. And I dare almost challenge any man to show me a page together which is correct in both. As for Ben Jonson, I am loath to name him, because he is a most judicious writer; yet he very often falls into these errors. And I once more beg the reader's pardon for accusing him of them. Only let him consider that I live in an age where my least faults are severely censured; and that I have no way left to extenuate my failings but my showing as great in those whom we admire:

> cædimus, inque vicem præbemus cura sagittis.[2]

I cast my eyes but by chance on *Catiline*; and in the three or four first pages found enough to conclude that Jonson writ not correctly:

> Let the long-hid seeds
> Of treason, in thee, now shoot forth in deeds
> Ranker than horror.[3]

In reading some bombast speeches of *Macbeth*, which are not to be understood, he[4] used to say that it was horror; and I am much afraid that this is so.

> Thy parricide late on thy only son,
> After his mother, to make empty way
> For thy last wicked nuptials, worse than they
> That blaze that act of thy incestuous life,
> Which gained thee at once a daughter and a wife.[5]

[1] Quoted by Cicero, *Ad Atticum*, II.19: 'enough of acorns.'
[2] Persius, *Satires*, IV.42: 'We alternately strike, and expose our own legs to the arrows.'
[3] *Catiline*, I.25-7, from the opening soliloquy spoken by Sulla's ghost.
[4] I.e. Ben Jonson, though the remark has not survived in his writings.
[5] *Catiline*, I.32-6 ('which got thee at once . . .').

The sense is here extremely perplexed; and I doubt the word
they is false grammar.

>   And be free
> Not heaven itself from thy impiety.[1]

A *synchysis*, or ill placing of words, of which Tully so much
complains in *Oratory*.[2]

>   The waves and dens of beasts could not receive
>   The bodies that those souls were frighted from.[3]

The preposition in the end of the sentence; a common fault
with him, and which I have but lately observed in my own
writings.[4]

>   What all the several ills that visit earth,
>   Plague, famine, fire, could not reach unto,
>   The sword, nor surfeits; let thy fury do.[5]

Here are both the former faults: for, besides that the preposition
unto is placed last in the verse, and at the half period, and is
redundant, there is the former synchysis in the words *the
sword, nor surfeits*, which in construction ought to have been
placed before the other.

Catiline says of Cethegus that for his sake he would

>   Go on upon the gods, kiss lightning, wrest
>   The engine from the Cyclops, and give fire
>   At face of a full cloud, and stand his ire.[6]

To *go on upon* is only to go on twice. To *give fire at face of a full
cloud* was not understood in his own time; *and stand his ire*,
besides the antiquated word *ire*, there is the article *his*, which
makes false construction: and *giving fire at the face of a cloud*
is a perfect image of shooting, however it came to be known in
those days to Catiline.

>   Others there are,
>   Whom envy to the state draws and pulls on,
>   For contumelies received; and such are sure ones.[7]

---

[1] *Catiline*, 59-60.
[2] *De oratore*, lxiv, where word-order is discussed, though the term occurs
not here but in *Ad Atticum*, vi.9.
[3] *Catiline*, I.250-1 ('The maws and dens. . . .').
[4] Each instance of the solecism was corrected by Dryden for the second
edition (1684) of the essay *Of Dramatic Poesy*; cf. pp. 13, 23, etc., above.
[5] *Ibid.*, I.49, 51-2 ('Plagues . . .').   [6] *Ibid.*, I.143-5.
[7] *Ibid.*, I.146-8 ('draws and puts on').

Ones in the plural number:[1] but that is frequent with him; for he says, not long after,

> Cæsar and Crassus, if they be ill men,
> Are mighty ones.
> Such men, they do not succour more the cause, &c.[2]

They redundant.

> Though Heaven should speak with all his wrath at once,
> We should stand upright and unfear'd.[3]

His is ill syntax with *Heaven*; and by *unfear'd* he means *unafraid*: words of a quite contrary signification.

> The ports are open.[4]

He perpetually uses ports for gates; which is an affected error in him, to introduce Latin by the loss of the English idiom; as in the translation of Tully's speeches he usually does.

Well placing of words, for the sweetness of pronunciation, was not known till Mr Waller introduced it; and therefore 'tis not to be wondered if Ben Jonson has many such lines as these:

But being bred up in his father's needy fortunes, Brought up in's sister's prostitution, &c.[5]

But meanness of expression one would think not to be his error in a tragedy, which ought to be more high and sounding than any other kind of poetry; and yet, amongst others in *Catiline*, I find these four lines together:

> So Asia, thou art cruelly even
> With us, for all the blows thee given;
> When we, whose virtue conquered thee,
> Thus by thy vices ruin'd be.[6]

Be there is false English for *are*; though the rhyme hides it.

But I am willing to close the book, partly out of veneration to the author, partly out of weariness to pursue an argument which is so fruitful in so small a compass. And what correctness,

---

[1] This correction, too was made in the second edition of the essay *Of Dramatic Poesy*; cf. p. 22n., above.
[2] *Catiline*, IV.530-1; IV.56.   [3] *Ibid.*, IV.30,32.
[4] *Ibid.*, IV.302.   [5] *Ibid.*, IV.122-3.   [6] *Ibid.*, I.587-90.

after this, can be expected from Shakespeare or from Fletcher, who wanted that learning and care which Jonson had? I will therefore spare my own trouble of inquiring into their faults; who, had they lived now, had doubtless written more correctly. I suppose it will be enough for me to affirm (as I think I safely may), that these and the like errors which I taxed in the most correct of the last age, are such into which we do not ordinarily fall. I think few of our present writers would have left behind them such a line as this:

> Contain your spirit in more stricter bounds.[1]

But that gross way of two comparatives was then ordinary; and therefore more pardonable in Jonson.

As for the other part of refining, which consists in receiving new words and phrases, I shall not insist much on it. 'Tis obvious that we have admitted many: some of which we wanted, and therefore our language is the richer for them, as it would be by importation of bullion; others are rather ornamental than necessary, yet by their admission the language is become more courtly, and our thoughts are better dressed. These are to be found scattered in the writers of our age, and it is not my business to collect them. They, who have lately written with most care have, I believe, taken the rule of Horace for their guide; that is, not to be too hasty in receiving of words, but rather to stay till custom has made them familiar to us:

> quem penes arbitrium est, et jus, et norma loquendi.[2]

For I cannot approve of their way of refining, who corrupt our English idiom by mixing it too much with French:[3] that is a sophistication of language, not an improvement of it; a turning English into French, rather than a refining of English by French. We meet daily with those fops who value themselves on their

---

[1] *Every Man Out of His Humour*, Induction, l. 46. In his *English Grammar* (1640) II.iv, Jonson defends this duplication, common enough in Shakespeare, as 'a certain kind of English Atticism' used, as among the Greeks, 'for more emphasis.'

[2] *Ars poetica*, l. 72: 'to which belongs the rule, the law, the government of tongues.'

[3] Dryden, in spite of the anti-French prejudice that remained with him all his life, successfully adopted many French words into the language; cf. especially the speech of Lisideius in *Of Dramatic Poesy*, pp. 44-56 and p. 45n., above.

travelling, and pretend they cannot express their meaning in English because they would put off to us some French phrase of the last edition: without considering that, for aught they know, we have a better of our own. But these are not the men who are to refine us; their talent is to prescribe fashions, not words: at best, they are only serviceable to a writer so as Ennius was to Virgil. He may *aurum ex stercore colligere*.[1] For 'tis hard if, amongst many insignificant phrases, there happen not something worth preserving; though they themselves, like Indians, know not the value of their own commodity.

There is yet another way of improving language, which poets especially have practised in all ages: that is, by applying received words to a new signification. And this, I believe, is meant by Horace, in that precept which is so variously construed by expositors:

> dixeris egregie, notum si callida verbum
> reddiderit junctura novum.[2]

And, in this way, he himself had a particular happiness: using all the tropes, and particularly metaphors, with that grace which is observable in his Odes, where the beauty of expression is often greater than that of thought; as in that one example, amongst an infinite number of others: *et vultus nimium lubricus aspici*.[3]

And therefore, though he innovated little, he may justly be called a great refiner of the Roman tongue. This choice of words, and heightening of their natural signification, was observed in him by the writers of the following ages: for Petronius says of him, *et Horatii curiosa felicitas*.[4] By this graffing, as I may call it, on old words, has our tongue been beautified by the three fore-mentioned poets, Shakespeare, Fletcher, and Jonson: whose excellencies I can never enough admire. And in this they have been followed especially by Sir John Suckling and Mr Waller, who refined upon them. Neither have they who succeeded them been wanting in their endeavours to adorn our mother tongue: but it is not so lawful for me to praise my living contemporaries as to admire my dead predecessors.

---

[1] Latin proverb: 'pick up gold from the dung.'

[2] *Ars poetica*, ll. 47-8: 'You will speak well if a fresh setting restores new force to a familiar word.'

[3] *Odes*, I.xix.8: 'her face too dangerous to gaze on.'   [4] *Satyricon*, 118.

I should now speak of the refinement of wit;[1] but I have been so large on the former subject that I am forced to contract myself in this. I will therefore only observe to you that the wit of the last age was yet more incorrect than their language. Shakespeare, who many times has written better than any poet in any language, is yet so far from writing wit always, or expressing that wit according to the dignity of the subject, that he writes in many places below the dullest writer of ours, or of any precedent age. Never did any author precipitate himself from such heights of thought to so low expressions as he often does. He is the very Janus of poets; he wears almost everywhere two faces; and you have scarce begun to admire the one, ere you despise the other. Neither is the luxuriance of Fletcher (which his friends have taxed in him) a less fault than the carelessness of Shakespeare. He does not well always; and, when he does, he is a true Englishman; he knows not when to give over. If he wakes in one scene, he commonly slumbers in another; and if he pleases you in the first three acts, he is frequently so tired with his labour that he goes heavily in the fourth, and sinks under his burden in the fifth.

For Ben Jonson, the most judicious of poets, he always writ properly, and as the character required; and I will not contest farther with my friends who call that wit: it being very certain that even folly itself, well represented, is wit in a larger signification; and that there is fancy as well as judgment in it, though not so much or noble: because all poetry being imitation, that of folly is a lower exercise of fancy, though perhaps as difficult as the other, for 'tis a kind of looking downward in the poet, and representing that part of mankind which is below him.

In these low characters of vice and folly lay the excellency of that inimitable writer; who, when at any time he aimed at wit in the stricter sense, that is, sharpness of conceit, was forced either to borrow from the Ancients, as to my knowledge he did very much from Plautus; or, when he trusted himself alone, often fell into meanness of expression. Nay, he was not free from the

---

[1] This discussion confuses the old and the new significances of 'wit.' To the old sense, the propriety of words to subject, as Dryden defined it early in the preface to *Annus Mirabilis* (p. 98, above) it adds little. But the new and 'stricter sense,' which Dryden defines below as 'sharpness of conceit,' can only be applied to the comic, and is fatal to the older and more general usage.

lowest and most grovelling kind of wit, which we call clenches,[1] of which *Every Man in His Humour*[2] is infinitely full. And, which is worse, the wittiest persons in the drama speak them. His other comedies are not exempted from them. Will you give me leave to name some few? Asper, in which character he personates himself (and he neither was, nor thought himself, a fool), exclaiming against the ignorant judges of the age, speaks thus:

> How monstrous and detested is't, to see
> A fellow that has neither art nor brain,
> Sit like an Aristarchus, or stark-ass,
> Taking men's lines, with a tobacco face,
> In snuff, &c.[3]

And presently after: 'I mar'le whose wit 'twas to put a prologue in yond sackbut's mouth. They might well think he would be out of tune, and yet you'd play upon him too.'[4] Will you have another of the same stamp? 'O, I cannot abide these limbs of satin, or rather Satan.'[5]

But it may be you will object that this was Asper, Macilente, or Carlo Buffone: you shall, therefore, hear him speak in his own person, and that in the two last lines or sting of an epigram. 'Tis inscribed to Fine Grand who, he says, was indebted to him for many things which he reckons there; and concludes thus:

> Forty things more, dear Grand, which you know true,
> For which, or pay me quickly, or I'll pay you.[6]

This was then the mode of wit, the vice of the age, and not Ben Jonson's. For you see, a little before him, that admirable wit Sir Philip Sidney perpetually playing with his words. In his time, I believe, it ascended first into the pulpit, where (if you will give me leave to clench too) it yet finds the benefit of its clergy. For they are commonly the first corrupters of eloquence, and the last reformed from vicious oratory; as a famous Italian[7] has

---

[1] The first of Dryden's plays to be acted, *The Wild Gallant* (1669), performed in February 1663, contains a number of puns. But, on the whole, he avoided them forever after.
[2] But the examples Dryden proceeds to quote are all from *Every Man Out of His Humour* (1600).
[3] *Every Man Out of His Humour*, Induction, ll. 177-81.
[4] *Ibid.*, Prologue.   [5] *Ibid.*, IV.iv.   [6] Epigram no. lxxiii, ll. 21-2.
[7] Ker suggests, without much certainty, D. Emmanuele Tesauro, *Cannocchiale Aristotelico*, in the chapter 'De' concetti predicabili.' But the title ('The Aristotelian Prospect-Glass') bears no relation to the one mentioned by Dryden.

observed before me, in his *Treatise of the Corruption of the Italian Tongue*, which he principally ascribes to priests and preaching friars.

But, to conclude with what brevity I can, I will only add this, in defence of our present writers, that, if they reach not some excellencies of Ben Jonson (which no age, I am confident, ever shall) yet, at least, they are above that meanness of thought which I have taxed, and which is frequent in him.

That the wit of this age is much more courtly may easily be proved by viewing the characters of gentlemen which were written in the last. First, for Jonson, Truewit in the *Silent Woman* was his masterpiece. And Truewit was a scholar-like kind of man, a gentleman with an allay of pedantry, a man who seems mortified to the world by much reading. The best of his discourse is drawn not from the knowledge of the town, but books. And, in short, he would be a fine gentleman in an university. Shakespeare showed the best of his skill in his Mercutio; and he said himself that he was forced to kill him in the third act, to prevent being killed by him. But, for my part, I cannot find he was so dangerous a person: I see nothing in him but what was so exceeding harmless that he might have lived to the end of the play, and died in his bed, without offence to any man.

Fletcher's Don John[1] is our only bugbear; and yet I may affirm, without suspicion of flattery, that he now speaks better, and that his character is maintained with much more vigour in the fourth and fifth acts than it was by Fletcher in the three former. I have always acknowledged the wit of our predecessors, with all the veneration which becomes me; but, I am sure, their wit was not that of gentlemen; there was ever somewhat that was ill-bred and clownish in it, and which confessed the conversation of the authors.

And this leads me to the last and greatest advantage of our writing, which proceeds from conversation. In the age wherein those poets lived, there was less of gallantry than in ours; neither did they keep the best company of theirs. Their fortune has been much like that of Epicurus, in the retirement of his gardens: to live almost unknown, and to be celebrated after their

---

[1] The young hero in *The Chances* (first published in the 1647 folio), a comedy by John Fletcher.

decease. I cannot find that any of them were conversant in courts, except Ben Jonson: and his genius lay not so much that way as to make an improvement by it. Greatness was not then so easy of access, nor conversation so free, as now it is. I cannot, therefore, conceive it any insolence to affirm that, by the knowledge and pattern of their wit who writ before us, and by the advantage of our own conversation, the discourse and raillery of our comedies excel what has been written by them. And this will be denied by none but some few old fellows who value themselves on their acquaintance with the Blackfriars;[1] who, because they saw their plays, would pretend a right to judge ours. The memory of these grave gentlemen is their only plea for being wits. They can tell a story of Ben Jonson, and perhaps have had fancy enough to give a supper in Apollo[2] that they might be called his sons; and, because they were drawn in to be laughed at in those times, they think themselves now sufficiently entitled to laugh at ours. Learning I never saw in any of them, and wit no more than they could remember. In short, they were unlucky to have been bred in an unpolished age, and more unlucky to live to a refined one. They have lasted beyond their own, and are cast behind ours: and not contented to have known little at the age of twenty, they boast of their ignorance at threescore.

Now, if any ask me whence it is that our conversation is so much refined, I must freely, and without flattery, ascribe it to the Court; and, in it, particularly to the King, whose example gives a law to it. His own misfortunes, and the nation's, afforded him an opportunity which is rarely allowed to sovereign princes, I mean of travelling, and being conversant in the most polished courts of Europe; and thereby of cultivating a spirit which was formed by nature to receive the impressions of a gallant and generous education. At his return, he found a nation lost as much in barbarism as in rebellion. And as the excellency of his nature forgave the one, so the excellency of his manners reformed the other. The desire of imitating so great a pattern first wakened the dull and heavy spirits of the English from their natural

---

[1] The theatre built by Burbage (the second on the site) in 1596, and demolished in 1655.

[2] A large, upstairs room in the Devil Tavern at Temple Bar, and the haunt of Jonson and the 'tribe of Ben,' or younger poets whom he called his sons.

reservedness, loosened them from their stiff forms of conversation, and made them easy and pliant to each other in discourse. Thus, insensibly, our way of living became more free: and the fire of the English wit, which was before stifled under a constrained, melancholy way of breeding, began first to display its force, by mixing the solidity of our nation with the air and gaiety of our neighbours. This being granted to be true, it would be a wonder if the poets, whose work is imitation, should be the only persons in three kingdoms who should not receive advantage by it; or if they should not more easily imitate the wit and conversation of the present age than of the past.

Let us therefore admire the beauties and the heights of Shakespeare, without falling after him into a carelessness and (as I may call it) a lethargy of thought, for whole scenes together. Let us imitate, as we are able, the quickness and easiness of Fletcher, without proposing him as a pattern to us, either in the redundancy of his matter, or the incorrectness of his language. Let us admire his wit and sharpness of conceit; but let us at the same time acknowledge that it was seldom so fixed, and made proper to his characters, as that the same things might not be spoken by any person in the play. Let us applaud his scenes of love; but let us confess that he understood not either greatness or perfect honour in the parts of any of his women. In fine, let us allow that he had so much fancy as when he pleased he could write wit: but that he wanted so much judgment as seldom to have written humour, or described a pleasant folly. Let us ascribe to Jonson the height and accuracy of judgment in the ordering of his plots, his choice of characters, and maintaining what he had chosen to the end. But let us not think him a perfect pattern of imitation; except it be in his humour: for love, which is the foundation of all comedies in other languages, is scarcely mentioned in any of his plays. And for humour itself, the poets of this age will be more wary than to imitate the meanness of his persons. Gentlemen will now be entertained with the follies of each other: and though they allow Cob and Tib to speak properly, yet they are not much pleased with their tankard or with their rags: and surely their conversation can be no jest to them on the theatre, when they would avoid it in the street.

To conclude all, let us render to our predecessors what is their due, without confining ourselves to a servile imitation of

all they writ: and, without assuming to ourselves the title of
better poets, let us ascribe to the gallantry and civility of our
age the advantage which we have above them; and to our
knowledge of the customs and manners of it, the happiness we
have to please beyond them.

TO MY MOST HONOURED FRIEND,
SIR CHARLES SEDLEY, Baronet

Prefixed to *The Assignation* (1673)

FAILURE OF THE COMEDY—LITERARY FRIENDSHIPS—
AN ATTACK ON THE WITS

Text: 4°, 1673.

The play was first produced, unsuccessfully, late in 1672, and the quarto followed early in the following year. Dryden's preface, addressed to Sir Charles Sedley (1639?-1701), playwright and poet, and probably the Lisideius of the dialogue *Of Dramatic Poesy*, is interesting mainly for its glimpse of intimate literary friendships, even of discussion-groups, enjoyed by Dryden, and for its attack upon the Wits, who had joined together to ridicule him in *The Rehearsal* (1672) and who were subjecting him to a pamphlet campaign. The attack is resumed, in more personal vein, in the preface to *All for Love*, pp. 221-31, below.

SIR,

THE design of dedicating plays is as common and unjust as that of desiring seconds in a duel. 'Tis engaging our friends (it may be) in a senseless quarrel, where they have much to venture without any concernment of their own. I have declared thus much beforehand, to prevent you from suspicion that I intend to interest either your judgment or your kindness in defending the errors of this comedy. It succeeded ill in the representation, against the opinion of many of the best judges of our age, to whom you know I read it ere it was presented publicly. Whether the fault was in the play itself, or in the lameness of the action, or in the number of its enemies, who came resolved to damn it for the title, I will not now dispute: that would be too like the little satisfaction which an unlucky gamester finds in the relation of every cast by which he came to lose his money. I have had formerly so much success that the miscarriage of this play was only my giving Fortune her revenge: I owed it her; and she was indulgent that she exacted not the payment long before. I will therefore deal more reasonably with you than any poet has ever done with any patron: I do not so much as oblige you for my sake to pass two ill hours in reading of my play. Think, if you please, that this dedication is only an occasion I have taken to do myself the greatest honour imaginable with posterity; that is, to be recorded in the number of those men whom you have favoured with your friendship and esteem. For I am well assured that besides the present satisfaction I have, it will gain me the greatest part of my reputation with after-ages, when they shall find me valuing myself on your kindness to me: I may have reason to suspect my own credit with them, but I have none to doubt of yours. And they who perhaps would forget me in my poems, would remember me in this epistle.

This was the course which has formerly been practised by the poets of that nation who were masters of the universe. Horace and Ovid,[1] who had little reason to distrust their immortality, yet took occasion to speak with honour of Virgil, Varius, Tibullus, and Propertius their contemporaries: as if they sought in the testimony of their friendship a farther evidence of their fame. For my own part, I, who am the least amongst the poets, have yet the fortune to be honoured with the best patron, and the best friend. For (to omit some great persons of our court to whom I am many ways obliged, and who have taken care of me, even amidst the exigencies of a war), I can make my boast to have found a better Maecenas in the person of my Lord Treasurer Clifford,[2] and a more elegant Tibullus in that of Sir Charles Sedley. I have chosen that poet to whom I would resemble you, not only because I think him at least equal, if not superior to Ovid in his elegies: nor because of his quality, for he was (you know) a Roman knight as well as Ovid: but for his candour, his wealth, his way of living, and particularly because of this testimony which is given him by Horace, which I have a thousand times in my mind applied to you:

[1] Horace, *Odes*, I.iii, xxiv, IV.xii, etc.; Ovid, *Amores*, I.xv, III.ix, *Tristia*, II.447-66, IV.x.

[2] Cf. the tribute to the elder Clifford in the preface addressed to his son in the 1697 Virgil, vol. II, p. 217 and n., below.

non tu corpus eras sine pectore; dii tibi formam,
dii tibi divitias dederunt, artemque fruendi.
quid voveat dulci nutricula majus alumno
qui sapere, et fari possit quæ sentiat, et cui
gratia, forma, valetudo contingat abunde;
et mundus victus, non deficiente crumina?[1]

Certainly the poets of that age enjoyed much happiness in the
conversation and friendship of one another. They imitated the
best way of living, which was to pursue an innocent and in-
offensive pleasure; that which one of the Ancients called
eruditam voluptatem.[2] We have, like them, our genial nights,
where our discourse is neither too serious, nor too light, but
always pleasant, and for the most part instructive: the raillery
neither too sharp upon the present, nor too censorious on the
absent; and the cups only such as will raise the conversation of
the night, without disturbing the business of the morrow. And
thus far not only the philosophers, but the Fathers of the
Church have gone, without lessening their reputation of good
manners or of piety. For this reason I have often laughed at
the ignorant and ridiculous descriptions which some pedants
have given of the Wits (as they are pleased to call them): which
are a generation of men as unknown to them as the people of
Tartary or the *terra Australis* are to us. And therefore, as we
draw giants and anthropophagi in those vacancies of our maps,
where we have not travelled to discover better; so those
wretches paint lewdness, atheism, folly, ill-reasoning, and all
manner of extravagances amongst us, for want of understanding
what we are. Oftentimes it so falls out that they have a particular pique to some one amongst us; and then they immediately interest Heaven in their quarrel; as 'tis an usual trick in
courts, when one designs the ruin of his enemy, to disguise
his malice with some concernment of the King's; and to revenge
his own cause with pretence of vindicating the honour of his
master. Such wits as they describe, I have never been so
unfortunate to meet in your company: but have often heard

[1] Horace, *Epistles*, I.iv.6-11: 'You used not to be a body without a soul.
The gods have given you beauty, and the wealth and knowledge to enjoy
life. What could any kind nurse wish more for her sweet child who can think,
and tell what he feels, and has abundantly favour, grace, and health, and a
good table, and a wallet that never lacks?'

[2] Quintilian, I.xii.18 ('ex illis ineruditis voluptatibus'): 'instructed
pleasure.'

much better reasoning at your table, than I have encountered
in their books. The wits they describe are the fops we banish:
for blasphemy and atheism, if they were neither sin nor ill
manners, are subjects so very common, and worn so threadbare,
that people who have sense avoid them, for fear of being suspected to have none. It calls the good name of their wit in
question, as it does the credit of a citizen when his shop is filled
with trumperies, and painted tiles instead of wares: we conclude
them bankrupt to all manner of understanding; and that to use
blasphemy is a kind of applying pigeons to the soles of the
feet:[1] it proclaims their fancy as well as judgment to be in a
desperate condition. I am sure for your own particular, if any
of these judges had once the happiness to converse with you,
to hear the candour of your opinions; how freely you commend
that wit in others, of which you have so large a portion yourself,
how unapt you are to be censorious; with how much easiness
you speak so many things, and those so pointed that no other
man is able to excel, or perhaps to reach by study; they would,
instead of your accusers, become your proselytes. They would
reverence so much good sense, and so much good nature, in the
same person; and come, like the Satyr,[2] to warm themselves
at that fire of which they are ignorantly afraid when they stood
at distance.

But you have too great a reputation to be wholly free from
censure: 'tis a fine which Fortune sets upon all extraordinary
persons, and from which you should not wish to be delivered
till you are dead. I have been used by my critics much more
severely, and have more reason to complain, because I am deeper
toned for a less estate. I am ridiculously enough accused to be a
contemner of universities, that is, in other words, an enemy of
learning: without the foundation of which I am sure no man can
pretend to be a poet. And if this be not enough, I am made a
detractor from my predecessors, whom I confess to have been my

---

[1] As a cure of the plague, it had been prescribed that a live pigeon be
cut in two and applied to the feet.

[2] Plutarch (*De capienda ex inimicis utilitate*, ch. 2), tells a story in the
opposite sense, of a Satyr all too familiar with fire, on its first being brought
by Prometheus to earth from heaven. Summers quotes Sir Edward Dyer's
sonnet on the story, printed in Sidney's *Arcadia*, which tells how a Satyr,
on first seeing fire,

Gave it a kiss, as it like sweet had been.

masters in the art.[1] But this latter was the accusation of the best
judge, and almost the best poet, in the Latin tongue. You find
Horace complaining that, for taxing some verses in Lucilius, he
himself was blamed by others,[2] though his design was no other
than mine now, to improve the knowledge of poetry: and it was no
defence to him, amongst his enemies, any more than it is for me,
that he praised Lucilius where he deserved it: *pagina laudatur
eadem.*[3] 'Tis for this reason I will be no more mistaken for my
good meaning: I know I honour Ben Jonson more than my little
critics, because without vanity I may own I understand him
better. As for the errors they pretend to find in me, I could easily
show them that the greatest part of them are beauties: and for
the rest, I could recriminate upon the best poets of our nation,
if I could resolve to accuse another of little faults, whom at the
same time I admire for greater excellencies.

But I have neither concernment enough upon me to write
any thing in my own defence, neither will I gratify the ambition
of two wretched scribblers[4] who desire nothing more than to be
answered. I have not wanted friends, even amongst strangers,
who have defended me more strongly than my contemptible
pedant could attack me. For the other: he is only like Fungoso
in the play, who follows the fashion at a distance, and adores
the Fastidius Brisk of Oxford.[5] You can bear me witness that I
have not consideration enough for either of them to be angry.
Let Maevius and Bavius admire each other: I wish to be hated

---

[1] Probably a reference to the accounts of Shakespeare, Jonson, and Beaumont and Fletcher in the essay *Of Dramatic Poesy*, pp. 67f., above.

[2] *Satires*, I.x.

[3] *Ibid.*, l. 4 ('charta laudatur eadem'): 'In the same poem he is praised.'

[4] Probably the actor Richard Leigh (b. 1649), formerly of the Queen's
College, Oxford, and author of an anonymous pamphlet, *The Censure of the
Rota on Mr Dryden's Conquest of Granada* (1673); and Martin Clifford
(d. 1677), Master of the Charterhouse since 1671 and part-author of *The
Rehearsal* (1672). *DNB* quotes a letter from Clifford to Dryden dated
1 July 1672: 'Since I cannot draw you to make a reply to me, assure yourself
that after this letter you shall hear no further from me.' Summers also
suggests Edward Ravenscroft (d. 1697), who certainly replied to this attack
in his prologue to *The Careless Lovers* (1673). He had already abused Dryden's heroic plays, in the prologue to his adaptation of Molière's *Le bourgeois
gentilhomme*, as 'plays of rhyme and noise.' Dryden retorted in his prologue
to *Marriage a-la-mode* (1673), again (perhaps) here, and in the prologue to
The Assignation. Macdonald suggests the unknown author of *The Friendly
Vindication of Mr Dryden from the Censure of the Rota* (1673), another
pamphlet of the day.

[5] Fungoso is the student imitator of the foppish courtier Briske in
Jonson's *Every Man Out of His Humour* (1600).

by them and their fellows, by the same reason for which I desire to be loved by you. And I leave it to the world, whether their judgment of my poetry ought to be preferred to yours; though they are much prejudiced by their malice, as I desire you should be led by your kindness, to be partial to,

Sir,
Your most humble
and most faithful servant,
JOHN DRYDEN.

PROLOGUE, EPILOGUE, etc.

to *Aureng-Zebe: a Tragedy* (1676)

A PROJECTED EPIC—
WEARINESS WITH RHYME—ADMIRATION FOR SHAKESPEARE
—CONTEMPT FOR THE THEATRE—
RESTORATION AUDIENCES

Text: 4°, 1676.

Dryden's heroic play on the last of the Moguls, first performed in November 1675, is one of the finest of his achievements in the new fashion, but its dedicatory epistle to John Sheffield (1648-1721), Earl of Mulgrave and later (1694) Marquess of Normanby, as well as the Prologue and Epilogue, suggest in their bitterness a double dissatisfaction with his dramatic career: an urge to emulate Shakespeare's achievement in blank verse—the Prologue foreshadows the unrhymed *All for Love*—and a disgust with London theatres and their audiences.

The following paragraph, which occurs midway in the complimentary epistle to Sheffield, 'To John, Earl of Mulgrave,' is our first hint of Dryden's unfulfilled dream of an English epic. The 1697 *Aeneis*, suitably dedicated to Sheffield, may have been undertaken in partial fulfilment.

THE truth is, the consideration of so vain a creature as man is not worth our pains. I have fool enough at home without looking for it abroad; and am a sufficient theatre to myself of ridiculous actions without expecting company, either in a court, a town, or playhouse. 'Tis on this account that I am weary with drawing the deformities of life and lazars of the people, where every figure of imperfection more resembles me than it can do others. If I must be condemned to rhyme, I should find some ease in my change of punishment. I desire to be no longer the Sisyphus of the stage: to roll up a stone with endless labour (which, to follow the proverb, gathers no moss) and which is perpetually falling down again. I never thought myself very fit for an employment where many of my predecessors have excelled me in all kinds; and some of my contemporaries, even in my own partial judgment, have outdone me in comedy. Some little hopes I have yet remaining, and those too, considering my abilities, may be vain, that I may make the world some part of amends for many ill plays by an heroic poem. Your Lordship has been long acquainted with my design, the subject of which you know is great, the story English, and neither too far distant from the present age, nor too near approaching it. Such it is, in my opinion, that I could not have wished a nobler occasion to do honour by it to my king, my country, and my friends; most of our ancient nobility being concerned in the action.[1] And your Lordship has one particular reason to promote this under-taking, because you were the first who gave me the opportunity of discoursing it to his Majesty and his Royal Highness. They were then pleased both to commend the design, and to en-courage it by their commands. But the unsettledness of my condition has hitherto put a stop to my thoughts concerning it. As I am no successor to Homer in his wit, so neither do I desire to be in his poverty. I can make no rhapsodies, nor go a-begging at the Grecian doors, while I sing the praises of their ancestors. The times of Virgil please me better, because he had an Augus-tus for his patron. And to draw the allegory nearer you, I am sure I shall not want a Maecenas with him. 'Tis for your Lord-ship to stir up that remembrance in his Majesty, which his many avocations of business have caused him, I fear, to lay aside. And (as himself and his royal brother are the heroes of the poem) to represent to them the images of their warlike predecessors; as Achilles is said to be roused to glory with the sight of the combat before the ships.[2] For my own part, I am satisfied to have offered the design; and it may be to the advant-age of my reputation to have it refused me.

[1] Probably the Black Prince's expedition to Spain in 1367, which he mentions as an alternative to an Arthurian epic in the preface to Juvenal, vol. II, p. 92, below. Johnson, in his Life of Dryden, complains that 'he mentions his design in terms so obscure that he seems afraid lest his plan should be purloined.'
[2] *Iliad,* xvi.

PROLOGUE

Our author by experience finds it true,
'Tis much more hard to please himself than you:
And out of no feigned modesty, this day
Damns his laborious trifle of a play.
Not that it's worse than what before he writ,   5
But he has now another taste of wit;
And to confess a truth (though out of time)
Grows weary of his long-loved mistress, Rhyme.
Passion's too fierce to be in fetters bound,
And Nature flies him like enchanted ground.   10
What verse can do, he has performed in this,
Which he presumes the most correct of his.
But spite of all his pride, a secret shame
Invades his breast at Shakespeare's sacred name:
Awed when he hears his godlike Romans rage,   15
He, in a just despair, would quit the stage,
And to an age less polished, more unskill'd,
Does with disdain the foremost honours yield.
As with the greater dead he dares not strive,
He would not match his verse with those who live.   20
Let him retire, betwixt two ages cast,
The first of this, and hindmost of the last.
A losing gamester, let him sneak away;
He bears no ready money from the play.
The fate which governs poets thought it fit   25
He should not raise his fortunes by his wit.
The clergy thrive, and the litigious bar;
Dull heroes fatten with the spoils of war;
All southern vices, Heaven be praised, are here;
But wit's a luxury you think too dear.   30
When you to cultivate the plant are loath,
'Tis a shrewd sign 'twas never of your growth:
And wit in northern climates will not blow,
Except, like orange-trees, 'tis housed from snow.
There needs no care to put a playhouse down,   35
'Tis the most desert place of all the town.
We and our neighbours, to speak proudly, are

Like monarchs ruined with expensive war;
While, like wise English, unconcerned, you sit,
And see us play the tragedy of wit.   40

EPILOGUE

A pretty task! And so I told the fool
Who needs would undertake to please by rule:
He thought that if his characters were good,
The scenes entire, and freed from noise and blood,
The action great, yet circumscribed by time,   5
The words not forced, but sliding into rhyme,
The passions raised and calmed by just degrees,
As tides are swelled, and then retire to seas;
He thought, in hitting these, his business done,
Though he, perhaps, has failed in every one.   10
But, after all, a poet must confess
His art's like physic, but a happy guess.
Your pleasure on your fancy must depend:
The lady's pleased, just as she likes her friend.
No song! no dance! no show! he fears you'll say;   15
You love all naked beauties but a play.
He much mistakes your methods to delight
And, like the French, abhors our target-fight:[1]
But those damned dogs can never be i' th' right.
True English hate your Monsieur's paltry arts;   20
For you are all silk-weavers[2] in your hearts.
Bold Britons at a brave bear-garden fray
Are roused and, clattering sticks, cry Play, play, play.
Meantime your filthy foreigner will stare,
And mutter to himself, *Ha, gens barbare!*   25
And Gad, 'tis well he mutters; well for him;
Our butchers else would tear him limb from limb.

---

[1] Dryden had just satisfied this traditional hunger of London audiences for noise, though he had condemned it as early as the essay *Of Dramatic Poesy*. The text of Act II of *Aureng-Zebe* is headed with the direction: 'Betwixt the acts, a warlike tune is played, shooting off guns, and shouts of soldiers are heard, as in an assault.'

[2] I.e. anti-French, like the English silk-weavers in their hatred of French competition.

'Tis true, the time may come your sons may be
Infected with this French civility;
But this in after-ages will be done: 30
Our poet writes a hundred years too soon.
This age comes on too slow, or he too fast:
And early springs are subject to a blast!
Who would excel when few can make a test
Betwixt indifferent writing and the best?   35
For favours cheap and common who would strive,
Which like abandoned prostitutes you give?
Yet scattered here and there I some behold
Who can discern the tinsel from the gold:
To these he writes; and if by them allow'd,   40
'Tis their prerogative to rule the crowd.
For he more fears (like a presuming man)
Their votes who cannot judge, than theirs who can.

THE AUTHOR'S APOLOGY FOR
HEROIC POETRY AND POETIC LICENCE

Prefixed to *The State of Innocence: an Opera* (1677)

CRITICS—IMAGERY—POETIC LICENCE—WIT

Text: 4°, 1677.

This opera, hastily adapted from *Paradise Lost* with Milton's approval, may have been designed for the wedding of the Duke of York (later James II) and Mary of Modena in November 1673, but was never used. The story fits Aubrey's well-known record, in his Life of Milton, that the old poet gave Dryden 'leave to tag his verses,' i.e. put them into rhyme: Milton did not die until November 1674. But publication was delayed until the beginning of 1677, and only then undertaken, according to Dryden, because of the growing corruption of manuscript copies.

The 'Apology' is a rambling essay, but marks Dryden's discovery of Longinus. Boileau's translation of his treatise *On the Sublime* had appeared in 1674, and by the end of the century Longinus was established with Aristotle and Horace as one of the three classical authorities on aesthetics. His influence might have led Dryden into a freer and more adventurous poetic, as the 'Apology' suggests, had not Rymer's *Tragedies of the Last Age* (1678) recalled him to defend neo-classical positions. As it is, the 'Apology'—which, for all its title, is in no sense a treatise on the epic—is Dryden's most daring advocacy of 'hard' metaphors and 'strong' hyperboles since his early abandonment of the metaphysical conceit.

To satisfy the curiosity of those who will give themselves the trouble of reading the ensuing poem, I think myself obliged to render them a reason why I publish an opera which was never acted. In the first place, I shall not be ashamed to own that my chiefest motive was the ambition which I acknowledged in the Epistle.[1] I was desirous to lay at the feet of so beautiful and excellent a Princess a work which, I confess, was unworthy her, but which I hope she will have the goodness to forgive. I was

[1] 'To her Royal Highness, the Duchess,' i.e. Mary, Duchess of York, which precedes complimentary verses by Lee and 'The Author's Apology.'

also induced to it in my own defence; many hundred copies of it being dispersed abroad without my knowledge or consent:[1] so that every one gathering new faults, it became at length a libel against me; and I saw, with some disdain, more nonsense than either I, or as bad a poet, could have crammed into it at a month's warning; in which time 'twas wholly written, and not since revised. After this, I cannot, without injury to the deceased author of *Paradise Lost*, but acknowledge that this poem has received its entire foundation, part of the design, and many of the ornaments, from him.[2] What I have borrowed will be so easily discerned from my mean productions, that I shall not need to point the reader to the places: and truly I should be sorry, for my own sake, that any one should take the pains to compare them together; the original being undoubtedly one of the greatest, most noble, and most sublime poems which either this age or nation has produced.[3] And though I could not refuse the partiality of my friend[4] who is pleased to commend me in his verses, I hope they will rather be esteemed the effect of his love to me than of his deliberate and sober judgment. His genius is able to make beautiful what he pleases: yet, as he has been too favourable to me, I doubt not but he will hear of his kindness from many of our contemporaries. For we are fallen into an age of illiterate, censorious, and detracting people who, thus qualified, set up for critics.

In the first place, I must take leave to tell them that they wholly mistake the nature of criticism[5] who think its business is principally to find fault. Criticism, as it was first instituted by

---

[1] At least three transcripts have survived, one in the British Museum, one in the Bodleian, and a third (containing Dryden's own corrections) at Harvard.

[2] Milton, according to Aubrey, received Dryden as a 'familiar learned acquaintance,' though we do not know how often Dryden visited the ageing poet, who was 65, and in the last year of his life, when Dryden adapted *Paradise Lost* (1667). There is a reference to their conversation in the preface to the *Fables*, vol. II, p. 271, below.

[3] There is a late tradition, reported in *Explanatory Notes and Remarks on Paradise Lost* (1734) by the two Jonathan Richardsons (father and son), p. cxix, that Dryden, on reading *Paradise Lost*, remarked to Dorset: 'This man ... cuts us all out.' But his support failed to give the poem much success in its early years.

[4] Nathaniel Lee, who contributed complimentary verse to the 1677 quarto 'To Mr Dryden, on his Poem of Paradise.'

[5] The earliest recorded use of the word as a literary term. Dryden later coined the word 'witticism' (p. 204 and n., below) by analogy.

Aristotle, was meant a standard of judging well; the chiefest part of which is to observe those excellencies which should delight a reasonable reader. If the design, the conduct, the thoughts, and the expressions of a poem be generally such as proceed from a true genius of poetry, the critic ought to pass his judgment in favour of the author. 'Tis malicious and unmanly to snarl at the little lapses of a pen from which Virgil himself stands not exempted. Horace acknowledges that honest Homer nods sometimes:[1] he is not equally awake in every line; but he leaves it also as a standing measure for our judgments,

> non, ubi plura nitent in carmine, paucis
> offendar maculis, quas aut incuria fudit,
> aut humana parum cavit natura.[2]

And Longinus, who was undoubtedly, after Aristotle, the greatest critic amongst the Greeks, in his twenty-seventh chapter ΠΕΡΙ 'ΥΨΟΥΣ,[3] has judiciously preferred the sublime genius that sometimes errs to the middling or indifferent one which makes few faults, but seldom or never rises to any excellence. He compares the first to a man of large possessions who has not leisure to consider of every slight expense, will not debase himself to the management of every trifle: particular sums are not laid out or spared to the greatest advantage in his economy, but are sometimes suffered to run to waste, while he is only careful of the main. On the other side, he likens the mediocrity of wit to one of a mean fortune, who manages his store with extreme frugality, or rather parsimony; but who, with fear of running into profuseness, never arrives to the magnificence of living. This kind of genius writes indeed correctly. A wary man he is in grammar: very nice as to solecism or barbarism, judges to a hair of little decencies, knows better than any man what is not to be written, and never hazards himself so far as to fall, but plods

---

[1] *Ars poetica*, l. 359.   [2] *Ibid.* (*verum, ubi. . .*). Cf. p. 77n., above.
[3] *On the Sublime*, the treatise on excellence in poetry and oratory attributed to Longinus (1st century A.D.?), was translated into English by a certain John Hall as early as 1652 (*Of the Height of Eloquence*), but achieved fame only with the French version of Boileau (1674). Its vogue among English aestheticians of the eighteenth century was enormous, but its influence on Dryden was largely confined to the present essay, or the brief interval between Boileau's version and the appearance of Rymer's *Tragedies of the Last Age* in 1678. Cf. T. R. Henn, *Longinus and English Criticism* (1934); Samuel H. Monk, *The Sublime* (1935); and Allen Tate, 'Longinus and the New Criticism,' in his *The Man of Letters in the Modern World* (1955).

on deliberately and, as a grave man ought, is sure to put his staff before him; in short, he sets his heart upon it, and with wonderful care makes his business sure; that is, in plain English, neither to be blamed nor praised. I could, says my author, find out some blemishes in Homer;[1] and am, perhaps, as naturally inclined to be disgusted at a fault as another man; but after all, to speak impartially, his failings are such as are only marks of human frailty: they are little mistakes, or rather negligences, which have escaped his pen in the fervour of his writing; the sublimity of his spirit carries it with me against his carelessness; and though Apollonius his *Argonauts*, and Theocritus his *Eidullia*, are more free from errors, there is not any man of so false a judgment who would choose rather to have been Apollonius or Theocritus than Homer.

'Tis worth our consideration a little to examine how much these hypercritics of English poetry differ from the opinion of the Greek and Latin judges of antiquity; from the Italians and French who have succeeded them; and, indeed, from the general taste and approbation of all ages. Heroic poetry, which they contemn, has ever been esteemed, and ever will be, the greatest work of human nature: in that rank has Aristotle placed it; and Longinus is so full of the like expressions that he abundantly confirms the other testimony. Horace as plainly delivers his opinion, and particularly praises Homer in these verses:

> Trojani Belli scriptorem, Maxime Lolli,
> dum tu declamas Romæ, Præneste relegi:
> qui quid sit pulchrum, quid turpe, quid utile, quid non,
> planius ac melius Chrysippo et Crantore dicit.[2]

And in another place, modestly excluding himself from the number of poets, because he only writ odes and satires, he tells you a poet is such an one,

> cui mens divinior, atque os
> magna sonaturum.[3]

Quotations are superfluous in an established truth: otherwise

---

[1] Ch. xxxiii.

[2] *Epistles*, I.ii.1-4: 'My dear Lollius Maximus, while you study the art of speaking in Rome, at Praeneste I have reread the poet of the Trojan war; who shows more fully and with better effect than Chrysippus and Crantor what is noble and what base, what useful and what not.'

[3] *Satires*, I.iv.43-4: 'whose soul is more divine, and whose mouth gives forth noble thoughts.'

I could reckon up, amongst the moderns, all the Italian commentators on Aristotle's book of poetry;[1] and amongst the French, the greatest of this age, Boileau and Rapin; the latter of which is alone sufficient, were all other critics lost, to teach anew the rules of writing. Any man who will seriously consider the nature of an epic poem, how it agrees with that of poetry in general, which is to instruct and to delight; what actions it describes, and what persons they are chiefly whom it informs, will find it a work which indeed is full of difficulty in the attempt, but admirable when 'tis well performed. I write not this with the least intention to undervalue the other parts of poetry: for comedy is both excellently instructive, and extremely pleasant: satire lashes vice into reformation, and humour represents folly so as to render it ridiculous. Many of our present writers are eminent in both these kinds; and particularly the author of the *Plain Dealer*,[2] whom I am proud to call my friend, has obliged all honest and virtuous men by one of the most bold, most general, and most useful satires which has ever been presented on the English theatre. I do not dispute the preference of tragedy; let every man enjoy his taste: but 'tis unjust that they who have not the least notion of heroic writing should therefore condemn the pleasure which others receive from it, because they cannot comprehend it. Let them please their appetites in eating what they like; but let them not force this dish on all the table. They who would combat general authority with particular opinion must first establish themselves a reputation of understanding better than other men. Are all the flights of heroic poetry to be concluded bombast, unnatural, and mere madness, because they are not affected with their excellencies? 'Tis just as reasonable as to conclude there is no day because a blind man cannot distinguish of light and colours. Ought they not rather, in modesty, to doubt of their own judgments, when they think this or that expression in Homer, Virgil, Tasso, or Milton's *Paradise* to be too far strained, than positively to conclude that 'tis all fustian, and mere nonsense? 'Tis true, there are limits to be set betwixt the boldness and rashness of a poet; but he must understand those limits who pretends to judge as well as he who

[1] Rapin, in his *Réflexions* (1674), had listed many of them, including Castelvetro, Minturno, and Piccolomini.

[2] William Wycherley (1640?-1716). His comedy *The Plain Dealer* was also published in 1677.

undertakes to write: and he who has no liking to the whole ought, in reason, to be excluded from censuring of the parts. He must be a lawyer before he mounts the tribunal; and the judicature of one court, too, does not qualify a man to preside in another. He may be an excellent pleader in the Chancery, who is not fit to rule the Common Pleas. But I will presume for once to tell them that the boldest strokes of poetry, when they are managed artfully, are those which most delight the reader.

Virgil and Horace, the severest writers of the severest age, have made frequent use of the hardest metaphors, and of the strongest hyperboles: and in this case the best authority is the best argument. For generally to have pleased, and through all ages, must bear the force of universal tradition. And if you would appeal from thence to right reason, you will gain no more by it in effect than, first, to set up your reason against those authors; and, secondly, against all those who have admired them. You must prove why that ought not to have pleased, which has pleased the most learned and the most judicious; and to be thought knowing, you must first put the fool upon all mankind. If you can enter more deeply than they have done into the causes and resorts of that which moves pleasure in a reader, the field is open, you may be heard: but those springs of human nature are not so easily discovered by every superficial judge. It requires philosophy as well as poetry to sound the depth of all the passions; what they are in themselves, and how they are to be provoked; and in this science the best poets have excelled. Aristotle raised the fabric of his *Poetry* from observation of those things in which Euripides, Sophocles, and Aeschylus pleased: he considered how they raised the passions, and thence has drawn rules for our imitation.[1] From hence have sprung the tropes and figures for which they wanted a name who first practised them, and succeeded in them. Thus I grant you that the knowledge of nature was the original rule; and that all poets ought to study her, as well as Aristotle and Horace, her interpreters. But then this also undeniably follows, that those things which delight all ages must have been an imitation of nature;

---

[1] Like all his contemporaries, Dryden assumes that the *Poetics* offers 'laws' in the sense of precepts. In fact Aristotle seems concerned rather to offer laws in the scientific sense, i.e. generalizations based upon observation of existing Greek drama.

which is all I contend. Therefore is rhetoric made an art; therefore the names of so many tropes and figures were invented: because it was observed they had such and such effect upon the audience. Therefore catachreses and hyperboles have found their place amongst them; not that they were to be avoided, but to be used judiciously, and placed in poetry as heightenings and shadows are in painting, to make the figure bolder, and cause it to stand off to sight.

> nec retia cervis
> ulla dolum meditantur,[1]

says Virgil in his *Eclogues*: and speaking of Leander in his *Georgics*,

> cæca nocte natat serus freta, quem super ingens
> porta tonat coeli, et scopulis inlisa reclamant
> æquora.[2]

In both of these, you see he fears not to give voice and thought to things inanimate.

Will you arraign your master Horace for his hardness of expression when he describes the death of Cleopatra, and says she did *asperos tractare serpentes, ut atrum corpore combiberet venenum*,[3] because the body in that action performs what is proper to the mouth?

As for hyperboles, I will neither quote Lucan, nor Statius, men of an unbounded imagination, but who often wanted the poise of judgment. The divine Virgil was not liable to that exception; and yet he describes Polyphemus thus:

> graditurque per aequor
> jam medium; necdum fluctus latera ardua tingit.[4]

In imitation of this place, our admirable Cowley thus paints Goliah:

---

[1] *Eclogues*, V.60-1: 'nets plan no snare for stags.'

[2] *Georgics*, III.260-2: 'Above him Heaven's great portal thunders, and the billows, dashing upon the cliffs, echo the cry.'

[3] *Odes*, I.xxxvii,26-8: 'to handle fierce snakes, to imbibe into her body black poison.'

[4] *Aeneid*, III.664-5 ('. . . tinxit'): 'He strides through the sea; nor has the wave yet wetted his mighty sides.'

> The valley, now, this monster seem'd to fill;
> And we, methought, look'd up to him from our hill,[1]

where the two words *seemed* and *methought* have mollified the figure, and yet if they had not been there, the fright of the Israelites might have excused their belief of the giant's stature.

In the 8th of the Æneids, Virgil paints the swiftness of Camilla thus:

> illa vel intactæ segetis per summa volaret
> gramina, nec teneras cursu læsisset aristas;
> vel mare per medium, fluctu suspensa tumenti,
> ferret iter, celeres nec tingeret æquore plantas.[2]

You are not obliged, as in history, to a literal belief of what the poet says; but you are pleased with the image, without being cozened by the fiction.

Yet even in history, Longinus quotes Herodotus on this occasion of hyperboles.[3] The Lacedemonians, says he, at the straits of Thermopylæ, defended themselves to the last extremity; and when their arms failed them, fought it out with their nails and teeth; till at length (the Persians shooting continually upon them) they lay buried under the arrows of their enemies. It is not reasonable (continues the critic) to believe that men could defend themselves with their nails and teeth from an armed multitude; nor that they lay buried under a pile of darts and arrows; and yet there wants not probability for the figure: because the hyperbole seems not to have been made for the sake of the description, but rather to have been produced from the occasion.

---

[1] *Davideis* (1656), III.385-6 ('And we, methoughts . . .'). Cowley, in a note to this passage, defends himself from the charge of 'too swelling an hyperbole,' and quotes classical precedents, including 'graditur per aequor . . .', above.

[2] *Aeneid*, vii.808-11:

> Outstripp'd the winds in speed upon the plain,
> Flew o'er the fields, nor hurt the bearded grain:
> She swept the seas, and as she skimm'd along,
> Her flying feet unbath'd on billows hung.
>   (Dryden's version, 1100-3.)

These lines are approvingly paraphrased by Pope in the *Essay on Criticism*, ll. 372-4, as an example of onomatopoeia:

> Not so when swift Camilla scours the plain,
> Flies o'er th'unbending corn, and skims along the main.

[3] Ch. xxxviii. Cf. Herodotus, vii.225.

'Tis true, the boldness of the figures are to be hidden sometimes by the address of the poet, that they may work their
effect upon the mind without discovering the art which caused
it. And therefore they are principally to be used in passion;
when we speak more warmly, and with more precipitation, than
at other times: for then, *si vis me flere, dolendum est primum
ipsi tibi*;[1] the poet must put on the passion he endeavours
to represent: a man in such an occasion is not cool enough,
either to reason rightly, or to talk calmly. Aggravations are then
in their proper places; interrogations, exclamations, hyperbata,[2]
or a disordered connection of discourse, are graceful there
because they are natural. The sum of all depends on what before
I hinted, that this boldness of expression is not to be blamed
if it be managed by the coolness and discretion which is necessary to a poet.

Yet before I leave this subject, I cannot but take notice how
disingenuous our adversaries appear: all that is dull, insipid,
languishing, and without sinews, in a poem, they call an imitation of nature: they only offend our most equitable judges, who
think beyond them; and lively images and elocution are never
to be forgiven.

What fustian, as they call it, have I heard these gentlemen
find out in Mr Cowley's *Odes*! I acknowledge myself unworthy
to defend so excellent an author, neither have I room to do it
here; only in general I will say that nothing can appear more
beautiful to me than the strength of those images which they
condemn.

Imaging is, in itself, the very height and life of poetry. It is,
as Longinus describes it, a discourse which, by a kind of
enthusiasm, or extraordinary emotion of the soul, makes it
seem to us that we behold those things which the poet paints,
so as to be pleased with them, and to admire them.[3]

If poetry be imitation, that part of it must needs be best
which describes most lively our actions and passions, our
virtues and our vices, our follies and our humours: for neither
is comedy without its part of imaging; and they who do it best
are certainly the most excellent in their kind. This is too plainly

---

[1] Horace, *Ars poetica*, ll. 102-3: 'If you wish me to grieve, you must first
grieve yourself.'
[2] I.e. transpositions. Cf. Longinus, ch. xxii.   [3] Longinus, ch. xv.

proved to be denied. But how are poetical fictions, how are hippocentaurs and chimeras, or how are angels and immaterial substances to be imaged; which, some of them, are things quite out of nature; others, such whereof we can have no notion? This is the last refuge of our adversaries; and more than any of them have yet had the wit to object against us. The answer is easy to the first part of it. The fiction of some beings which are not in nature (second notions, as the logicians call them) has been founded on the conjunction of two natures which have a real separate being. So hippocentaurs were imagined by joining the natures of a man and horse together; as Lucretius tell us, who has used this word of *image* oftener than any of the poets:

> nam certe ex vivo centauri non fit imago,
> nulla fuit quoniam talis natura animantis:
> verum ubi equi atque hominis, casu, convenit imago,
> hærescit facile extemplo, etc.[1]

The same reason may also be alleged for chimeras and the rest. And poets may be allowed the like liberty for describing things which really exist not, if they are founded on popular belief. Of this nature are fairies, pigmies, and the extraordinary effects of magic; for 'tis still an imitation, though of other men's fancies: and thus are Shakespeare's *Tempest*, his *Midsummer Night's Dream*, and Ben Jonson's *Masque of Witches*[2] to be defended. For immaterial substances, we are authorized by Scripture in their description: and herein the text accommodates itself to vulgar apprehension, in giving angels the likeness of beautiful young men. Thus, after the pagan divinity, has Homer drawn his gods with human faces: and thus we have notions of things above us, by describing them like other beings more within our knowledge.

I wish I could produce any one example of excellent imaging in all this poem: perhaps I cannot; but that which comes nearest it is in these four lines, which have been sufficiently canvassed by my well-natured censors:

[1] *De rerum natura*, iv.739-42: 'The image of a centaur is certainly not drawn from life, since no living creature like it ever existed. But where images of horse and man meet by chance, they may readily combine.'

[2] *The Masque of Queens*, first performed in 1609 and first printed in the 1616 folio.

> Seraph and cherub, careless of their charge,
> And wanton, in full ease now live at large:
> Unguarded leave the passes of the sky,
> And all dissolved in hallelujahs lie.[1]

I have heard (says one of them) of anchoves dissolved in sauce; but never of an angel in hallelujahs. A mighty witticism[2] (if you will pardon a new word!) but there is some difference between a laugher and a critic. He might have burlesqued Virgil too, from whom I took the image: *invadunt urbem, somno vinoque sepultam*.[3] A city's being buried is just as proper on occasion as an angel's being dissolved in ease and songs of triumph.

Mr Cowley lies as open too in many places:

> Where their vast courts the mother waters keep, etc.[4]

For if the mass of waters be the mothers, then their daughters, the little streams, are bound, in all good manners, to make courtesy to them, and ask them blessing. How easy 'tis to turn into ridicule the best descriptions, when once a man is in the humour of laughing, till he wheezes at his own dull jest! But an image which is strongly and beautifully set before the eyes of the reader, will still be poetry when the merry fit is over: and last when the other is forgotten.

I promised to say somewhat of poetic licence,[5] but have in part anticipated my discourse already. Poetic licence I take to be the liberty, which poets have assumed to themselves in all ages, of speaking things in verse which are beyond the severity of prose. 'Tis that particular character which distinguishes and sets the bounds betwixt *oratio soluta*[6] and poetry. This, as to what regards the thought or imagination of a poet, consists in fiction: but then those thoughts must be expressed; and here

---

[1] *The State of Innocence*, I.i.
[2] This coinage, on the analogy of 'criticism,' apparently took well, and Dryden used it a few years later in *The Vindication [of] The Duke of Guise* (1683). Cf. vol. II, p. 82, below.
[3] *Aeneid*, II.265: 'They storm the city, buried in sleep and wine.'
[4] *Davideis* (1656), I.79. Dryden later parodied the line in *Mac Flecknoe* (1682), ll. 72-3:
> Where their vast courts the mother-strumpets keep,
> And, undisturb'd by watch, in silence sleep.
[5] Dryden's discussion is too perfunctory to be of much importance, but he is committed to it by the terms of his own title.
[6] Cicero's term for prose, as against verse (*oratio poemata*).

arise two other branches of it: for if this licence be included in a single word, it admits of tropes; if in a sentence or proposition, of figures; both which are of a much larger extent, and more forcibly to be used in verse than prose. This is that birthright which is derived to us from our great forefathers, even from Homer down to Ben. And they who would deny it to us have, in plain terms, the fox's quarrel to the grapes: they cannot reach it.

How far these liberties are to be extended, I will not presume to determine here, since Horace does not. But it is certain that they are to be varied, according to the language and age in which an author writes. That which would be allowed to a Grecian poet, Martial tells you, would not be suffered in a Roman.[1] And 'tis evident that the English does more nearly follow the strictness of the latter than the freedoms of the former. Connection of epithets, or the conjunction of two words in one, are frequent and elegant in the Greek, which yet Sir Philip Sidney, and the translator of Du Bartas, have unluckily attempted in the English;[2] though this, I confess, is not so proper an instance of poetic licence, as it is of variety of idiom in languages.

Horace a little explains himself on this subject of *licentia poetica*, in these verses:

> pictoribus atque poetis
> quidlibet audendi semper fuit æqua potestas:
> sed non, ut placidis coeant immitia, non ut
> serpentes avibus geminentur, tigribus hædi.[3]

He would have a poem of a piece; not to begin with one thing and end with another: he restrains it so far that thoughts of an unlike nature ought not to be joined together. That were indeed

---

[1] *Epigrams*, ix.12.

[2] Rapin had already censured Ronsard and du Bartas for their compound epithets, which on the whole passed out of favour in the eighteenth century, though Keats revived them. Ker quotes Joseph Hall, *Satires* (1597-8), vi.1f.:
> He knows the grace of that new elegance
> Which sweet Philisides fetch'd of late from France,
> That well beseem'd his high-styl'd *Arcady*·
> Tho' others mar it with much liberty,
> In epithets to join two words in one.

[3] *Ars poetica*, ll. 9-10, 12-13: 'Painters and poets have always had an equal right to audacity. . . . But not to mate the savage with the tame, to pair serpents with birds and kids with tigers.'

to make a chaos. He taxed not Homer, nor the divine Virgil, for interesting their gods in the wars of Troy and Italy; neither, had he now lived, would he have taxed Milton, as our false critics[1] have presumed to do, for his choice of a supernatural argument: but he would have blamed my author, who was a Christian, had he introduced into his poem heathen deities, as Tasso is condemned by Rapin on the like occasion; and as Camoens, the author of the *Lusiads*, ought to be censured by all his readers when he brings in Bacchus and Christ into the same adventure of his fable.[2]

From that which has been said, it may be collected that the definition of wit (which has been so often attempted, and ever unsuccessfully by many poets) is only this: that it is a propriety of thoughts and words; or, in other terms, thoughts and words elegantly adapted to the subject.[3] If our critics will join issue on this definition, that we may *convenire in aliquo tertio*;[4] if they will take it as a granted principle, 'twill be easy to put an end to this dispute. No man will disagree from another's judgment concerning the dignity of style in heroic poetry; but all reasonable men will conclude it necessary that sublime subjects ought to be adorned with the sublimest, and (consequently often) with the most figurative expressions. In the meantime, I will not run into their fault of imposing my opinions on other men, any more than I would my writings on their taste: I have only laid down, and that superficially enough, my present thoughts; and shall be glad to be taught better by those who pretend to reform our poetry.

[1] This probably refers only to verbal critics of *Paradise Lost*: Rymer's attack on Milton, promised at the end of his *Tragedies of the Last Age* (1678), was never written. But the objection was natural to any Englishman of Milton's day, even to his friends; cf. Marvell's introductory verses prefixed to the epic:

> the argument
> Held me a while misdoubting his intent,
> That he would ruin (for I saw him strong)
> The sacred truths to fable and old song.

[2] Rapin in the *Réflexions*, xiii, condemns Camoens on this account, but not Tasso. The *Lusiad* had recently been translated from the Portuguese by Sir Richard Fanshawe (1655).

[3] Cf. preface to *Annus Mirabilis*, p. 98, above.

[4] I.e. agree upon some third (and intermediate) position.

LETTER TO CHARLES, EARL OF DORSET
c. Sept. 1677

RYMER'S *TRAGEDIES OF THE LAST AGE*

Texts: The ms. is in the R.B. Adam Johnsonian Library at the University of Rochester, New York, and is reprinted with a facsimile in the *Catalogue* (1929), III.87-8; and in *Ward*, no. 6.

The letter lacks address and date, but the reference to Rymer's first treatise places it in the autumn of 1677, while the mention of Northamptonshire makes it seem likely that it was addressed to the Earl of Dorset (1638-1706), the 'Eugenius' of the essay *Of Dramatic Poesy.* Dryden was evidently staying on Dorset's estate there. The letter leaves no doubt that Dryden's admiration for Rymer as a critic was sincere.

I AM now settled in the country; and having given two of three days to idleness, parsons, and my cousin's discourse, which is the worst of the three evils, am going to drudge for the winter. But your Lordship's secret is no longer so to me: for, by this tattle which I have had here, I am confirmed that there is a certain lady called Mrs B. Trissham, who is yet at London, and who is expected down this week, without her mother. The choice is not amiss; for she is held the flower of Northamptonshire: one of the housemaids here has served her formerly: and my wise cousin should have married her: but that being broken off, I doubt, not very handsomely on his side, a breach has ensued; and I find by him he is like to marry elsewhere ere long. If your parson's be not private enough, here you may be as unknown as you please, and much more conveniently than where you design; this house not being above a little half mile distant from the blessed abode; for I can easily see it from my window. And my cousin is to be managed as I please; being sufficiently easy as well in all other things as in his understanding: he talks nothing all day long to me in French and Italian to show his breeding.

Mr Rymer sent me his book,[1] which has been my best entertainment hitherto: 'tis certainly very learned, and the best piece of criticism in the English tongue; perhaps in any other of the modern. If I am not altogether of his opinion, I am so in most of what he says: and think myself happy that he has not fallen upon me as severely and as wittily as he has upon Shakespeare and Fletcher.[2] For he is the only man I know capable of finding out a poet's blind sides: and if he can hold here, without exposing his *Edgar*[3] to be censured by his enemies, I think there is no man will dare to answer him, or can.

I am in pain to know how your Lordship has your health; though I must not beg to hear it from you, because I had rather see it confirmed by my own eyes.

I am, my Lord,

Your Lordship's most obedient humble servant,

J. DRYDEN

By Bringis the carrier, who lodges at the Bell in Smithfield, and goes out on Thursday morning: from Mr Elmes his house at Lilford.

---

[1] *The Tragedies of the Last Age* was published in the late summer of 1677, with '1678' on its title-page.

[2] Much of Rymer's treatise consists of attacks upon *Rollo, Duke of Normandy*—i.e. *The Bloody Brother* (1639), now thought to be by Chapman, Fletcher, Jonson, and Massinger—and upon Beaumont and Fletcher's *A King and No King* (1619) and *The Maid's Tragedy* (1619), with occasional slighting references to Shakespearean tragedy. The bulk of his attack upon Shakespeare, however, he reserved for the second of his two major critical works, *A Short View of Tragedy* (1693), notably his notorious critique of *Othello*.

[3] Rymer was not so wise. His unacted play *Edgar: an Heroic Tragedy* was published some days or weeks after Dryden's letter, late in 1677, though it had been written well before *The Tragedies of the Last Age*. Its absurdities exposed Rymer to many attacks by his enemies, as Dryden predicted.

HEADS OF AN ANSWER TO RYMER

(written in 1677)

ARISTOTLE ON TRAGEDY—THE PLOT—PITY AND TERROR—
DEFENCE OF SHAKESPEARE AND FLETCHER

Text: The 'Heads,' scribbled by Dryden in the end-papers of the copy of *The Tragedies of the Last Age* sent him by Rymer late in 1677 (cf. p. 209, above), were first printed by Tonson in his 1711 edition of Beaumont and Fletcher. Nearly seventy years later, Johnson appended them to his Life of Dryden (1779), unaware that they had ever been published before. Johnson, who like Tonson transcribed from ms.—the volume had by then aptly passed into the possession of David Garrick, and was destroyed by fire a few years after—offered an utterly different order of text from Tonson's. His text also reveals a few verbal variants, recorded here in footnotes.

A comparison of the order of the two texts reveals seven sections or units observed by both Tonson and Johnson: paragraphs 1-6, 7-28, 29-33, 34, 35-38, 39-50, 51-3. Johnson published these sections in the following order: 4th, 7th, 5th, 1st, 3rd, 6th, 2nd. An examination of surviving copies of Rymer's book suggests that Dryden had, at most, ten leaves at the beginning and end on which to scribble—for both Tonson and Johnson speak of 'blank leaves', never of marginalia—and this count includes one page before the title-page, bearing the words 'Licensed by R. L'estrange.' Since Tonson's opening (para. 1, below) is so evidently Dryden's own, it seems likely that it did not appear upon the first blank leaf of the volume, since no editor (and certainly not Johnson) would have rejected it upon sight as the true opening. I suggest that Dryden began to write on the final end-papers of the book, immediately after the text (paras 1-33?) and then, exhausting the space there, returned to the beginning of the volume (paras 34-53?). This would explain why Johnson, who was working under pressure to write the *Lives of the English Poets* in four years, began his text with para. 34. His other variants from Tonson's order may have been forced upon him in his attempt to make sense of a text the true opening of which he had mistaken.

Tonson's order is superior in every way, and I have adopted it here; and in nearly every case Tonson's readings seem preferable to Johnson's. It is altogether likely that his claim is true: 'Just as he [Dryden] left them, be pleased to take them here *verbatim* inserted' (*The Works of Beaumont and Fletcher*, I.xii). Cf. J. M. Osborn, *Dryden: Some Biographical Facts and Problems* (1940), pp. 267-9;

Curt A. Zimansky, *The Critical Works of Rymer* (1956), pp. xxxiii-xxxix, who prefers Johnson's order; and George Watson, *Review of English Studies*, new ser. xiv (1963).

The 'Heads' are a first draft for 'The Grounds of Criticism in Tragedy' (pp. 243-61, below), and far superior in interest. They are more outspoken, and more combatively anti-Rymer, though still oddly respectful. Dryden never dared to repeat in public this lucid exposure of 'Aristotelianism' (cf., e.g., para. 40, below). His adaptations of Shakespeare for the Restoration stage, and his reverential baiting of Rymer in the 'Grounds of Criticism,' seemed to him a more prudent method of defending the English dramatic tradition.

(I)

1] He who undertakes to answer this excellent critique[1] of Mr Rymer, in behalf of our English poets against the Greek, ought to do it in this manner.

2] Either by yielding to him the greatest part of what he contends for, which consists in this, that the μῦθος, i.e. the design and conduct of it, is more conducing in the Greeks to those ends of tragedy which Aristotle and he propose, namely to cause terror and pity; yet the granting this does not set the Greeks above the English poets.

3] But the answerer ought to prove two things: first, that the fable is not the greatest masterpiece of a tragedy, tho' it be the foundation of it.

4] Secondly, that other ends as suitable to the nature of tragedy may be found in the English, which were not in the Greek.

5] Aristotle places the fable first;[2] not *quoad dignitatem*, *sed quoad fundamentum*;[3] for a fable, never so movingly contrived to those ends of his, pity and terror, will operate nothing on our affections, except the characters, manners, thoughts, and words are suitable.

---

[1] The earliest recorded use of the word, apart from a letter by Wycherley to the Earl of Mulgrave of about the same date (20 August 1677), referring to the same treatise by Rymer. Cf. *The Critical Works of Rymer*, ed. Zimansky, p. 193. The word, one of many French borrowings, was no doubt current in Restoration London.

[2] *Poetics*, ch. vi.

[3] 'on account of its dignity, but on account of its priority.'

6] So that it remains for Mr Rymer to prove that in all those, or the greatest part of them, we are inferior to Sophocles and Euripides; and this he has offered at in some measure but, I think, a little partially to the Ancients.

(II)

7] To make a true judgment in this competition between[1] the Greek poets and the English in tragedy, consider

    I. How Aristotle has defined a tragedy.
   II. What he assigns the end of it to be.
 III. What he thinks the beauties of it.
 IV. The means to attain the end proposed.

Compare the Greek and English tragic poets justly and without partiality, according to those rules.

8] Then, secondly, consider whether Aristotle has made a just definition of tragedy, of its parts, of its ends, of its beauties;[2] and whether he, having not seen any others but those of Sophocles, Euripides, etc., had or truly could determine what all the excellencies of tragedy are, and wherein they consist.

9] Next show in what ancient tragedy was deficient: for example, in the narrowness of its plots, and fewness of persons, and try whether that be not a fault in the Greek poets; and whether their excellency was so great when the variety was visibly so little; or whether what they did was not very easy to do.

10] Then make a judgment on what the English have added to their beauties: as, for example, not only more plot, but also new passions; as namely, that of love, scarce touched on by the Ancients, except in this one example of Phaedra, cited by Mr Rymer; and in that how short they were of Fletcher.

11] Prove also that love, being an heroic passion, is fit for tragedy, which cannot be denied, because of the example alleged of Phaedra; and how far Shakespeare has outdone them in friendship, etc.

12] To return to the beginning of this enquiry:[3] consider if pity and terror be not enough for tragedy to move; and I

---

[1] 'betwixt' in Johnson.   [2] 'and of its beauties' in Johnson.
[3] Para. 2, above.

believe, upon a true definition of tragedy, it will be found that
its work extends farther, and that it is to reform manners by
delightful representation of human life in great persons, by
way of dialogue. If this be true, then not only pity and terror
are to be moved as the only means to bring us to virtue, but
generally love to virtue and hatred to vice; by shewing the
rewards of one, and punishments of the other; at least by rendering virtue always amiable, though it be shown unfortunate; and
vice detestable, tho' it be shown triumphant.

13] If then the encouragement of virtue and discouragement
of vice be the proper ends of poetry in tragedy: pity and terror,
tho' good means, are not the only. For all the passions in their
turns are to be set in a ferment: as joy, anger, love, fear are
to be used as the poet's commonplaces; and a general concernment for the principal actors is to be raised by making them
appear such in their characters, their words, and actions, as
will interest the audience in their fortunes.

14] And if after all, in a larger sense, pity comprehends this
concernment for the good, and terror includes detestation for
the bad, then let us consider whether the English have not
answered this end of tragedy as well as the Ancients, or perhaps
better.

15] And here Mr Rymer's objections against these plays are
to be impartially weighed, that we may see whether they are of
weight enough to turn the balance against our countrymen.

16] 'Tis evident those plays which he arraigns[1] have moved
both those passions in a high degree upon the stage.

17] To give the glory of this away from the poet, and to place
it upon the actors, seems unjust.[2]

18] One reason is, because whatever actors they have found,
the event has been the same, that is, the same passions have
been always moved; which shows that there is something of
force and merit in the plays themselves, conducing to the design
of raising these two passions: and suppose them ever to have

---

[1] *The Bloody Brother* (*Rollo*), *A King and No King*, and *The Maid's
Tragedy*.
[2] Cf. Rymer: 'These say (for instance) *A King and No King* pleases . . . I
say that Mr Hart pleases; most of the business falls to his share, and what
he delivers, every one takes upon content; their eyes are prepossessed and
charmed by his action, before aught of the poet's can approach their ears. . . .'
(*Critical Works*, ed. Zimansky, p. 19.)

been excellently acted, yet action only adds grace, vigour, and more life upon the stage; but cannot give it wholly where it is not first. But secondly, I dare appeal to those who have never seen them acted, if they have not found those two passions moved within them; and if the general voice will carry it, Mr Rymer's prejudice will take off his single testimony.

19] This, being matter of fact, is reasonably to be established by this appeal; as if one man says 'tis night, when[1] the rest of the world conclude it to be day, there needs no further argument against him that it is so.

20] If he urge that the general taste is depraved, his arguments to prove this can at best but evince that our poets took not the best way to raise those passions; but experience proves against him that those[2] means which they have used have been successful and have produced them.

21] And one reason of that success is, in my opinion, this, that Shakespeare and Fletcher have written to the genius of the age and nation in which they lived; for tho' nature, as he objects, is the same in all places, and reason too the same,[3] yet the climate, the age, the dispositions of the people to whom a poet writes, may be so different that what pleased the Greeks would not satisfy an English audience.

22] And if they proceeded upon a foundation of truer reason to please the Athenians than Shakespeare and Fletcher to please the English, it only shows that the Athenians were a more judicious people; but the poet's business is certainly to please the audience.

23] Whether our English audience have been pleased hitherto with acorns, as he calls it, or with bread,[4] is the next question; that is, whether the means which Shakespeare and Fletcher have used in their plays to raise those passions before named, be better applied to the ends by the Greek poets than by them; and perhaps we shall not grant him this wholly. Let it be yielded[5] that a writer is not to run down with the stream, or

---

[1] 'when' omitted in Johnson.   [2] 'these' in Johnson.

[3] Rymer: 'Nature is the same, and man is the same [in Athens and London]; he loves, grieves, hates, envies, has the same affections and passions in both places . . .' (ibid.).

[4] Rymer: 'I cannot be persuaded that the people are so very mad of acorns, but that they could be well content to eat the bread of civil persons' (ibid., p. 20).

[5] 'granted' in Johnson.

to please the people by their own usual methods, but rather to reform their judgments: it still remains to prove that our theatre needs this total reformation.

24] The faults which he has found in their designs are rather wittily aggravated in many places than reasonably urged; and as much may be returned on the Greeks by one who were as witty as himself.

25] Secondly, they destroy not, if they are granted, the foundation of the fabric, only take away from the beauty of the symmetry: for example, the faults in the character of the King and No King are not, as he makes them, such as render him detestable, but only imperfections which accompany human nature, and for the most part[1] excused by the violence of his love; so that they destroy not our pity or concernment for him. This answer may be applied to most of his objections of that kind.

26] And Rollo committing many murders, when he is answerable but for one, is too severely arraigned by him; for it adds to our horror and detestation of the criminal; and poetic justice[2] is not neglected neither, for we stab him in our minds for every offence which he commits; and the point which the poet is to gain on the audience is not so much in the death of an offender, as the raising an horror of his crimes.

27] That the criminal should neither be wholly guilty, nor wholly innocent, but so participating of both as to move both pity and terror, is certainly a good rule, but not perpetually to be observed; for that were to make all tragedies too much alike; which objection he foresaw, but has not fully answered.

28] To conclude, therefore: if the plays of the Ancients are more correctly plotted, ours are more beautifully written; and if we can raise passions as high on worse foundations, it shows our genius in tragedy is greater, for in all other parts of it the English have manifestly excelled them.

(III)

29] For the fable itself, 'tis in the English more adorned with episodes, and larger than in the Greek poets; consequently

---

[1] 'and are for the most part' in Johnson.   [2] Cf. p. 245 and n., below.

more diverting. For, if the action be but one, and that plain, without any counter-turn of design or episode, i.e. under-plot, how can it be so pleasing as the English, which have both under-plot and a turned design, which keeps the audience in expectation of the catastrophe? whereas in the Greek poets we see through the whole design at first.

30] For the characters, they are neither so many nor so various in Sophocles and Euripides as in Shakespeare and Fletcher; only they are more adapted to those ends of tragedy which Aristotle commends to us: pity and terror.

31] The manners flow from the characters, and consequently must partake of their advantages and disadvantages.

32] The thoughts and words, which are the fourth and fifth beauties of tragedy, are certainly more noble and more poetical in the English than in the Greek, which must be proved by comparing them somewhat more equitably than Mr Rymer has done.

33] After all, we need not yield that the English way is less conducing to move pity and terror, because they often shew virtue oppressed and vice punished: where they do not both, or either, they are not to be defended.

(IV[1])

34] That we may the less wonder why pity and terror are not now the only springs on which our tragedies move, and that Shakespeare may be more excused, Rapin confesses that the French tragedies now all run on the *tendre*;[2] and gives the reason, because love is the passion which most predominates in our souls, and that therefore the passions represented become insipid, unless they are conformable to the thoughts of the audience. But it is to be concluded that this passion works not now among the French so strongly as the other two did amongst the Ancients. Amongst us, who have a stronger genius for writing, the operations from the writing are much stronger: for the raising of Shakespeare's passions are[3] more from the excellency of the words and thoughts than the justness of the

---

[1] The first section in Johnson's version. Cf. p. 210, above.
[2] *Réflexions sur la poétique d'Aristote* (1674), II.x.   [3] 'is' in Johnson.

occasion; and if he has been able to pick single occasions, he has never founded the whole reasonably; yet by the genius of poetry, in writing he has succeeded.

(V)

35] The parts of a poem, tragic or heroic, are:

   I. The fable itself.

  II. The order or manner of its contrivance in relation of the parts to the whole.

 III. The manners or decency of the characters in speaking or acting what is proper for them, and proper to be shewn by the poet.

 IV. The thoughts which express the manners.

  V. The words which express those thoughts.[1]

36] In the last of these Homer excels Virgil, Virgil all other ancient poets, and Shakespeare all modern poets.

37] For the second of these, the order: the meaning is that a fable ought to have a beginning, middle, and an end,[2] all just and natural, so that that part[3] which is the middle, could not naturally be the beginning or end, and so of the rest: all are depending on one another, like the links of a curious chain.[4]

38] If terror and pity are only to be raised, certainly this author follows Aristotle's rules, and Sophocles's and Euripides's example; but joy may be raised too, and that doubly, either by seeing a wicked man punished, or a good man at last fortunate; or perhaps indignation, to see wickedness prosperous and goodness depressed:[5] both these may be profitable to the end of tragedy, reformation of manners; but the last improperly,

---

[1] Dryden used this scheme, which owes something to Aristotle's *Poetics*, and more to Rymer's translation of Rapin's *Réflexions* (1674), in writing 'The Grounds of Criticism in Tragedy,' but left himself no room to fulfil the last two undertakings. Cf. p. 260, below.

[2] Aristotle, *Poetics*, ch. vii.   [3] 'that part, *e.g.*,' in Johnson.

[4] 'all depend' in Johnson. Tonson has 'chair,' Johnson 'chain.'

[5] Dryden, following Rapin and Rymer, largely neglects Aristotle's metaphor of 'catharsis' (*Poetics*, ch. vi), and writes as if drama *induces* emotions in the audience rather than purges them. But Aristotle's own later discussion of tragedy is open to this interpretation. Cf. para. 46, below.

only as it begets pity in the audience: tho' Aristotle, I confess, places tragedies of this kind in the second form.[1]

(VI)

39] And, if we should grant that the Greeks performed this better, perhaps it may admit a[2] dispute whether pity and terror are either the prime, or at least the only ends of tragedy.

40] 'Tis not enough that Aristotle has said so, for Aristotle drew his models of tragedy from Sophocles and Euripides; and if he had seen ours, might have changed his mind.

41] And chiefly we have to say (what I hinted on pity and terror in the last paragraph save one[3]) that the punishment of vice and reward of virtue are the most adequate ends of tragedy, because most conducing to good example of life. Now pity is not so easily raised for a criminal (as[4] the ancient tragedy always represents its chief person such) as it is for an innocent man, and the suffering of innocence and punishment of the offender is of the nature of English tragedy: contrarily,[5] in the Greek, innocence is unhappy often, and the offender escapes.

42] Then, we are not touched with the sufferings of any sort of men so much as of lovers; and this was almost unknown to the Ancients; so that they neither administered poetical justice[6] (of which Mr Rymer boasts) so well as we; neither knew they the best commonplace of pity, which is love.

43] He therefore unjustly blames us for not building on what the Ancients left us, for it seems, upon consideration of the premisses, that we have wholly finished what they began.

44] My judgment on this piece is this, that it is extremely learned; but that the author of it is better read in the Greek than in the English poets; that all writers ought to study this critique as the best account I have ever seen of the Ancients; that the model of tragedy he has here given is excellent and extreme correct; but that it is not the only model of all tragedy,

---

[1] *Poetics*, ch. xiii.   [2] 'of' in Johnson.
[3] Evidently para. 38, above. In Johnson's arrangement, Section III preceded this.
[4] 'and' in Johnson, who omits brackets and makes nonsense of the passage.
[5] 'contrary' in Tonson, 'contrarily' in Johnson. Cf. 'The Grounds of Criticism in Tragedy,' p. 245 and n., below.

because it is too much circumscribed in plot, characters, etc.;
and lastly, that we may be taught here justly to admire and
imitate the Ancients, without giving them the preference with
this author in prejudice to our own country.

45] Want of method in this excellent treatise makes the thoughts
of the author sometimes obscure.

46] His meaning, that pity and terror are to be moved, is that
they are to be moved as the means conducing to the ends of
tragedy, which are pleasure and instruction.

47] And these two ends may be thus distinguished. The chief
end[1] of the poet is to please; for his immediate reputation
depends on it.

48] The great end of the poem is to instruct, which is performed by making pleasure the vehicle of that instruction; for
poetry is an art, and all arts are made to profit.[2]

49] The pity which the poet is to labour for is for the criminal,
not for those, or him, whom he has murdered, or who have
been the occasion of the tragedy. The terror is likewise in the
punishment of the same criminal who, if he be represented too
great an offender, will not be pitied; if altogether innocent, his
punishment will be unjust.[3]

50] Another obscurity is, where he says Sophocles perfected
tragedy by introducing the third actor;[4] that is, he meant three
kinds of action, one company singing or speaking,[5] another
playing on the music, a third dancing.

(VII)

51] Rapin attributes more to the *dictio*, that is, to the words
and discourses[6] of a tragedy, than Aristotle had done, who places
them in the last rank of beauties; perhaps only last in order,
because they are the last product of the design, of the disposition
or connection of its parts; of the characters, of the manners of

---

[1] Tonson misprints 'ends'.
[2] Johnson, who has 'poesy' for 'poetry' in this sentence, adds the word
'Rapin' (cf. *Réflexions*, I.ix).
[3] Cf. Aristotle, *Poetics*, ch. xiii.
[4] *Critical Works*, ed. Zimansky, p. 22.
[5] Johnson omits 'speaking.'   [6] 'discourse' in Johnson.

those characters, and of the thoughts proceeding[1] from those manners.

52] Rapin's words are remarkable: ''Tis not the admirable intrigue, the surprising events, the[2] extraordinary incidents that make the beauty of a tragedy; 'tis the discourses when they are natural and passionate'.[3]

53] So are Shakespeare's.

[1] Tonson has 'of proceeding'. [2] and' in Johnson.
[3] *Réflexions*, I.xxvi.

PREFACE

to *All for Love: or The World Well Lost* (1678)

Text: 4°, 1678.

All for Love, a blank verse tragedy adapted from Shakespeare's *Antony and Cleopatra*, was first performed in December 1677, and the quarto probably appeared a few weeks later, early in 1678. The preface, which follows a dedicatory epistle 'To Thomas, Earl of Danby,' begins with a vindication of the plot of the play, and ends by enlarging the statement made on the title-page that it was 'Written in Imitation of Shakespeare's Style.' More interesting, though less apt to the occasion, are the renewed attack upon the French dramatic tradition (this time with Racine himself as the chief target) and the angry reply to Rochester's satirical 'Allusion' which marks Dryden's break with the Court wits, whose favours he had once sought. The cavalier dismissal of rhyme towards the end of the preface strikes a new note in his criticism, and one to be heard often in his later career: a confident indifference to public favour, except as it may affect his pocket, and a readiness to indulge his own current interests in his prefaces without much regard for relevance.

THE death of Antony and Cleopatra is a subject which has been treated by the greatest wits of our nation, after Shakespeare;[1] and by all so variously that their example has given me the confidence to try myself in this bow of Ulysses amongst the crowd of suitors; and, withal, to take my own measures, in

---

[1] Apart from the *Antonie* (1592) of Mary, Countess of Pembroke, an adaptation from the French of Garnier, there was one precursor of Shakespeare's tragedy from which Dryden certainly borrowed, especially in his Act V: Samuel Daniel's stilted *Tragedy of Cleopatra* (1594). *The False One*, probably by John Fletcher and Massinger, first performed 1619-22, has Cleopatra's youth for its subject. More recently, in February 1677 Sir Charles Sedley's *Antony and Cleopatra* (1677), a tragedy in the new heroic manner, had been performed with success.

aiming at the mark. I doubt not but the same motive has prevailed with all of us in this attempt: I mean the excellency of the moral. For the chief persons represented were famous patterns of unlawful love; and their end accordingly was unfortunate. All reasonable men have long since concluded that the hero of the poem ought not to be a character of perfect virtue, for then he could not, without injustice, be made unhappy; nor yet altogether wicked, because he could not then be pitied.[1] I have therefore steered the middle course; and have drawn the character of Antony as favourably as Plutarch, Appian, and Dion Cassius would give me leave: the like I have observed in Cleopatra. That which is wanting to work up the pity to a greater height was not afforded me by the story; for the crimes of love which they both committed were not occasioned by any necessity, or fatal ignorance, but were wholly voluntary;[2] since our passions are, or ought to be, within our power. The fabric of the play is regular enough, as to the inferior parts of it; and the unities of time, place, and action more exactly observed than, perhaps, the English theatre requires. Particularly, the action is so much one that it is the only of the kind without episode, or under-plot; every scene in the tragedy conducing to the main design, and every act concluding with a turn of it.[3] The greatest error in the contrivance seems to be in the person of Octavia: for though I might use the privilege of a poet to introduce her into Alexandria, yet I had not enough considered that the compassion she moved to herself and children was destructive to that which I reserved for Antony and Cleopatra; whose mutual love, being founded upon vice, must lessen the favour of the audience to them when virtue and innocence were oppressed by it. And, though I justified Antony in some measure by making Octavia's departure to proceed wholly from herself; yet the force of the first machine still remained; and the dividing of pity, like the cutting of a river into many channels, abated the strength of the natural stream. But this is an objection which none of my critics have urged against me; and therefore I might have let it pass, if I could have resolved to have been partial to myself. The faults my enemies have found are rather cavils concerning

[1] Aristotle, *Poetics*, ch. xiii.
[2] This had been one of Rymer's requirements for tragedy in his *Tragedies of the Last Age* (1678).
[3] Aristotle, *Poetics*, ch. xiii.

little, and not essential decencies; which a Master of the Ceremonies may decide betwixt us. The French poets, I confess, are
strict observers of these punctilios: they would not, for example,
have suffered Cleopatra and Octavia to have met; or, if they had
met, there must have only passed betwixt them some cold civilities, but no eagerness of repartee, for fear of offending against
the greatness of their characters, and the modesty of their sex.
This objection I foresaw, and at the same time contemned; for
I judged it both natural and probable that Octavia, proud of her
new-gained conquest, would search out Cleopatra to triumph
over her; and that Cleopatra, thus attacked, was not of a spirit
to shun the encounter: and 'tis not unlikely that two exasperated rivals should use such satire as I have put into their mouths;
for after all, though the one were a Roman, and the other a
queen, they were both women. 'Tis true, some actions, though
natural, are not fit to be represented; and broad obscenities in
words ought in good manners to be avoided: expressions therefore are a modest clothing of our thoughts, as breeches and petti-
coats are of our bodies. If I have kept myself within the bounds
of modesty, all beyond it is but nicety and affectation; which is
no more but modesty depraved into a vice: they betray themselves who are too quick of apprehension in such cases, and leave
all reasonable men to imagine worse of them than of the poet.[1]

Honest Montaigne goes yet further: *Nous ne sommes que
cérémonie; la cérémonie nous emporte, et laissons la substance des
choses. Nous nous tenons aux branches, et abandonnons le tronc et le
corps. Nous avons appris aux dames de rougir, oyant seulement
nommer ce qu'elles ne craignent aucunement à faire. Nous n'osons
appeler à droit nos membres, et ne craignons pas de les employer à
toute sorte de débauche. La cérémonie nous défend d'exprimer par
paroles les choses licites et naturelles, et nous l'en croyons; la raison
nous défend de n'en faire point d'illicites et mauvaises, et personne
ne l'en croit.*[2] My comfort is that by this opinion my enemies are

---

[1] Cf. Rymer, *op. cit.*: 'Here [in Euripides's *Hippolytus*] is a scene of madness, but not of Bedlam-madness; here is nature, not the obscenities, not the
blind-sides of nature which are represented when Arbaces and Panthea go
loose together [the brother and sister in *A King and No King*]' (*Critical
Works*, ed. Zimansky, p. 50).
[2] *Essais* (1580), II.17, 'De la présomption.' This remarkable passage is so
inaptly quoted here that it seems doubtful whether Dryden understood it.
Florio translates: 'We are nought but ceremony: ceremony doth transport
us, and we leave the substance of things; we hold fast by the boughs, and

but sucking critics, who would fain be nibbling ere their teeth are come.

Yet in this nicety of manners does the excellency of French poetry consist: their heroes are the most civil people breathing; but their good breeding seldom extends to a word of sense. All their wit is in their ceremony; they want the genius which animates our stage; and therefore 'tis but necessary, when they cannot please, that they should take care not to offend. But as the civillest man in the company is commonly the dullest, so these authors, while they are afraid to make you laugh or cry, out of pure good manners make you sleep. They are so careful not to exasperate a critic that they never leave him any work; so busy with the broom, and make so clean a riddance, that there is little left either for censure or for praise: for no part of a poem is worth our discommending where the whole is insipid; as when we have once tasted of palled wine, we stay not to examine it glass by glass. But while they affect to shine in trifles, they are often careless in essentials. Thus their Hippolytus is so scrupulous in point of decency that he will rather expose himself to death than accuse his stepmother to his father;[1] and my critics, I am sure, will commend him for it: but we of grosser apprehensions are apt to think that this excess of generosity is not practicable but with fools and madmen. This was good manners with a vengeance; and the audience is like to be much concerned at the misfortunes of this admirable hero: but take Hippolytus out of his poetic fit, and I suppose he would think it a wiser part to set the saddle on the right horse, and choose rather to live with the reputation of a plain-spoken, honest man, than to die with the infamy of an incestuous villain. In the meantime we may take notice that where the poet ought to have preserved the character as it was delivered to us by antiquity, when he should have given us the picture of a rough young man, of the Amazonian strain, a jolly huntsman, and both by his profession and his early rising a mortal enemy to love, he has chosen to give him the

leave the trunk or body. We have taught ladies to blush only by hearing that named which they nothing fear to do. We dare not call our members by their proper names, and fear not to employ them in all kinds of dissoluteness. Ceremony forbids us by words to express lawful and natural things; and we believe it. Reason willeth us to do no bad or unlawful things, and no man giveth credit unto it.'

[1] Racine, *Phèdre*, IV.ii. The first edition of the play (1677) was entitled *Phèdre et Hippolyte*.

turn of gallantry, sent him to travel from Athens to Paris, taught him to make love, and transformed the Hippolytus of Euripides[1] into Monsieur Hippolyte. I should not have troubled myself thus far with French poets, but that I find our Chedreux[2] critics wholly form their judgments by them. But for my part, I desire to be tried by the laws of my own country; for it seems unjust to me that the French should prescribe here till they have conquered. Our little sonneteers who follow them have too narrow souls to judge of poetry. Poets themselves are the most proper, though I conclude not the only critics. But till some genius as universal as Aristotle shall arise, one who can penetrate into all arts and sciences without the practice of them, I shall think it reasonable that the judgment of an artificer in his own art should be preferable to the opinion of another man; at least where he is not bribed by interest, or prejudiced by malice: and this, I suppose, is manifest by plain induction. For first, the crowd cannot be presumed to have more than a gross instinct of what pleases or displeases them: every man will grant me this; but then, by a particular kindness to himself, he draws[3] his own stake first, and will be distinguished from the multitude of which other men may think him one. But, if I come closer to those who are allowed for witty men,[4] either by the advantage of their quality, or by common fame, and affirm that neither are they qualified to decide sovereignly concerning poetry, I shall yet have

---

[1] Rymer's stock example of Greek tragedy in his *Tragedies of the Last Age* (1678), and Racine's avowed source for Phèdre.

[2] I.e. foppish, modish. Chedreux was a fashionable wig-maker often mentioned in Restoration plays. Cf. Etherege, *The Man of Mode* (1676), III.ii; Dryden, *The Kind Keeper* (1680), II.i.

[3] I.e. withdraws—a gaming term.

[4] A veiled counter-attack against John Wilmot, Earl of Rochester (1647-80), to whom Dryden had formerly dedicated his comedy *Marriage a-la-Mode* (1673). In the meantime, Rochester had circulated in manuscript his satire 'An Allusion to Horace, the 10th Satire of the 1st Book,' probably written in the spring of 1675, though it was not published till the *Poems on Several Occasions* (1680?). The 'Allusion' makes fun of Dryden as a poet, playwright, and critic. The following lines are apparently provoked by the 'Epilogue to the Second Part of [*The Conquest of*] *Granada*' and the 'Defence of the Epilogue' (1672):

But does not D—— find ev'n Jonson dull?
Fletcher and Beaumont uncorrect, and full
O[f] 'lewd lines,' as he calls 'em? Shakespeare's style
Stiff and affected; to his own the while
Allowing all the justness, that his pride
So arrogantly had to those denied?

a strong party of my opinion; for the most of them severally will exclude the rest, either from the number of witty men, or at least of able judges. But here again they are all indulgent to themselves; and every one who believes himself a wit, that is, every man, will pretend at the same time to a right of judging. But to press it yet farther, there are many witty men, but few poets; neither have all poets a taste of tragedy. And this is the rock on which they are daily splitting. Poetry, which is a picture of nature, must generally please; but 'tis not to be understood that all parts of it must please every man; therefore is not tragedy to be judged by a witty man, whose taste is only confined to comedy. Nor is every man who loves tragedy a sufficient judge of it: he must understand the excellencies of it too, or he will only prove a blind admirer, not a critic. From hence it comes that so many satires on poets, and censures of their writings, fly abroad. Men of pleasant conversation (at least esteemed so), and endued with a trifling kind of fancy, perhaps helped out with some smattering of Latin, are ambitious to distinguish themselves from the herd of gentlemen by their poetry:

rarus enim ferme sensus communis in illa fortuna.[1]

And is not this a wretched affectation, not to be contented with what fortune has done for them, and sit down quietly with their estates, but they must call their wits in question, and needlessly expose their nakedness to public view? Not considering that they are not to expect the same approbation from sober men which they have found from their flatterers after the third bottle. If a little glittering in discourse has passed them on us for witty men, where was the necessity of undeceiving the world? Would a man who has an ill title to an estate, but yet is in possession of it, would he bring it of his own accord to be tried at Westminster? We who write, if we want the talent, yet have the excuse that we do it for a poor subsistence; but what can be urged in their defence who, not having the vocation of poverty to scribble, out of mere wantonness take pains to make themselves ridiculous? Horace was certainly in the right where he said that *no man is satisfied with his own condition*. A poet is not pleased, because he is not rich; and the rich are discontented,

[1] Juvenal, *Satires*, viii.73: 'For in those high places, concern for others is rare indeed.'

because the poets will not admit them of their number. Thus the case is hard with writers: if they succeed not, they must starve; and if they do, some malicious satire is prepared to level them for daring to please without their leave. But while they are so eager to destroy the fame of others, their ambition is manifest in their concernment: some poem of their own is to be produced, and the slaves are to be laid flat with their faces on the ground, that the monarch[1] may appear in the greater majesty.

Dionysius and Nero had the same longings, but with all their power they could never bring their business well about. 'Tis true, they proclaimed themselves poets by sound of trumpet; and poets they were, upon pain of death to any man who durst call them otherwise. The audience had a fine time on't, you may imagine; they sat in a bodily fear, and looked as demurely as they could: for 'twas a hanging matter to laugh unseasonably and the tyrants were suspicious, as they had reason, that their subjects had 'em in the wind; so, every man in his own defence set as good a face upon the business as he could. 'Twas known beforehand that the monarchs were to be crowned laureates; but when the show was over, and an honest man was suffered to depart quietly, he took out his laughter which he had stifled, with a firm resolution never more to see an Emperor's play, though he had been ten years a-making it. In the meantime the true poets were they who made the best markets, for they had wit enough to yield the prize with a good grace, and not contend with him who had thirty legions.[2] They were sure to be rewarded if they confessed themselves bad writers, and that was somewhat better than to be martyrs for their reputation. Lucan's example was enough to teach them manners; and after he was put to death, for overcoming Nero, the Emperor carried it without dispute for the best poet in his dominions. No man was ambitious of that grinning honour;[3] for if he heard the malicious trumpeter

---

[1] Probably Rochester again, who soon after his appearance at Court in 1665, at the age of eighteen, became the leader of the 'Court Wits,' including the dramatist Thomas Killigrew, Sir Charles Sedley, Charles Sackville (Earl of Dorset), and George Villiers, Duke of Buckingham, later satirized as Zimri in *Absalom and Achitophel*, ll. 543f.

[2] Cf. p. 111n., above.

[3] Cf. Shakespeare, *I Henry IV*, V.iii. This allusion, and the following one, suggest that Dryden had been reading more of Shakespeare than *Antony and Cleopatra*—perhaps with a view to a general refutation of Rymer's attack on the Elizabethans.

proclaiming his name before his betters, he knew there was but one way with him.[1] Mæcenas took another course, and we know he was more than a great man, for he was witty too: but finding himself far gone in poetry, which Seneca assures us was not his talent,[2] he thought it his best way to be well with Virgil and with Horace; that at least he might be a poet at the second hand; and we see how happily it has succeeded with him; for his own bad poetry is forgotten, and their panegyrics of him still remain. But they who should be our patrons are for no such expensive ways to fame; they have much of the poetry of Mæcenas, but little of his liberality. They are for persecuting Horace and Virgil, in the persons of their successors (for such is every man who has any part of their soul and fire, though in a less degree). Some of their little zanies yet go further; for they are persecutors even of Horace himself, as far as they are able, by their ignorant and vile imitations of him;[3] by making an unjust use of his authority, and turning his artillery against his friends. But how would he disdain to be copied by such hands! I dare answer for him, he would be more uneasy in their company than he was with Crispinus, their forefather, in the Holy Way; and would no more have allowed them a place amongst the critics than he would Demetrius the mimic, and Tigellius the buffoon:

> Demetri, teque, Tigelli,
> discipulorum inter jubeo plorare cathedras.[4]

With what scorn would he look down on such miserable translators who make doggerel of his Latin, mistake his meaning, misapply his censures, and often contradict their own? He is fixed as a landmark to set out the bounds of poetry:

> saxum antiquum, ingens, . . .
> limes agro positus, litem ut discerneret arvis.[5]

---

[1] Cf. *Henry V*, II.iii.   [2] *Epistula*, 114.
[3] The clearest of all references in the preface to Rochester, and especially to his 'Allusion to Horace.'
[4] *Satires*, I.x.90 (*discipularum* . . .): 'Demetrius, and you, Tigellius, go and whine among the seats of your pupils.' Like Ben Jonson before him, in the *Poetaster*, Dryden assumes that the bore Horace met on the Via Sacra (*Satires*, I.ix) was the Crispinus of I.i.120, etc.
[5] *Aeneid*, xii, 897-8:
> An antique stone he saw: the common bound
> Of neighbouring fields; and barrier of the ground.
>   (Dryden's *Aeneis*, xii, 1300-1.)

But other arms than theirs, and other sinews, are required to raise the weight of such an author; and when they would toss him against their enemies,

> genua labant, gelidus concrevit frigore sanguis.
> tum lapis ipse, viri vacuum per inane volutus,
> nec spatium evasit totum, nec pertulit ictum.[1]

For my part, I would wish no other revenge, either for myself or the rest of the poets, from this rhyming judge of the twelve-penny gallery,[2] this legitimate son of Sternhold,[3] than that he would subscribe his name to his censure, or (not to tax him beyond his learning) set his mark: for, should he own himself publicly, and come from behind the lion's skin, they whom he condemns would be thankful to him, they whom he praises would choose to be condemned; and the magistrates[4] whom he has elected would modestly withdraw from their employment, to avoid the scandal of his nomination. The sharpness of his satire, next to himself, falls most heavily on his friends, and they ought never to forgive him for commending them perpetually the wrong way, and sometimes by contraries. If he have a friend whose hastiness in writing is his greatest fault, Horace would have taught him to have minced the matter, and to have called it readiness of thought, and a flowing fancy; for friendship will allow a man to christen an imperfection by the name of some neighbour virtue:

---

[1] *Aeneid*, xii, 905-7 (*neque pertulit ictum*):

> His knocking knees are bent beneath to load:
> And shivering cold congeals his vital blood.
> The stone drops from his arms: and falling short,
> For want of vigour mocks his vain effort.

[2] The upper gallery in Restoration theatres consisted of shilling seats. Cf. Dryden's prologue to Nahum Tate's *The Loyal General* (1680):

> Remove your benches, you apostate pit,
> And take above twelve pennyworth of wit.
>   (ll. 8-9).

[3] Thomas Sternhold (d. 1549), part-author of a doggerel version of the Psalms. Cf. p. 86n., above.

[4] Rochester, 'Allusion,' *op. cit.*, ll. 120-4:

> I loathe the rabble, 'tis enough for me,
> If S[edley], S[hadwell], S[heppard], W[ycherley],
> G[odolphin], B[utler], B[uckhurst], B[uckingham],
> And some few more, whom I omit to name,
> Approve my sense . . .

> vellem in amicitia sic erraremus; et isti
> errori nomen virtus posuisset honestum.[1]

But he would never have allowed him to have called a slow man
hasty, or a hasty writer a slow drudge,[2] as Juvenal explains it:

> canibus pigris, scabieque vetusta
> laevibus, et siccae lambentibus ora lucernae,
> nomen erit, Pardus, Tigris, Leo; si quid adhuc est
> quod fremit in terris violentius.[3]

Yet Lucretius laughs at a foolish lover, even for excusing the
imperfections of his mistress:

> nigra μελίχροος est, immunda et foetida ἄκοσμος.
> balba loqui, non quit, τραυλίζει; muta pudens est, etc.[4]

But to drive it *ad Æthiopem cygnum*[5] is not to be endured. I
leave him to interpret this by the benefit of his French version
on the other side, and without farther considering him than I
the rest of my illiterate censors, whom I have disdained to
answer, because they are not qualified for judges. It remains
that I acquaint the reader that I have endeavoured in this play
to follow the practice of the Ancients, who, as Mr Rymer has
judiciously observed, are and ought to be our masters. Horace
likewise gives it for a rule in his art of poetry:

---

[1] *Satires*, I.iii.41-2: 'I wish that we might sin like this in friendship, and
that good sense had put an honourable name on errors such as these.'

[2] Rochester, 'Allusion,' *op. cit.*, ll. 41-3:

> Of all our modern wits none seems to me
> Once to have touched upon true comedy,
> But hasty Shadwell, and slow Wycherley.

The line is referred to by Pope in his imitation of Horace's first epistle of
the second book, l. 85. As Warburton pointed out, Dryden has misrepre-
sented Rochester. The line, says Warburton, 'gives to each his epithet, not
to design the difference of their talents, but the number of their productions.'

[3] *Satires*, viii, 34-7: 'Lazy dogs, bald with chronic mange, who lick the
edges of a dry lamp, will be called "Pard," "Tiger," "Lion," or by any other
animal there is that roars more fiercely.'

[4] *De rerum natura*, IV.1160,1164:

> The sallow skin is for the swarthy put . . .
> She stammers: oh, what grace in lisping lies;
> If she says nothing, to be sure she's wise.

(Dryden's version from *Sylvæ*, 'Concerning the Nature of Love,' ll. 145,
151-2).

[5] Juvenal, *Satires*, VIII, 33: 'to a pitch-black swan.'

vos exemplaria Græca
nocturna versate manu, versate diurna.[1]

Yet, though their models are regular, they are too little for
English tragedy, which requires to be built in a larger compass.
I could give an instance in the *Oedipus Tyrannus*, which was the
masterpiece of Sophocles; but I reserve it for a more fit occasion,
which I hope to have hereafter.[2] In my style I have professed to
imitate the divine Shakespeare; which that I might perform more
freely, I have disencumbered myself from rhyme. Not that I
condemn my former way, but that this is more proper to my
present purpose.[3] I hope I need not to explain myself that I
have not copied my author servilely: words and phrases must
of necessity receive a change in succeeding ages. But 'tis almost
a miracle that much of his language remains so pure; and that he
who began dramatic poetry amongst us, untaught by any and, as
Ben Jonson tells us, without learning,[4] should by the force of his
own genius perform so much that in a manner he has left no
praise for any who come after him. The occasion is fair, and the
subject would be pleasant to handle: the difference of styles
betwixt him and Fletcher, and wherein, and how far, they are
both to be imitated. But since I must not be over-confident in
my own performance after him, it will be prudence in me to be
silent. Yet I hope I may affirm, and without vanity, that by
imitating him I have excelled myself throughout the play: and
particularly that I prefer the scene betwixt Antony and Ventidius
in the first act to anything which I have written in this kind.

---

[1] *Ars poetica*, ll. 268-9: 'Look to your Greek models by night and day.'
[2] An adaptation of this play, in collaboration with Nathaniel Lee, was one
of Dryden's next tasks. Cf. pp. 232-7, below.
[3] This empirical attitude to rhyme marks the second stage in the evolution
of Dryden's ideas, following his advocacy of rhyme in the essay *Of Dramatic
Poesy* and in the 'Defence of *An Essay*.' For the third stage, cf. 'To the Earl
of Roscommon,' vol. II, pp. 14-17, below.
[4] Cf. *Of Dramatic Poesy*, p. 67n., above.

PREFACE, PROLOGUE, EPILOGUE

to *Oedipus: a Tragedy* (1679)

CORNEILLE'S, SENECA'S ADAPTATIONS OF SOPHOCLES—
THE GREEK THEATRE

Text: 4°, 1679.

This adaptation from Sophocles—Dryden's only attempt to adapt a Greek play—is acknowledged on the title-page (cf. Epilogue, ll.1-4, below) as a collaboration with Nathaniel Lee. Several years later, in his *Vindication* [*of*] *The Duke of Guise* (1683), Dryden claimed to have written 'the first and third acts,' as well as 'the scenery [i.e. scenario] of the whole play' (p. 42). It was performed with great success in September 1678. The Prologue and Epilogue are hardly more than contemptuous injunctions to the audience at Dorset Garden to show a proper respect for Greek drama, but the preface, which bears the stamp of Dryden's talent rather than Lee's, is his most extended and enthusiastic account of Greek drama. Here, and in his adaptations from Shakespeare of the same period, Dryden's object was probably to justify the programme drafted in his 'Heads of an Answer to Rymer' to combine in Restoration drama the best of the classical and English traditions of the stage.

PREFACE

THOUGH it be dangerous to raise too great an expectation, especially in works of this nature, where we are to please an unsatiable audience, yet 'tis reasonable to prepossess them in favour of an author, and therefore both the Prologue and Epilogue informed you that *Oedipus* was the most celebrated piece of all antiquity; that Sophocles, not only the greatest wit, but one of the greatest men in Athens, made it for the stage at the public cost, and that it had the reputation of being his master-piece, not only amongst the seven of his which are still remaining, but of the greater number which are perished. Aristotle has more than once admired it in his *Book of Poetry*,[1] Horace has mentioned it:[2] Lucullus, Julius Caesar,[3] and other noble Romans, have written on the same subject, though their poems are wholly lost; but Seneca's is still preserved. In our own age, Corneille has attempted it, and it appears, by his preface, with great success.[4] But a judicious reader will easily observe how much the copy is inferior to the original. He tells you himself that he owes a great part of his success to the happy episode of Theseus and Dirce: which is the same thing as if we should acknowledge that we were indebted for our good fortune to the under-plot of Adrastus, Eurydice, and Creon. The truth is, he miserably failed in the character of his hero: if he desired that Oedipus should be pitied, he should have made him a better man. He forgot that Sophocles had taken care to shew him, in his first entrance, a just, a merciful, a successful, a religious prince and, in short, a father of his country: instead of these, he has drawn him suspicious, designing, more anxious of keeping the Theban crown than solicitous for the safety of his people: hectored by Theseus,[5] contemned by Dirce,[6] and scarce maintaining a second part in his own tragedy. This was an error in the first concoction; and therefore never to be mended in the second or the third. He introduced a greater hero than Oedipus himself: for when Theseus was once there, that companion of Hercules must yield to none. The poet was obliged to furnish him with business, to make him an equipage suitable to his dignity, and by following him too close, to lose his other King of Branford[7] in the crowd.

Seneca, on the other side, as if there were no such thing as nature to be minded in a play, is always running after pompous expression, pointed sentences, and philosophical notions more proper for the study than the stage. The Frenchman followed a wrong scent; and the Roman was absolutely at cold hunting.

[1] *Poetics*, chh. xi, xvi.

[2] Horace nowhere mentions the *Oedipus* of Sophocles.

[3] There is no record of Lucullus writing on the subject; but Suetonius, in his Life of Julius Caesar (lvi) mentions Caesar's knowledge of the play.

[4] *Oedipe* (1659). In the preface 'Au lecteur,' Corneille claimed: 'Cette tragédie a plu assez au Roi pour me faire recevoir de véritables et solides marques de son approbation.'

[5] *Oedipe*, I.2.   [6] *Ibid.*, II.1.

[7] *The Rehearsal* (1672), by the second Duke of Buckingham and others, contains two Kings of Brentford, brother kings who converse in a style 'never yet upon the stage' (II.2).

All we could gather out of Corneille was that an episode must be, but not his way: and Seneca supplied us with no new hint, but only a relation which he makes of his Tiresias raising the ghost of Laius:[1] which is here performed in view of the audience, the rites and ceremonies so far his as he agreed with antiquity, and the religion of the Greeks: but he himself was beholding to Homer's Tiresias[2] in the *Odysses* for some of them; and the rest have been collected from Heliodore's *Æthiopiques*,[3] and Lucan's *Erictho*.[4] Sophocles indeed is admirable everywhere: and therefore we have followed him as close as we possibly could. But the Athenian theatre (whether more perfect than ours is not now disputed) had a perfection differing from ours. You see there in every act a single scene (or two at most) which manage the business of the play, and after that succeeds the chorus, which commonly takes up more time in singing than there had been employed in speaking. The principal person appears almost constantly through the play; but the inferior parts seldom above once in the whole tragedy. The conduct of our stage is much more difficult, where we are obliged never to lose any considerable character which we have once presented. Custom likewise has obtained that we must form an under-plot of second persons, which must be depending on the first, and their by-walks must be like those in a labyrinth, which all of 'em lead into the great parterre: or like so many several lodging chambers, which have their outlets into the same gallery. Perhaps, after all, if we could think so, the ancient method, as 'tis the easiest, is also the most natural and the best. For variety, as 'tis managed, is too often subject to breed distraction: and while we would please too many ways, for want of art in the conduct, we please in none.

But we have given you more already than was necessary for a preface and, for aught we know, may gain no more by our instructions than that politic nation[5] is like to do, who have taught their enemies to fight so long, that at last they are in a condition to invade them.

[1] Seneca, *Oedipus*, II.390f.　　[2] *Odyssey*, xi.
[3] This Greek romance by Heliodorus (3rd century A.D.?), first printed in 1535, was first translated into English by Thomas Underdowne (1569?). Dryden's debt is to the necromantic scene at the end of Book vi.
[4] *Pharsalia*, vi.507f.
[5] Probably a jibe at the French. In August 1678 Louis XIV's forces were defeated at Mons by Dutch and British forces under the Prince of Orange. Cf. Prologue, l. 25, below.

PROLOGUE

When Athens all the Grecian State did guide,
And Greece gave laws to all the world beside,
Then Sophocles with Socrates did sit,
Supreme in wisdom one, and one in wit:
And wit from wisdom differed not in those,   5
But as 'twas sung in verse, or said in prose.
Then *Oedipus*, on crowded theatres,
Drew all admiring eyes and listening ears;
The pleas'd spectator shouted every line,
The noblest, manliest, and the best design!   10
And every critic of each learned age
By this just model has reform'd the stage.
Now, should it fail (as Heav'n avert our fear!)
Damn it in silence, lest the world should hear.
For were it known this poem did not please,   15
You might set up for perfect salvages:
Your neighbours would not look on you as men,
But think the nation all turn'd Picts again.
Faith, as you manage matters, 'tis not fit
You should suspect yourselves of too much wit.   20
Drive not the jest too far, but spare this piece;
And, for this once, be not more wise than Greece.
See twice! Do not pell-mell to damning fall,
Like true-born Britons who ne'er think at all:
Pray be advised; and though at Mons[1] you won,   25
On pointed cannon do not always run.
With some respect to ancient wit proceed;
You take the four first Councils for your creed.[2]
But, when you lay tradition wholly by,
And on the private spirit alone rely,   30
You turn fanatics in your poetry.
If, notwithstanding all that we can say,
You needs will have your pen'worths of the play,

[1] On 17 August 1678, when British regiments, with the Prince of Orange's forces, attacked the French army besieging Mons—an enterprise, according to Scott, 'needless as well as desperate.'
[2] The first four councils of the Christian church, establishing the Athanasian creed, were all held in the eastern or Greek empire.

And come resolv'd to damn, because you pay,
Record it, in memorial of the fact,   35
The first play bury'd since the Woollen Act.[1]

EPILOGUE

What Sophocles could undertake alone,
Our poets found a work for more than one;
And therefore two lay tugging at the piece,
With all their force, to draw the ponderous mass from Greece.
A weight that bent ev'n Seneca's strong Muse,   5
And which Corneille's shoulders did refuse.[2]
So hard it is, th' Athenian harp to string!
So much two Consuls yield to one just King.
Terror and pity this whole poem sway;
The mightiest machines that can mount a play;   10
How heavy will those vulgar souls be found
Whom two such engines cannot move from ground?
When Greece and Rome have smil'd upon this birth,
You can but damn for one poor spot of earth;
And when your children find your judgment such   15
They'll scorn their sires, and wish themselves born Dutch;
Each haughty poet will infer with ease
How much his wit must under-write to please.
As some strong churl would brandishing advance
The monumental sword that conquer'd France;[3]   20
So you, by judging this, your judgments teach
Thus far you like, that is, thus far you reach.
Since then the vote of full two thousand years
Has crown'd this plot, and all the dead are theirs;
Think it a debt you pay, not alms you give,   25
And in your own defence let his play live.
Think 'em not vain, when Sophocles is shown,
To praise his worth, they humbly doubt their own.

[1] A very recent Act, passed in 1678, requiring that burial shrouds be made only of wool as protection to the industry.
[2] Cf. preface, above.
[3] The sword of the Black Prince, over his tomb in Canterbury Cathedral. Cromwell is said to have drawn it.

Yet as weak States each others' pow'r assure,
Weak poets by conjunction are secure.   30
Their treat is what your palates relish most,
Charm! song! and show! a murder and a ghost!
We know not what you can desire or hope
To please you more, but burning of a Pope.

PREFACE, THE GROUNDS OF CRITICISM IN TRAGEDY

Both prefixed to *Troilus and Cressida* (1679)

REFINEMENT OF ENGLISH—SOURCES OF PLAY
ARISTOTLE ON TRAGEDY—SHAKESPEARE AND FLETCHER—
PLOT AND MANNERS OF TRAGEDY

Text: 4°, 1679.

Dryden's adaptation of Shakespeare's tragedy was first performed in the spring of 1679, and the quarto—which marked the beginning of his connection with the publisher Tonson, ended only by the poet's death—followed before the end of the year. The brief preface introduces, by an exception, not only the play itself, but a separate critical essay, 'The Grounds of Criticism in Tragedy,' a cautious and diplomatic version of the 'Heads of an Answer to Rymer' (pp. 210-20, above), written in the previous year in the end-papers of Rymer's *Tragedies of the Last Age* (1678). Only Rymer's provocation can explain Dryden's regressive attitude here: his critical doctrines seem less liberal and less 'English' than in his early period, out of concern for Rymer's severe neoclassicism, and the essay is more frankly prescriptive in tone than most of his criticism. Dryden, evidently, was genuinely impressed by the force of Rymer's attack upon the English dramatic tradition, and concerned lest his own critical respectability should suffer. The 'Grounds,' accordingly, is much less radical, much less frankly anti-Rymer, than the unpublished 'Heads,' and concedes more than it should. But its importance is capital, none the less: for Dryden, in conceding Rymer's principle of the dignity of the tragic hero, slyly demonstrates that the Greek tragedians themselves observe it only imperfectly, and that Shakespeare and 'Fletcher' had many virtues which the Greeks lacked.

THE poet Æschylus was held in the same veneration by the Athenians of after ages as Shakespeare is by us; and Longinus has judged, in favour of him, that he had a noble boldness of expression, and that his imaginations were lofty and heroic;[1] but, on the other side, Quintilian affirms that he was daring to

---

[1] *On the Sublime,* xv.5-6.

238

extravagance.[1] 'Tis certain that he affected pompous words, and that his sense too often was obscured by figures; notwithstanding these imperfections, the value of his writings after his decease was such that his countrymen ordained an equal reward to those poets who could alter his plays to be acted on the theatre, with those whose productions were wholly new, and of their own. The case is not the same in England; though the difficulties of altering are greater, and our reverence for Shakespeare much more just, than that of the Grecians for Æschylus. In the age of that poet, the Greek tongue was arrived to its full perfection; they had then amongst them an exact standard of writing and of speaking. The English language is not capable of such a certainty; and we are at present so far from it that we are wanting in the very foundation of it, a perfect grammar.[2] Yet it must be allowed to the present age that the tongue in general is so much refined since Shakespeare's time that many of his words, and more of his phrases, are scarce intelligible. And of those which we understand, some are ungrammatical, others coarse; and his whole style is so pestered with figurative expressions, that it is as affected as it is obscure. 'Tis true, that in his

[1] *Institutio*, X.i.66.

[2] A disparagement of the several English grammars that had appeared earlier in the century, including the *English Grammar* of Ben Jonson, published posthumously in 1640, and the *Short Institution of Grammar* (1647) of Dryden's old master at Westminster, Richard Busby. Dryden's plea for linguistic standards in English to match the discipline of French is renewed in the complimentary letter of dedication 'To Robert, Earl of Sunderland,' which precedes the preface. His call for a dictionary on historical principles was hardly realized until Johnson (1755), and that for a British Academy under royal patronage not until the present century. 'You know, my Lord,' he wrote to Sunderland, citing Richelieu's Académie Française, 'how low he laid the foundations of so great a work: that he began it with a *Grammar* and a *Dictionary*; without which all those remarks and observations which have since been made had been performed to as little purpose as it would be to consider the furniture of rooms before the contrivance of the house. Propriety must first be stated, ere any measures of elegance can be taken . . . ,' and he goes on to demand lexicographers with a knowledge of the sources of English. 'For I am often put to a stand, in considering whether what I write be the idiom of the tongue, or false grammar and nonsense couched beneath that specious name of *anglicism*; and have no other way to clear my doubts but by translating my English into Latin, and thereby trying what sense the words will bear in a more stable language.' He goes on to complain that English 'has the disadvantage to be founded on the Dutch. We are full of monosyllables, and those clogged with consonants, and our pronunciation is effeminate; all which are enemies to a sounding language. 'Tis true that, to supply our poverty, we have trafficked with our neighbour nations; by which means we abound as much in words as Amsterdam does in religions.'

later plays he had worn off somewhat of the rest; but the tragedy which I have undertaken to correct was, in all probability, one of his first endeavours on the stage.[1]

The original story was written by one Lollius, a Lombard, in Latin verse, and translated by Chaucer into English; intended, I suppose, a satire on the inconstancy of women: I find nothing of it among the Ancients; not so much as the name once Cressida mentioned.[2] Shakespeare (as I hinted), in the apprenticeship of his writing, modelled it into that play which is now called by the name of *Troilus and Cressida*; but so lamely is it left to us, that it is not divided into acts; which fault I ascribe to the actors who printed it after Shakespeare's death; and that too so carelessly, that a more uncorrect copy I never saw.[3] For the play itself, the author seems to have begun it with some fire; the characters of Pandarus and Thersites are promising enough; but as if he grew weary of his task, after an entrance or two, he lets 'em fall: and the later part of the tragedy is nothing but a confusion of drums and trumpets, excursions and alarms. The chief persons, who give name to the tragedy, are left alive; Cressida is false, and is not punished. Yet, after all, because the play was Shakespeare's, and that there appeared in some places of it the admirable genius of the author, I undertook to remove that heap of rubbish under which many excellent thoughts lay wholly buried. Accordingly, I new modelled the plot; threw out many unnecessary persons; improved those characters which were begun and left unfinished, as Hector, Troilus, Pandarus, and Thersites; and added that of Andromache. After this I made, with no small trouble, an order and connection of all the scenes;[4] removing them from the places where they were inartificially set; and though it was impossible to keep 'em all unbroken, because the scene must be sometimes in the city and sometimes in the camp, yet I have so ordered them that there is a coherence

---

[1] *Troilus and Cressida* was probably written in about 1602, in mid-career. But the chronology of Shakespeare's plays was not settled with even relative certainty until Malone's edition of 1790.

[2] The story of Troilus and Cressida is altogether post-classical; and though 'Chryseida' is an accusative of the Greek 'Chryseis,' it was not attached to the present heroine before Boccaccio, who in his *Filostrato* substituted 'Criseida' for the 'Briseida' of the *Roman de Troie*.

[3] The text of the First Folio (1623), edited by the actors John Heminge and Henry Condell, lacks scene-divisions, as does the quarto of 1609.

[4] Corneille's 'liaison des scène' in the Examen of *La Suivante*: cf. *Of Dramatic Poesy*, p. 37, above.

of 'em with one another, and a dependence on the main design: no leaping from Troy to the Grecian tents, and thence back again in the same act; but a due proportion of time allowed for every motion. I need not say that I have refined his language, which before was obsolete; but I am willing to acknowledge that as I have often drawn his English nearer to our times, so I have sometimes conformed my own to his; and consequently, the language is not altogether so pure as it is significant. The scenes of Pandarus and Cressida, of Troilus and Pandarus, of Andromache with Hector and the Trojans, in the second act, are wholly new; together with that of Nestor and Ulysses with Thersites, and that of Thersites with Ajax and Achilles. I will not weary my reader with the scenes which are added of Pandarus and the lovers, in the third; and those of Thersites, which are wholly altered; but I cannot omit the last scene in it, which is almost half the act, betwixt Troilus and Hector. The occasion of raising it was hinted to me by Mr Betterton: the contrivance and working of it was my own. They who think to do me an injury by saying that it is an imitation of the scene betwixt Brutus and Cassius, do me an honour by supposing I could imitate the incomparable Shakespeare; but let me add that if Shakespeare's scene, or the faulty copy of it in *Amintor and Melantius*, had never been, yet Euripides had furnished me with an excellent example in his *Iphigenia*,[1] between Agamemnon and Menelaus; and from thence, indeed, the last turn of it is borrowed. The occasion which Shakespeare, Euripides, and Fletcher have all taken is the same; grounded upon friendship: and the quarrel of two virtuous men, raised by natural degrees to the extremity of passion, is conducted in all three to the declination of the same passion, and concludes with a warm renewing of their friendship. But the particular groundwork which Shakespeare has taken is incomparably the best; because he has not only chosen two of the greatest heroes of their age, but has likewise interested the liberty of Rome, and their own honours who were the redeemers of it, in this debate. And if he has made Brutus, who was naturally a patient man, to fly into excess at first, let it be remembered in his defence that, just before, he has received

[1] *Iphigenia in Aulis.* A comparison between Euripides's quarrel-scene and that of Beaumont and Fletcher in *The Maid's Tragedy* (1619), iii, between the friends Amintor and Melantius, had already been made by Rymer in his *Tragedies of the Last Age* (1678), as Dryden later confesses (p. 242, below).

the news of Portia's death; whom the poet, on purpose neglecting a little chronology, supposes to have died before Brutus, only to give him an occasion of being more easily exasperated.[1] Add to this that the injury he had received from Cassius had long been brooding in his mind; and that a melancholy man, upon consideration of an affront, especially from a friend, would be more eager in his passion than he who had given it, though naturally more choleric.

Euripides, whom I have followed, has raised the quarrel betwixt two brothers who were friends. The foundation of the scene was this: the Grecians were windbound at the port of Aulis, and the oracle had said that they could not sail, unless Agamemnon delivered up his daughter to be sacrificed: he refuses; his brother Menelaus urges the public safety; the father defends himself by arguments of natural affection, and hereupon they quarrel. Agamemnon is at last convinced, and promises to deliver up Iphigenia, but so passionately laments his loss that Menelaus is grieved to have been the occasion of it and, by a return of kindness, offers to intercede for him with the Grecians, that his daughter might not be sacrificed. But my friend Mr Rymer has so largely, and with so much judgment, described this scene, in comparing it with that of Melantius and Amintor, that it is superfluous to say more of it; I only named the heads of it, that any reasonable man might judge it was from thence I modelled my scene betwixt Troilus and Hector. I will conclude my reflexions on it with a passage of Longinus, concerning Plato's imitation of Homer: 'We ought not to regard a good imitation as a theft, but as a beautiful idea of him who undertakes to imitate, by forming himself on the invention and the work of another man; for he enters into the lists like a new wrestler, to dispute the prize with the former champion. This sort of emulation, says Hesiod, is honourable, ἀγαθὴ δ' ἔρις ἐστὶ βροτοῖσιν[2], when we combat for victory with a hero, and are not without glory even in our overthrow. Those great men whom we propose to ourselves as patterns of our imitation serve us as a torch, which is lifted up before us to enlighten our passage;

---

[1] *Julius Caesar*, IV, where Brutus receives the news of his wife's death before the battle of Philippi. In fact, Portia killed herself after hearing of her husband's death in the battle.

[2] *Works and Days*, l. 24: 'this strife is wholesome to men'.

and often elevate our thoughts as high as the conception we have of our author's genius.'[1]

I have been so tedious in three acts that I shall contract myself in the two last. The beginning scenes of the fourth act are either added or changed wholly by me; the middle of it is Shakespeare altered, and mingled with my own; three or four of the last scenes are altogether new. And the whole fifth act, both the plot and the writing, are my own additions.

But having written so much for imitation of what is excellent, in that part of the preface which related only to myself, methinks it would neither be unprofitable nor unpleasant to inquire how far we ought to imitate our own poets, Shakespeare and Fletcher, in their tragedies: and this will occasion another inquiry how those two writers differ between themselves. But since neither of these questions can be solved unless some measures be first taken by which we may be enabled to judge truly of their writings, I shall endeavour, as briefly as I can, to discover the grounds and reason of all criticism, applying them in this place only to tragedy. Aristotle with his interpreters, and Horace, and Longinus, are the authors to whom I owe my lights; and what part soever of my own plays, or of this, which no mending could make regular, shall fall under the condemnation of such judges, it would be impudence in me to defend. I think it no shame to retract my errors, and am well pleased to suffer in the cause, if the art may be improved at my expense: I therefore proceed to

THE GROUNDS OF CRITICISM IN TRAGEDY.

Tragedy is thus defined by Aristotle[2] (omitting what I thought unnecessary in his definition). 'Tis an imitation of one entire, great, and probable action; not told, but represented; which, by moving in us fear and pity, is conducive to the purging of those two passions in our minds. More largely thus, tragedy describes or paints an action, which action must have all the properties above named. First, it must be one or single, that is, it must not be a history of one man's life; suppose of Alexander the Great, or Julius Caesar, but one single action of theirs. This condemns all Shakespeare's historical plays, which are rather chronicles represented than tragedies, and all double action of plays. As to avoid a satire upon others, I will make bold with

[1] *On the Sublime*, xiii.4.   [2] In *Poetics*, ch. vi (freely rendered).

my own *Marriage a-la-Mode*, where there are manifestly two actions, not depending on one another: but in *Oedipus* there cannot properly be said to be two actions, because the love of Adrastus and Eurydice has a necessary dependence on the principal design, into which it is woven. The natural reason of this rule is plain; for two different independent actions distract the attention and concernment of the audience, and consequently destroy the intention of the poet: if his business be to move terror and pity, and one of his actions be comical, the other tragical, the former will divert the people, and utterly make void his greater purpose. Therefore, as in perspective, so in tragedy, there must be a point of sight in which all the lines terminate; otherwise the eye wanders, and the work is false. This was the practice of the Grecian stage. But Terence made an innovation in the Roman: all his plays have double actions; for it was his custom to translate two Greek comedies, and to weave them into one of his, yet so that both the actions were comical, and one was principal, the other but secondary or subservient. And this has obtained on the English stage, to give us the pleasure of variety.

As the action ought to be one, it ought, as such, to have order in it, that is, to have a natural beginning, a middle, and an end. A natural beginning, says Aristotle, is that which could not necessarily have been placed after another thing, and so of the rest.[1] This consideration will arraign all plays after the new model of Spanish plots,[2] where accident is heaped upon accident, and that which is first might as reasonably be last: an inconvenience not to be remedied but by making one accident naturally produce another, otherwise 'tis a farce and not a play. Of this nature is the *Slighted Maid*,[3] where there is no scene in the first act which might not by as good reason be in the fifth. And if the action to be one, the tragedy ought likewise to conclude with the action of it. Thus in *Mustapha*,[4] the play should naturally have ended with the death of Zanger, and not have given us the grace cup after dinner of Solyman's divorce from Roxolana.

The following properties of the action are so easy that they need not my explaining. It ought to be great, and to consist of great persons, to distinguish it from comedy, where the action

---

[1] *Poetics*, ch. vii.   [2] Cf. *Of Dramatic Poesy*, p. 48 and n., above.
[3] A romantic comedy, published in 1663, by Sir Robert Stapylton (d. 1669).
[4] By Lord Orrery. Cf. preface to *The Rival Ladies*, p. 1, above.

is trivial, and the persons of inferior rank. The last quality of the action is that it ought to be probable, as well as admirable and great. 'Tis not necessary that there should be historical truth in it; but always necessary that there should be a likeness of truth, something that is more than barely possible, *probable* being that which succeeds or happens oftener than it misses. To invent therefore a probability, and to make it wonderful, is the most difficult undertaking in the art of poetry; for that which is not wonderful is not great; and that which is not probable will not delight a reasonable audience. This action, thus described, must be represented and not told, to distinguish dramatic poetry from epic: but I hasten to the end or scope of tragedy, which is, to rectify or purge our passions, fear and pity.[1]

To instruct delightfully is the general end of all poetry. Philosophy instructs, but it performs its work by precept: which is not delightful, or not so delightful as example. To purge the passions by example is therefore the particular instruction which belongs to tragedy. Rapin, a judicious critic, has observed from Aristotle that pride and want of commiseration are the most predominant vices in mankind;[2] therefore, to cure us of these two, the inventors of tragedy have chosen to work upon two other passions, which are fear and pity. We are wrought to fear by their setting before our eyes some terrible example of misfortune, which happened to persons of the highest quality; for such an action demonstrates to us that no condition is privileged from the turns of fortune; this must of necessity cause terror in us, and consequently abate our pride. But when we see that the most virtuous, as well as the greatest, are not exempt from such misfortunes, that consideration moves pity in us, and insensibly works us to be helpful to, and tender over, the distressed, which is the noblest and most god-like of moral virtues. Here 'tis observable that it is absolutely necessary to make a man virtuous, if we desire he should be pitied: we lament not, but detest, a wicked man, we are glad when we behold his crimes are punished, and that poetical justice[3] is done upon him.

[1] *Poetics*, ch. xiii.   [2] Rapin, *Réflexions*, xvii.
[3] The earliest recorded use of the phrase is by Rymer in *The Tragedies of the Last Age* (1678): 'A poet must of necessity see justice exactly administered, if he intended to please.' 'No poetical justice could have touched them [Rollo and Otto]: guilty they were to be in enjoying their father's crime, but not of committing any new' (*Critical Works*, ed. Zimansky, pp. 22, 26). Cf. 'Heads of an Answer to Rymer,' paras. 26, 42, above.

Euripides was censured by the critics of his time for making his chief characters too wicked: for example, Phædra, though she loved her son-in-law with reluctancy, and that it was a curse upon her family for offending Venus, yet was thought too ill a pattern for the stage. Shall we therefore banish all characters of villainy? I confess I am not of that opinion; but it is necessary that the hero of the play be not a villain; that is, the characters which should move our pity ought to have virtuous inclinations, and degrees of moral goodness in them. As for a perfect character of virtue, it never was in nature, and therefore there can be no imitation of it; but there are allays of frailty to be allowed for the chief persons, yet so that the good which is in them shall outweigh the bad, and consequently leave room for punishment on the one side, and pity on the other.

After all, if any one will ask me whether a tragedy cannot be made upon any other grounds than those of exciting pity and terror in us, Bossu,[1] the best of modern critics, answers thus in general: that all excellent arts, and particularly that of poetry, have been invented and brought to perfection by men of a transcendent genius; and that therefore they who practise afterwards the same arts are obliged to tread in their footsteps, and to search in their writings the foundation of them; for it is not just that new rules should destroy the authority of the old. But Rapin writes more particularly thus: that no passions in a story are so proper to move our concernment as fear and pity; and that it is from our concernment we receive our pleasure, is undoubted; when the soul becomes agitated with fear for one character, or hope for another, then it is that we are pleased in tragedy by the interest which we take in their adventures.[2]

Here, therefore, the general answer may be given to the first question, how far we ought to imitate Shakespeare and Fletcher in their plots; namely, that we ought to follow them so far only as they have copied the excellencies of those who invented and brought to perfection dramatic poetry: those things only excepted which religion, customs of countries, idioms of languages, etc., have altered in the superstructures, but not in the foundation of the design.

How defective Shakespeare and Fletcher have been in all their plots, Mr Rymer has discovered in his criticisms: neither

[1] Le Bossu (1631-89), *Du poème épique* (1675).   [2] Rapin, *Réflexions,* xviii.

can we who follow them be excused from the same or greater errors; which are the more unpardonable in us, because we want their beauties to countervail our faults. The best of their designs, the most approaching to antiquity, and the most conducing to move pity, is the *King and No King*; which, if the farce of Bessus were thrown away, is of that inferior sort of tragedies which end with a prosperous event. 'Tis probably derived from the story of Oedipus, with the character of Alexander the Great, in his extravagancies, given to Arbaces. The taking of this play, amongst many others, I cannot wholly ascribe to the excellency of the action; for I find it moving when it is read: 'tis true, the faults of the plot are so evidently proved that they can no longer be denied. The beauties of it must therefore lie either in the lively touches of the passion: or we must conclude, as I think we may, that even in imperfect plots there are less degrees of nature, by which some faint emotions of pity and terror are raised in us: as a less engine will raise a less proportion of weight, though not so much as one of Archimedes' making; for nothing can move our nature, but by some natural reason, which works upon passions. And since we acknowledge the effect, there must be something in the cause.

The difference between Shakespeare and Fletcher in their plotting seems to be this: that Shakespeare generally moves more terror, and Fletcher more compassion. For the first had a more masculine, a bolder and more fiery genius; the second, a more soft and womanish. In the mechanic beauties of the plot, which are the observation of the three unities, time, place, and action, they are both deficient; but Shakespeare most. Ben Jonson reformed those errors in his comedies, yet one of Shakespeare's was regular before him; which is, *The Merry Wives of Windsor*.[1] For what remains concerning the design, you are to be referred to our English critic. That method which he has prescribed to raise it from mistake, or ignorance of the crime, is certainly the best, though 'tis not the only: for amongst all the tragedies of Sophocles, there is but one, *Oedipus*, which is wholly built after that model.

After the plot, which is the foundation of the play, the next thing to which we ought to apply our judgment is the manners, for now the poet comes to work above ground: the ground-work

[1] But the action of this comedy is spread over some three days.

indeed is that which is most necessary, as that upon which depends the firmness of the whole fabric; yet it strikes not the eye so much as the beauties or imperfections of the manners, the thoughts, and the expressions.

The first rule which Bossu prescribes to the writer of an heroic poem, and which holds too by the same reason in all dramatic poetry, is to make the moral of the work, that is, to lay down to yourself what that precept of morality shall be, which you would insinuate into the people; as namely Homer's (which I have copied in my *Conquest of Granada*) was that union preserves a commonwealth, and discord destroys it; Sophocles, in his *Oedipus*, that no man is to be accounted happy before his death. 'Tis the moral that directs the whole action of the play to one centre; and that action or fable is the example built upon the moral, which confirms the truth of it to our experience: when the fable is designed, then, and not before, the persons are to be introduced with their manners, characters, and passions.

The manners in a poem are understood to be those inclinations, whether natural or acquired, which move and carry us to actions, good, bad, or indifferent, in a play; or which incline the persons to such or such actions.[1] I have anticipated part of this discourse already, in declaring that a poet ought not to make the manners perfectly good in his best persons; but neither are they to be more wicked in any of his characters than necessity requires. To produce a villain, without other reason than a natural inclination to villainy is, in poetry, to produce an effect without a cause; and to make him more a villain than he has just reason to be, is to make an effect which is stronger than the cause.

The manners arise from many causes; and are either distinguished by complexion, as choleric and phlegmatic, or by the differences of age or sex, of climates, or quality of the persons, or their present condition: they are likewise to be gathered from the several virtues, vices, or passions, and many other commonplaces which a poet must be supposed to have learned from natural philosophy, ethics, and history; of all which whosoever is ignorant, does not deserve the name of poet.

[1] Cf. a later definition of 'manners' in the preface to the *Fables*, vol. II, p. 278, below.

But as the manners are useful in this art, they may be all comprised under these general heads: first, they must be apparent; that is, in every character of the play, some inclinations of the person must appear; and these are shown in the actions and discourse. Secondly, the manners must be suitable, or agreeing to the persons; that is, to the age, sex, dignity, and the other general heads of manners: thus, when a poet has given the dignity of a king to one of his persons, in all his actions and speeches, that person must discover majesty, magnanimity, and jealousy of power, because these are suitable to the general manners of a king. The third property of manners is resemblance; and this is founded upon the particular characters of men, as we have them delivered to us by relation or history; that is, when a poet has the known character of this or that man before him, he is bound to represent him such, at least not contrary to that which fame has reported him to have been. Thus, it is not a poet's choice to make Ulysses choleric, or Achilles patient, because Homer has described 'em quite otherwise. Yet this is a rock on which ignorant writers daily split; and the absurdity is as monstrous as if a painter should draw a coward running from a battle, and tell us it was the picture of Alexander the Great.

The last property of manners is that they be constant and equal, that is, maintained the same through the whole design: thus, when Virgil had once given the name of *pious* to Æneas,[1] he was bound to show him such, in all his words and actions through the whole poem. All these properties Horace has hinted to a judicious observer: 1. *notandi sunt tibi mores*; 2. *aut famam sequere*; 3. *aut sibi convenientia finge*; 4. *servetur ad imum, qualis ab incepto processerit, et sibi constet.*[2]

From the manners, the characters of persons are derived; for indeed the characters are no other than the inclinations, as they appear in the several persons of the poem; a character being thus defined, that which distinguishes one man from another. Not to repeat the same things over again which have been said of the manners, I will only add what is necessary here. A character, or that which distinguishes one man from all others, cannot be

[1] 'sum pius Aeneas'—*Aeneid*, I.379.
[2] *Ars poetica*, ll. 156, 119, 126-7: 'You must remark the manners of each age'; 'either follow tradition, or create your own convention'; 'let each character be maintained as it began, and remain consistent with itself.'

supposed to consist of one particular virtue, or vice, or passion only; but 'tis a composition of qualities which are not contrary to one another in the same person; thus the same man may be liberal and valiant, but not liberal and covetous; so in a comical character or humour (which is an inclination to this or that particular folly), Falstaff is a liar, and a coward, a glutton, and a buffoon, because all these qualities may agree in the same man; yet it is still to be observed that one virtue, vice, and passion ought to be shown in every man, as predominant over all the rest; as covetousness in Crassus, love of his country in Brutus; and the same in characters which are feigned.

The chief character or hero in a tragedy, as I have already shown, ought in prudence to be such a man who has so much more in him of virtue than of vice, that he may be left amiable to the audience, which otherwise cannot have any concernment for his sufferings; and 'tis on this one character that the pity and terror must be principally, if not wholly, founded. A rule which is extremely necessary, and which none of the critics that I know have fully enough discovered to us. For terror and compassion work but weakly when they are divided into many persons. If Creon had been the chief character in *Oedipus*, there had neither been terror nor compassion moved; but only detestation of the man and joy for his punishment; if Adrastus and Eurydice had been made more appearing characters, then the pity had been divided, and lessened on the part of Oedipus: but making Oedipus the best and bravest person, and even Jocasta but an underpart to him, his virtues and the punishment of his fatal crime drew both the pity and the terror to himself.

By what had been said of the manners, it will be easy for a reasonable man to judge whether the characters be truly or falsely drawn in a tragedy; for if there be no manners appearing in the characters, no concernment for the persons can be raised; no pity or horror can be moved, but by vice or virtue; therefore, without them, no person can have any business in the play. If the inclinations be obscure, 'tis a sign the poet is in the dark, and knows not what manner of man he presents to you; and consequently you can have no idea, or very imperfect, of that man; nor can judge what resolutions he ought to take; or what words or actions are proper for him. Most comedies made up of accidents or adventures are liable to fall into this error; and tragedies with many turns are subject to it; for the manners never can be evident where the surprises of fortune take up all the business of the stage; and where the poet is more in pain to tell you what happened to such a man than what he was. 'Tis one of the excellencies of Shakespeare that the manners of his persons are generally apparent, and you see their bent and inclinations. Fletcher comes far short of him in this, as indeed he does almost in every thing: there are but glimmerings of manners in most of his comedies, which run upon adventures; and in his tragedies, Rollo,[1] Otto,[2] the King and No King, Melantius,[3] and many others of his best, are but pictures shown you in the twilight; you know not whether they resemble vice or virtue, and they are either good, bad, or indifferent, as the present scene requires it. But of all poets, this commendation is to be given to Ben Jonson, that the manners even of the most inconsiderable persons in his plays are everywhere apparent.

By considering the second quality of manners, which is that they be suitable to the age, quality, country, dignity, etc., of the character, we may likewise judge whether a poet has followed nature. In this kind, Sophocles and Euripides have more excelled among the Greeks than Æschylus; and Terence more than Plautus among the Romans. Thus Sophocles gives to Oedipus the true qualities of a king, in both those plays which bear his name; but in the latter, which is the Oedipus Colonœus, he lets fall on purpose his tragic style; his hero speaks not in the arbitrary tone; but remembers, in the softness of his complaints, that he is an unfortunate blind old man; that he is banished from his country, and persecuted by his next relations. The present French poets are generally accused that wheresoever they lay the scene, or in whatsoever age, the manners of their heroes are wholly French. Racine's Bajazet is bred at Constantinople; but his civilities are conveyed to him, by some secret passage, from Versailles into the Seraglio. But our Shakespeare, having ascribed to Henry the Fourth the character of a king and of a father, gives him the perfect manners of each relation, when either he transacts with his son or with his subjects. Fletcher, on the other side, gives neither to Arbaces,

---

[1] Cf. p. 48n., above.   [2] The name of Rollo's brother.
[3] I.e. The Maid's Tragedy (1619).

nor to his King in the *Maid's Tragedy*, the qualities which are
suitable to a monarch; though he may be excused a little in the
latter, for the King there is not uppermost in the character; 'tis
the lover of Evadne, who is King only in a second consideration;
and though he be unjust, and has other faults which shall be
nameless, yet he is not the hero of the play. 'Tis true, we find
him a lawful prince (though I never heard of any King that was
in Rhodes), and therefore Mr Rymer's criticism stands good;
that he should not be shown in so vicious a character.[1] Sophocles has been more judicious in his *Antigona*; for though he
represents in Creon a bloody prince, yet he makes him not a
lawful king, but an usurper, and Antigona herself is the heroine
of the tragedy. But when Philaster wounds Arethusa and the boy;
and Perigot his mistress, in the *Faithful Shepherdess*, both these
are contrary to the character of manhood.[2] Nor is Valentinian
managed much better, for though Fletcher has taken his picture
truly, and shown him as he was, an effeminate, voluptuous man,
yet he has forgotten that he was an Emperor, and has given him
none of those royal marks which ought to appear in a lawful
successor of the throne. If it be inquired what Fletcher should
have done on this occasion; ought he not to have represented
Valentinian as he was? Bossu shall answer this question for me,
by an instance of the like nature: Mauritius, the Greek Emperor,
was a prince far surpassing Valentinian, for he was endued
with many kingly virtues; he was religious, merciful, and valiant,
but withal he was noted of extreme covetousness, a vice which
is contrary to the character of a hero, or a prince: therefore, says
the critic, that emperor was no fit person to be represented in a
tragedy, unless his good qualities were only to be shown, and
his covetousness (which sullied them all) were slurred over by
the artifice of the poet.[3] To return once more to Shakespeare:
no man ever drew so many characters, or generally distinguished
'em better from one another, excepting only Jonson. I will
instance but in one, to show the copiousness of his intention:
'tis that of Caliban, or the Monster in the *Tempest*. He seems

[1] Rymer, in *The Tragedies of the Last Age*, had condemned the nameless
king of *The Maid's Tragedy*: 'Certainly God never made a king with so little
wit, nor the devil with so little grace, as is this King Anonymous' (*Critical
Works*, ed. Zimansky, p. 61).
[2] Cf. 'Defence of an Epilogue,' p. 172 and n., above.
[3] *Traité du poème épique* (1675), IV.vii.

there to have created a person which was not in nature, a boldness which at first sight would appear intolerable; for he makes
him a species of himself, begotten by an incubus on a witch;
but this, as I have elsewhere proved, is not wholly beyond the
bounds of credibility, at least the vulgar still believe it. We
have the separated notions of a spirit, and of a witch; (and spirits,
according to Plato, are vested with a subtle body; according to
some of his followers, have different sexes[1]); therefore, as from
the distinct apprehensions of a horse, and of a man, imagination
has formed a centaure; so from those of an incubus and a sor-
ceress, Shakespeare has produced his monster. Whether or no
his generation can be defended, I leave to philosophy; but of
this I am certain, that the poet has most judiciously furnished
him with a person, a language, and a character, which will suit
him, both by father's and mother's side: he has all the dis-
contents and malice of a witch, and of a devil, besides a convenient proportion of the deadly sins; gluttony, sloth, and lust
are manifest; the dejectedness of a slave is likewise given
him, and the ignorance of one bred up in a desert island. His
person is monstrous, as he is the product of unnatural lust;
and his language is as hobgoblin as his person; in all things he is
distinguished from other mortals. The characters of Fletcher
are poor and narrow, in comparison of Shakespeare's; I remember not one which is not borrowed from him; unless you will
accept that strange mixture of a man[2] in the *King and No King*;
so that in this part Shakespeare is generally worth our imitation;
and to imitate Fletcher is but to copy after him who was a
copier.

Under this general head of manners, the passions are naturally
included as belonging to the characters. I speak not of pity and
of terror, which are to be moved in the audience by the plot; but
of anger, hatred, love, ambition, jealousy, revenge, etc., as they
are shown in this or that person of the play. To describe these

---

[1] E.g. Henry More (1614-87), *The Immortality of the Soul* (1659), III.ix.4.
The view was commonly held by the Cambridge Platonists, as well as by
Milton; cf. p. 161 and n., above, and *Paradise Lost*, viii, 622f.:

Whatever pure thou in the body enjoy'st
(And pure thou wert created) we enjoy
In eminence, and obstacle find none
Of membrane, joint, or limb. . . .

[2] Probably Arbaces himself, though Ker suggests Bessus.

naturally, and to move then artfully, is one of the greatest
commendations which can be given to a poet: to write pathetically, says Longinus, cannot proceed but for a lofty genius.[1] A
poet must be born with this quality; yet, unless he help himself
by an acquired knowledge of the passions, what they are in their
own nature, and by what springs they are to be moved, he will
be subject either to raise them where they ought not to be
raised, or not to raise them by the just degrees of nature, or to
amplify them beyond the natural bounds, or not to observe the
crisis and turns of them, in their cooling and decay: all which
errors proceed from want of judgment in the poet, and from
being unskilled in the principles of moral philosophy. Nothing
is more frequent in a fanciful writer than to foil himself by not
managing his strength; therefore, as in a wrestler, there is first
required some measure of force, a well-knit body, and active
limbs, without which all instruction would be vain; yet, these
being granted, if he want the skill which is necessary to a wrestler,
he shall make but small advantage of his natural robustuousness:
so, in a poet, his inborn vehemence and force of spirit will only
run him out of breath the sooner, if it be not supported by the
help of art. The roar of passion, indeed, may please an audience,
three parts of which are ignorant enough to think all is moving
which is noise, and it may stretch the lungs of an ambitious
actor, who will die upon the spot for a thundering clap; but it
will move no other passion than indignation and contempt from
judicious men. Longinus, whom I have hitherto followed,
continues thus: *If the passions be artfully employed, the discourse
becomes vehement and lofty: if otherwise, there is nothing more
ridiculous than a great passion out of season*: and to this purpose
he animadverts severely upon Æschylus, who writ nothing in
cold blood, but was always in a rapture, and in fury with his
audience:[2] the inspiration was still upon him, he was ever tearing
it upon the tripos;[3] or (to run off as madly as he does, from one
similitude to another) he was always at high flood of passion,
even in the dead ebb and lowest water-mark of the scene. He
who would raise the passion of a judicious audience, says a
learned critic,[4] must be sure to take his hearers along with him;

[1] Longinus, ch. viii.   [2] Ibid., ch. iii.
[3] I.e. tripod, the three-legged vessel on which the priestess of Apollo's
shrine at Delphi delivered her raving oracles.
[4] Le Bossu, III.ix.

if they be in a calm, 'tis in vain for him to be in a huff: he must move them by degrees, and kindle with 'em; otherwise he will be in danger of setting his own heap of stubble on fire, and of burning out by himself without warming the company that stand about him. They who would justify the madness of poetry from the authority of Aristotle have mistaken the text, and consequently the interpretation: I imagine it to be false read, where he says of poetry that it is εὐφυοῦς ἢ μανικοῦ, that it had always somewhat in it either of a genius, or of a madman. 'Tis more probable that the original ran thus, that poetry was εὐφυοῦς οὐ μανικοῦ, that it belongs to a witty man, but not to a madman.[1] Thus then the passions, as they are considered simply and in themselves, suffer violence when they are perpetually maintained at the same height; for what melody can be made on that instrument, all whose strings are screwed up at first to their utmost stretch, and to the same sound? But this is not the worst: for the characters likewise bear a part in the general calamity, if you consider the passions as embodied in them; for it follows of necessity that no man can be distinguished from another by his discourse, when every man is ranting, swaggering, and exclaiming with the same excess: as if it were the only business of all the characters to contend with each other for the prize at Billingsgate; or that the scene of the tragedy lay in Bet'lem.[2] Suppose the poet should intend this man to be choleric, and that man to be patient; yet when they are confounded in the writing, you cannot distinguish them from one another: for the man who was called patient and tame is only so before he speaks; but let his clack be set a-going, and he shall tongue it as impetuously, and as loudly, as the errantest hero in the play. By this means, the characters are only distinct in name; but, in reality, all the men and women in the play are the same person. No man should pretend to write who cannot temper his fancy with his judgment: nothing is more dangerous to a raw horseman than a hot-mouthed jade without a curb.

'Tis necessary therefore for a poet who would concern an audience by describing of a passion, first to prepare it, and not to rush upon it all at once. Ovid has judiciously shown the

[1] Aristotle, *Poetics*, ch. xvii. Rapin (ch. v), whom Dryden follows here, had denied Castelvetro's claim that Aristotle held the poet to be mad as well as divinely inspired.
[2] I.e. Bedlam.

difference of these two ways, in the speeches of Ajax and Ulysses: Ajax, from the very beginning, breaks out into his exclamations, and is swearing by his Maker, *agimus, proh Jupiter, inquit*.[1] Ulysses, on the contrary, prepares his audience with all the submissiveness he can practise, and all the calmness of a reasonable man; he found his judges in a tranquillity of spirit, and therefore set out leisurely and softly with 'em, till he had warmed 'em by degrees; and then he began to mend his pace, and to draw them along with his own impetuousness: yet so managing his breath, that it might not fail him at his need, and reserving his utmost proofs of ability even to the last. The success, you see, was answerable; for the crowd only applauded the speech of Ajax:

> vulgique secutum
> ultima murmur erat:[2]

But the judges awarded the prize for which they contended to Ulysses:

> mota manus procerum est; et quid facundia posset
> tum patuit, fortisque viri tulit arma disertus.[3]

The next necessary rule is to put nothing into the discourse which may hinder your moving of the passions. Too many accidents, as I have said, encumber the poet, as much as the arms of Saul did David; for the variety of passions which they produce are ever crossing and jostling each other out of the way. He who treats of joy and grief together is in a fair way of causing neither of those effects. There is yet another obstacle to be removed, which is pointed wit, and sentences affected out of season; these are nothing of kin to the violence of passion: no man is at leisure to make sentences and similes when his soul is in an agony. I the rather name this fault that it may serve to mind me of my former errors; neither will I spare myself, but give an example of this kind from my *Indian Emperor*. Montezuma, pursued by his enemies, and seeking sanctuary, stands parleying without the fort, and describing his danger to Cydaria, in a simile of six lines:

---

[1] *Metamorphoses*, xiii.5.   [2] *Ibid.*, 123.
[3] *Ibid.*, 382-3 (*re patuit* ...): 'The assembly was much moved, and it was revealed what eloquence could do: and the expert orator carried off the hero's arms.'

> As on the sands the frighted traveller
> Sees the high seas come rolling from afar, etc.[1]

My Indian potentate was well skilled in the sea for an inland
prince, and well improved since the first act, when he sent his
son to discover it. The image had not been amiss from another
man, at another time: *sed nunc non erat hisce locus*:[2] he destroyed
the concernment which the audience might otherwise have had
for him; for they could not think the danger near when he had
the leisure to invent a simile.

If Shakespeare be allowed, as I think he must, to have made
his characters distinct, it will easily be inferred that he understood the nature of the passions: because it has been proved
already that confused passions make undistinguishable characters: yet I cannot deny that he has his failings; but they are
not so much in the passions themselves as in his manner of
expression: he often obscures his meaning by his words, and
sometimes makes it unintelligible. I will not say of so great a
poet that he distinguished not the blown puffy style from true
sublimity; but I may venture to maintain that the fury of his
fancy often transported him beyond the bounds of judgment,
either in coining of new words and phrases, or racking words
which were in use into the violence of a catachresis.[3] 'Tis not
that I would explode the use of metaphors from passions, for
Longinus thinks 'em necessary to raise it:[4] but to use 'em at
every word, to say nothing without a metaphor, a simile, an
image, or description, is I doubt to smell a little too strongly of
the buskin. I must be forced to give an example of expressing
passion figuratively; but that I may do it with respect to Shakespeare, it shall not be taken from any thing of his: 'tis an exclama-
tion against Fortune, quoted in his *Hamlet* but written by some
other poet:

> Out, out, thou strumpet Fortune! all you gods,
> In general synod, take away her power;
> Break all the spokes and felleys from her wheel,
> And bowl the round nave down the hill of Heav'n,
> As low as to the fiends.[5]

[1] Act V ('As when upon the sands the traveller . . .').
[2] Horace, *Ars poetica*, l. 19: 'But this was not the place.'
[3] Cf. *Of Dramatic Poesy*, p. 21n., above.
[4] Ch. xxxii; 'explode' is probably a misprint in *1679* for 'exclude'.
[5] *Hamlet*, II.ii.515-19.

And immediately after, speaking of Hecuba, when Priam was killed before her eyes:

> The mobbled queen ran up and down,
> Threatening the flame with bisson rheum; a clout about
>   that head
> Where late the diadem stood; and for a robe,
> About her lank and all o'er-teemed loins,
> A blanket in th' alarm of fear caught up.
> Who this had seen, with tongue in venom steep'd
> 'Gainst Fortune's state would treason have pronounced;
> But if the gods themselves did see her then,
> When she saw Pyrrhus make malicious sport
> In mincing with his sword her husband's limbs,
> The instant burst of clamour that she made
> (Unless things mortal move them not at all)
> Would have made milch the burning eyes of Heaven,
> And passion in the gods.[1]

What a pudder is here kept in raising the expression of trifling thoughts! Would not a man have thought that the poet had been bound prentice to a wheelwright, for his first rant? and had followed a ragman for the clout and blanket, in the second? Fortune is painted on a wheel, and therefore the writer, in a rage, will have poetical justice done upon every member of that engine: after this execution, he bowls the nave down hill, from Heaven to the fiends (an unreasonable long mark, a man would think); 'tis well there are no solid orbs to stop it in the way, or no element of fire to consume it: but when it came to the earth, it must be monstrous heavy, to break ground as low as to the centre. His making milch the burning eyes of Heaven was a pretty tolerable flight too: and I think no man ever drew milk out of eyes before him: yet, to make the wonder greater, these eyes were burning. Such a sight indeed were enough to have raised passion in the gods; but to excuse the effects of it, he tells you, perhaps they did not see it. Wise men would be glad to find a little sense couched under all these pompous words; for bombast is commonly the delight of that audience which loves poetry, but understands it not: and as commonly has been the practice of those writers who, not being able to infuse a natural passion into the mind, have made it their business to ply the ears and to stun their judges by the noise. But Shakespeare does

[1] *Ibid.*, 524, 528-41.

not often thus; for the passions in his scene between Brutus
and Cassius are extremely natural, the thoughts are such as
arise from the matter, the expression of 'em not viciously
figurative. I cannot leave this subject, before I do justice to that
divine poet by giving you one of his passionate descriptions:
'tis of Richard the Second when he was deposed, and led in
triumph through the streets of London by Henry of Bulling-
brook: the painting of it is so lively, and the words so moving,
that I have scarce read any thing comparable to it in any other
language. Suppose you have seen already the fortunate usurper
passing through the crowd, and followed by the shouts and
acclamations of the people; and now behold King Richard
entering upon the scene: consider the wretchedness of his
condition, and his carriage in it; and refrain from pity if you
can:

> As in a theatre, the eyes of men,
> After a well-graced actor leaves the stage,
> Are idly bent on him that enters next,
> Thinking his prattle to be tedious:
> Even so, or with much more contempt, men's eyes
> Did scowl on Richard: no man cried, God save him:
> No joyful tongue gave him his welcome home,
> But dust was thrown upon his sacred head,
> Which with such gentle sorrow he shook off,
> His face still combating with tears and smiles
> (The badges of his grief and patience),
> That had not God (for some strong purpose) steel'd
> The hearts of men, they must perforce have melted,
> And barbarism itself have pitied him.[1]

To speak justly of this whole matter: 'tis neither height of
thought that is discommended, nor pathetic vehemence, nor any
nobleness of expression in its proper place; but 'tis a false measure of all these, something which is like 'em, and is not them;
'tis the Bristol-stone,[2] which appears like a diamond; 'tis an
extravagant thought, instead of a sublime one; 'tis roaring
madness, instead of vehemence; and a sound of words, instead
of sense. If Shakespeare were stripped of all the bombast in his
passions, and dressed in the most vulgar words, we should find
the beauties of his thoughts remaining; if his embroideries were
burnt down, there would still be silver at the bottom of the

---

[1] *Richard II*, V.ii.23-36.   [2] I.e. rock-crystal.

melting-pot: but I fear (at least let me fear it for myself) that we who ape his sounding words have nothing of his thought, but are all outside; there is not so much as a dwarf within our giant's clothes. Therefore, let not Shakespeare suffer for our sakes; 'tis our fault, who succeed him in an age which is more refined, if we imitate him so ill that we copy his failings only, and make a virtue of that in our writings which in his was an imperfection.

For what remains, the excellency of that poet was, as I have said, in the more manly passions; Fletcher's in the softer: Shakespeare writ better betwixt man and man; Fletcher, betwixt man and woman: consequently, the one described friendship better; the other love: yet Shakespeare taught Fletcher to write love: and Juliet, and Desdemona, are originals. 'Tis true, the scholar had the softer soul; but the master had the kinder. Friendship is both a virtue and a passion essentially; love is a passion only in its nature, and is not a virtue but by accident: good nature makes friendship; but effeminacy love. Shakespeare had an universal mind, which comprehended all characters and passions; Fletcher a more confined and limited: for though he treated love in perfection, yet honour, ambition, revenge, and generally all the stronger passions, he either touched not, or not masterly. To conclude all, he was a limb of Shakespeare.

I had intended[1] to have proceeded to the last property of manners, which is that they must be constant, and the characters maintained the same from the beginning to the end; and from thence to have proceeded to the thoughts and expressions suitable to a tragedy: but I will first see how this will relish with the age. 'Tis, I confess, but cursorily written; yet the judgment which is given here is generally founded upon experience: but because many men are shocked at the name of rules, as if they were a kind of magisterial prescription upon poets, I will conclude with the words of Rapin, in his reflections on Aristotle's work of poetry: 'If the rules be well considered, we shall find them to be made only to reduce nature into method, to trace her step by step, and not to suffer the least mark of her to escape us: 'tis only by these that probability in fiction is maintained, which is the soul of poetry. They are founded upon good sense, and sound reason, rather than on authority; for

[1] Cf. 'Heads of an Answer to Rymer,' para. 35, p. 217, above.

though Aristotle and Horace are produced, yet no man must argue that what they write is true because they writ it; but 'tis evident, by the ridiculous mistakes and gross absurdities which have been made by those poets who have taken their fancy only for their guide, that if this fancy be not regulated, 'tis a mere caprice, and utterly incapable to produce a reasonable and judicious poem'.[1]

[1] *Réflexions*, xii.

THE PREFACE

to *Ovid's Epistles, Translated by Several Hands* (1680)

LIFE OF OVID—THE 'EPISTLES'—PRINCIPLES OF TRANS-
LATION (METAPHRASE, PARAPHRASE, IMITATION)

Text: 8°, 1680.

Dryden's first essay on translation—a subject to which he returned
five years later in the preface to *Sylvae* (vol. II, pp. 18-33, below)—was
hailed by Johnson a century later, in his Life of Dryden, as a decisive
document 'in breaking the shackles of verbal interpretation, which
must for ever debar it from elegance.' But the preface seems rather a
call for moderation than a liberating gesture. Dryden's object is to
create a tradition of English translation somewhere between the word-
for-word ('metaphrase') and Cowley's anarchic individualism in his
'Pindaric Odes' ('imitation'). These are Dryden's first thoughts in
the art of translation, which was his occasional diversion in the
1680's and his almost unceasing task in the last decade of his life.

Of the twenty-three Epistles, nos. 2 and 18 were contributed by
Dryden, no. 13 by Dryden and Mulgrave. The text used was the
Dutch variorum by Borchard Cnipping, published in Amsterdam in
1670. The octavo probably appeared very early in 1680.

THE Life of Ovid being already written in our language before
the translation of his *Metamorphoses*,[1] I will not presume so far
upon myself to think I can add any thing to Mr Sandys his
undertaking. The English reader may there be satisfied that he
flourished in the reign of Augustus Cæsar, that he was extracted
from an ancient family of Roman knights; that he was born to
the inheritance of a splendid fortune, that he was designed to
the study of the law; and had made considerable progress in it,
before he quitted that profession for this of poetry, to which he
was more naturally formed. The cause of his banishment is
unknown; because he was himself unwilling further to provoke

[1] The *Metamorphosis Englished* by George Sandys (1578-1644) had first
appeared complete in 1626.

the Emperor by ascribing it to any other reason than what was pretended by Augustus, which was the lasciviousness of his Elegies and his *Art of Love*. 'Tis true they are not to be excused in the severity of manners, as being able to corrupt a larger Empire, if there were any, than that of Rome; yet this may be said in behalf of Ovid, that no man has ever treated the passion of love with so much delicacy of thought, and of expression, or searched into the nature of it more philosophically than he. And the Emperor who condemned him had as little reason as another man to punish that fault with so much severity, if at least he were the author of a certain epigram[1] which is ascribed to him, relating to the cause of the first civil war betwixt himself and Mark Anthony the Triumvir, which is more fulsome than any passage I have met with in our poet. To pass by the naked familiarity of his expressions to Horace, which are cited in that author's life,[2] I need only mention one notorious act of his, in taking Livia to his bed when she was not only married, but with child by her husband, then living. But deeds, it seems, may be justified by arbitrary power, when words are questioned in a poet. There is another guess of the grammarians, as far from truth as the first from reason; they will have him banished for some favours which they say he received from Julia, the daughter of Augustus, whom they think he celebrates under the name of Corinna in his Elegies: but he who will observe the verses which are made to that mistress, may gather from the whole contexture of them that Corinna was not a woman of the highest quality. If Julia were then married to Agrippa, why should our poet make his petition to Isis for her safe delivery, and afterwards condole her miscarriage; which for aught he knew, might be by her own husband? Or indeed how durst he be so bold to make the least discovery of such a crime, which was no less than capital, especially committed against a person of Agrippa's rank? Or if it were before her marriage, he would surely have been more discreet than to have published an accident which must have been fatal to them both. But what most confirms me against this opinion is that Ovid himself complains that the true person of Corinna was found out by the fame of his verses to her; which if it had been Julia, he durst not have owned; and besides, an immediate punishment

---

[1] Martial, xi.20.   [2] By Suetonius.

must have followed. He seems himself more truly to have touched at the cause of his exile in those obscure verses:

cur aliquid vidi? cur noxia lumina feci? etc.[1]

namely, that he had either seen, or was conscious to somewhat which had procured him his disgrace. But neither am I satisfied that this was the incest of the Emperor with his own daughter: for Augustus was of a nature too vindicative to have contented himself with so small a revenge, or so unsafe to himself, as that of simple banishment, and would certainly have secured his crimes from public notice by the death of him who was witness to them. Neither have historians given us any sight into such an action of this Emperor: nor would he (the greatest politician of his time), in all probability, have managed his crimes with so little secrecy as not to shun the observation of any man. It seems more probable that Ovid was either the confidant of some other passion, or that he had stumbled by some inadvertency upon the privacies of Livia, and seen her in a bath: for the words

nudam sine veste Dianam,[2]

agree better with Livia, who had the fame of chastity, than with either of the Julias, who were both noted of incontinency. The first verses which were made by him in his youth, and recited publicly, according to the custom, were, as he himself assures us, to Corinna: his banishment happened not till the age of fifty; from which it may be deduced, with probability enough, that the love of Corinna did not occasion it: nay, he tells us plainly that his offence was that of error only, not of wickedness; and in the same paper of verses also, that the cause was notoriously known at Rome, though it be left so obscure to after ages.

But to leave conjectures on a subject so uncertain, and to write somewhat more authentic of this poet. That he frequented the court of Augustus, and was well received in it, is most undoubted: all his poems bear the character of a court, and appear to be written, as the French call it, *cavalièrement*. Add to this, that the titles of many of his Elegies, and more of his letters in his banishment, are addressed to persons well known to us, even at this distance, to have been considerable in that court.

[1] *Tristia*, II.103: 'Why did I see? Why cause harmful beams to shine?'
[2] *Tristia*, II.105: 'Diana naked and unclothed.'

Nor was his acquaintance less with the famous poets of his age than with the noblemen and ladies. He tells you himself, in a particular account of his own life,[1] that Macer, Horace, Tibullus, Propertius, and many others of them, were his familiar friends, and that some of them communicated their writings to him; but that he had only seen Virgil.

If the imitation of nature be the business of a poet, I know no author who can justly be compared with ours, especially in the description of the passions. And to prove this, I shall need no other judges than the generality of his readers: for all passions being inborn with us, we are almost equally judges when we are concerned in the representation of them. Now I will appeal to any man who has read this poet, whether he finds not the natural emotion of the same passion in himself which the poet describes in his feigned persons? His thoughts, which are the pictures and results of those passions, are generally such as naturally arise from those disorderly motions of our spirits. Yet, not to speak too partially in his behalf, I will confess that the copiousness of his wit was such that he often writ too pointedly for his subject, and made his persons speak more eloquently than the violence of their passion would admit: so that he is frequently witty out of season; leaving the imitation of nature, and the cooler dictates of his judgment, for the false applause of fancy. Yet he seems to have found out this imperfection in his riper age; for why else should he complain that his *Metamorphosis* was left unfinished? Nothing, sure, can be added to the wit of that poem, or of the rest; but many things ought to have been retrenched, which I suppose would have been the business of his age, if his misfortunes had not come too fast upon him. But take him uncorrected as he is transmitted to us, and it must be acknowledged, in spite of his Dutch friends the commentators, even of Julius Scaliger himself, that Seneca's censure will stand good against him:

nescivit quod bene cessit relinquere:[2]

he never knew how to give over when he had done well; but, continually varying the same sense an hundred ways, and taking up in another place what he had more than enough inculcated before, he sometimes cloys his readers instead of satisfying them;

[1] *Tristia,* IV.x.43-54.   [2] M. Annaeus Seneca, *Controversiae,* IX.v.17.

and gives occasion to his translators, who dare not cover him, to blush at the nakedness of their father. This, then, is the allay of Ovid's writings, which is sufficiently recompensed by his other excellencies: nay, this very fault is not without its beauties: for the most severe censor cannot but be pleased with the prodigality of his wit, though at the same time he could have wished that the master of it had been a better manager. Everything which he does becomes him, and if sometimes he appears too gay, yet there is a secret gracefulness of youth which accompanies his writings, though the staidness and sobriety of age be wanting. In the most material part, which is the conduct, 'tis certain that he seldom has miscarried: for if his Elegies be compared with those of Tibullus and Propertius, his contemporaries, it will be found that those poets seldom designed before they writ. And though the language of Tibullus be more polished, and the learning of Propertius, especially in his Fourth Book, more set out to ostentation, yet their common practice was to look no further before them than the next line; whence it will inevitably follow that they can drive to no certain point, but ramble from one subject to another, and conclude with somewhat which is not of a piece with their beginning:

> purpureus late qui splendeat, unus et alter
> adsuitur pannus,[1]

as Horace says: though the verses are golden, they are but patched into the garment. But our poet has always the goal in his eye, which directs him in his race; some beautiful design, which he first establishes, and then contrives the means which will naturally conduct it to his end. This will be evident to judicious readers in this work of his Epistles, of which somewhat, at least in general, will be expected.

The title of them in our late editions is *Epistolæ heroidum*, *The Letters of the Heroines*.[2] But Heinsius[3] has judged more

---

[1] *Ars poetica*, ll. 15-16.

[2] The term 'heroine' presumably evolved as a critical term in pace with 'hero,' first used in the sense of 'the chief character' in the 'Defence of the Epilogue,' p. 172 and n., above. Rymer had used 'heroine' in the critical sense two years before the Ovid, in *The Tragedies of the Last Age* (1678) (*Critical Works*, ed. Zimansky, p. 58)—the earliest recorded use. The present case is hardly explicit enough to be regarded as an example.

[3] Heinsius's edition had appeared in 1652, but had been largely incorporated into Cnipping's variorum of 1670.

truly that the inscription of our author was barely *Epistles*; which he concludes from his cited verses, where Ovid asserts this work as his own invention, and not borrowed from the Greeks, whom (as the masters of their learning) the Romans usually did imitate. But it appears not from their writers that any of the Grecians ever touched upon this way, which our poet therefore justly has vindicated to himself. I quarrel not at the word *heroidum*, because 'tis used by Ovid in his *Art of Love*:

Jupiter ad verteres supplex *heroidas* ibat.[1]

But sure he could not be guilty of such an oversight to call his work by the name of *Heroines*, when there are divers men, or heroes, as namely Paris, Leander, and Acontius, joined in it. Except Sabinus, who writ some answers to Ovid's letters,

(quam celer de toto rediit meus orbe Sabinus,[2])

I remember not any of the Romans who have treated this subject, save only Propertius, and that but once, in his Epistle of Arethusa to Lycotas, which is written so near the style of Ovid that it seems to be but an imitation, and therefore ought not to defraud our poet of the glory of his invention.

Concerning this work of the Epistles, I shall content myself to observe these few particulars. First, that they are generally granted to be the most perfect piece of Ovid, and that the style of them is tenderly passionate and courtly; two properties well agreeing with the persons which were heroines and lovers. Yet where the characters were lower, as in Œnone and Hero, he has kept close to nature, in drawing his images after a country life, though perhaps he has Romanized his Grecian dames too much, and made them speak sometimes as if they had been born in the city of Rome, and under the Empire of Augustus. There seems to be no great variety in the particular subjects which he has chosen; most of the Epistles being written from ladies who were forsaken by their lovers: which is the reason that many of the same thoughts come back upon us in divers letters. But of the general character of women, which is modesty, he has taken a most becoming care; for his amorous expressions go no

[1] *Ars amatoria*, I.713.   [2] *Amores*, II.xviii.27-8.

further than virtue may allow, and therefore may be read, as he intended them, by matrons without a blush.

Thus much concerning the poet, whom you find translated by divers hands,[1] that you may at least have that variety in the English which the subject denied to the author of the Latin: it remains that I should say somewhat of poetical translations in general, and give my opinion (with submission to better judgments), which way of version seems to me the most proper.

All translation, I suppose, may be reduced to these three heads.

First, that of metaphrase, or turning an author word by word, and line by line, from one language into another. Thus, or near this manner, was Horace his *Art of Poetry* translated by Ben Jonson.[2] The second way is that of paraphrase, or translation with latitude, where the author is kept in view by the translator, so as never to be lost, but his words are not so strictly followed as his sense, and that too is admitted to be amplified, but not altered. Such is Mr Waller's translation of Virgil's Fourth Æneid.[3] The third way is that of imitation, where the translator (if now he has not lost that name) assumes the liberty not only to vary from the words and sense, but to forsake them both as he sees occasion; and taking only some general hints from the original, to run division on the ground-work,[4] as he pleases. Such is Mr Cowley's practice in turning two Odes of Pindar, and one of Horace, into English.[5]

Concerning the first of these methods, our master Horace has given us this caution:

> nec verbum verbo curabis reddere, fidus
> interpres.[6]
> Nor word for word too faithfully translate;

as the Earl of Roscommon has excellently rendered it. Too faithfully is, indeed, pedantically: 'tis a faith like that which proceeds from superstition, blind and zealous. Take it in the

---

[1] Cf. p. 273n., below.
[2] First published in the 1640 folio. Roscommon, in the preface to his own translation of the *Ars poetica* of 1680, also criticized Jonson's literalism.
[3] *The Passion of Dido* (1658), by Edmund Waller and Sidney Godolphin.
[4] I.e. invent variations on a musical theme.
[5] The Pindaric Odes appeared in Cowley's *Poems* (1656). Cf. the preface to *Sylvae*, vol. II, p. 32, below.
[6] *Ars poetica*, ll. 133-4.

expression of Sir John Denham to Sir Richard Fanshawe, on
his version of the *Pastor Fido*:

> That servile path thou nobly dost decline,
> Of tracing word by word, and line by line:
> A new and nobler way thou dost pursue,
> To make translations and translators too:
> They but preserve the ashes, thou the flame
> True to his sense, but truer to his fame.[1]

'Tis almost impossible to translate verbally, and well, at the
same time; for the Latin (a most severe and compendious
language) often expresses that in one word which either the
barbarity or the narrowness of modern tongues cannot supply
in more. 'Tis frequent also that the conceit is couched in some
expression, which will be lost in English:

> atque idem venti vela fidemque ferent.[2]

What poet of our nation is so happy as to express this thought
literally in English, and to strike wit, or almost sense, out of it?

In short, the verbal copier is encumbered with so many
difficulties at once that he can never disentangle himself from
all. He is to consider at the same time the thought of his
author, and his words, and to find out the counterpart to each in
another language; and, besides this, he is to confine himself to
the compass of numbers, and the slavery of rhyme. 'Tis much
like dancing on ropes with fettered legs: a man may shun a fall
by using caution; but the gracefulness of motion is not to be
expected: and when we have said the best of it, 'tis but a foolish
task; for no sober man would put himself into a danger for the
applause of escaping without breaking his neck. We see Ben
Jonson could not avoid obscurity in his literal translation of
Horace, attempted in the same compass of lines: nay, Horace
himself could scarce have done it to a Greek poet:

> brevis esse laboro, obscurus fio:[3]

either perspicuity or gracefulness will frequently be wanting.

---

[1] From Denham's complimentary verses in Fanshawe's translation of
Guarini's *Pastor Fido* (1647), ll. 15-16, 21-4.

[2] Ovid, *Heroides*, vii.8:
> While you, with loosen'd sails and vows, prepare
> To seek a land that flies the searcher's care.
>   (Dryden.)

[3] *Ars poetica*, ll. 25-6: 'I labour to be brief, and become obscure.'

Horace has indeed avoided both these rocks in his translation
of the three first lines of Homer's Odysses, which he has con-
tracted into two:

> dic mihi, Musa, virum captæ post tempora Trojæ,
> qui mores hominum multorum vidit, et urbes.[1]

> Muse, speak the man who, since the siege of Troy,
> So many towns, such change of manners saw.
> EARL OF ROSC.

But then the sufferings of Ulysses, which are a considerable
part of that sentence, are omitted:

> Ὅς μάλα πολλὰ πλάγχθη.

The consideration of these difficulties, in a servile, literal
translation, not long since made two of our famous wits, Sir
John Denham and Mr Cowley, to contrive another way of turning
authors into our tongue, called by the latter of them *imitation*.
As they were friends, I suppose they communicated their thoughts
on this subject to each other, and therefore their reasons for it
are little different, though the practice of one[2] is much more
moderate. I take imitation of an author, in their sense, to be an
endeavour of a later poet to write like one who has written before
him on the same subject; that is, not to translate his words, or
to be confined to his sense, but only to set him as a pattern,
and to write, as he supposes that author would have done, had
he lived in our age, and in our country. Yet I dare not say that
either of them have carried this libertine way of rendering authors
(as Mr Cowley calls it) so far as my definition reaches; for in the
Pindaric Odes the customs and ceremonies of ancient Greece are
still preserved. But I know not what mischief may arise hereafter from the example of such an innovation, when writers of
unequal parts to him shall imitate so bold an undertaking. To
add and to diminish what we please, which is the way avowed
by him, ought only to be granted to Mr Cowley, and that too
only in his translation of Pindar, because he alone was able to

---

[1] *Ars poetica*, ll. 141-2.
[2] Denham. But his theories, as Dryden suggests, were very like Cowley's.
In the preface to *The Destruction of Troy*, a translation of part of the second
book of the *Æneid*, Denham had written: 'I conceive it a vulgar error in
translating poets to affect being *fidus interpres*: . . . for it is not his business
alone to translate language into language, but poesy into poesy.' The quotation is continued below, p. 271.

make him amends, by giving him better of his own whenever he refused his author's thoughts. Pindar is generally known to be a dark writer, to want connection (I mean as to our understanding), to soar out of sight, and leave his reader at a gaze. So wild and ungovernable a poet cannot be translated literally, his genius is too strong to bear a chain, and Samson-like he shakes it off. A genius so elevated and unconfined as Mr Cowley's was but necessary to make Pindar speak English, and that was to be performed by no other way than imitation. But if Virgil, or Ovid, or any regular, intelligible authors be thus used, 'tis no longer to be called their work, when neither the thoughts nor words are drawn from the original; but instead of them there is something new produced, which is almost the creation of another hand. By this way, 'tis true, somewhat that is excellent may be invented, perhaps more excellent than the first design; though Virgil must be still excepted, when that perhaps takes place. Yet he who is inquisitive to know an author's thoughts will be disappointed in his expectation. And 'tis not always that a man will be contented to have a present made him, when he expects the payment of a debt. To state it fairly, imitation of an author is the most advantageous way for a translator to shew himself, but the greatest wrong which can be done to the memory and reputation of the dead. Sir John Denham (who advised more liberty than he took himself), gives this reason for his innovation, in his admirable preface before the translation of the Second Æneid: 'Poetry is of so subtle a spirit that, in pouring out of one language into another, it will all evaporate; and, if a new spirit be not added in the transfusion, there will remain nothing but a *caput mortuum*.'[1] I confess this argument holds good against a literal translation; but who defends it? Imitation and verbal version are, in my opinion, the two extremes which ought to be avoided; and therefore, when I have proposed the mean betwixt them, it will be seen how far his argument will reach.

No man is capable of translating poetry who, besides a genius to that art, is not a master both of his author's language and of his own. Nor must we understand the language only of the poet, but his particular turn of thoughts and of expression, which are the characters that distinguish and, as it were, individuate him

[1] Cf. p. 270n., above.

from all other writers. When we are come thus far, 'tis time to
look into ourselves, to conform our genius to his, to give his
thought either the same turn, if our tongue will bear it or, if not,
to vary but the dress, not to alter or destroy the substance. The
like care must be taken of the more outward ornaments, the
words. When they appear (which is but seldom) literally graceful, it were an injury to the author that they should be changed.
But since every language is so full of its own proprieties, that
what is beautiful in one is often barbarous, nay sometimes nonsense, in another, it would be unreasonable to limit a translator
to the narrow compass of his author's words: 'tis enough if he
choose out some expression which does not vitiate the sense. I
suppose he may stretch his chain to such a latitude; but by
innovation of thoughts, methinks he breaks it. By this means
the spirit of an author may be transfused, and yet not lost: and
thus 'tis plain that the reason alleged by Sir John Denham has
no farther force than to expression; for thought, if it be translated truly, cannot be lost in another language; but the words
that convey it to our apprehension (which are the image and
ornament of that thought) may be so ill chosen as to make it
appear in an unhandsome dress, and rob it of its native lustre.
There is therefore a liberty to be allowed for the expression,
neither is it necessary that words and lines should be confined
to the measure of their original. The sense of an author, generally
speaking, is to be sacred and inviolable. If the fancy of Ovid be
luxuriant, 'tis his character to be so, and if I retrench it, he is
no longer Ovid. It will be replied that he receives advantage by
this lopping of his superfluous branches, but I rejoin that a
translator has no such right: when a painter copies from the
life, I suppose he has no privilege to alter features and lineaments,
under pretence that his picture will look better; perhaps the face
which he has drawn would be more exact, if the eyes or nose were
altered, but 'tis his business to make it resemble the original. In
two cases only there may a seeming difficulty arise, that is, if the
thought be notoriously trivial or dishonest. But the same answer
will serve for both, that then they ought not to be translated.

                              et quæ
          desperes tractata nitescere posse, relinquas.[1]

[1] Horace, *Ars poetica*, ll. 149-50: 'and leave those things you cannot hope
to excel in, however you may treat them.'

Thus I have ventured to give my opinion on this subject against the authority of two great men, but I hope without offence to either of their memories, for I both loved them living, and reverence them now they are dead. But if, after what I have urged, it be thought by better judges that the praise of a translation consists in adding new beauties to the piece, thereby to recompense the loss which it sustains by change of language, I shall be willing to be taught better, and to recant. In the meantime, it seems to me that the true reason why we have so few versions which are tolerable is not for the too close pursuing of the author's sense, but because there are so few who have all the talents which are requisite for translation; and that there is so little praise and so small encouragement for so considerable a part of learning.

To apply, in short, what has been said, to this present work, the reader will here find most of the translations with some little latitude or variation from the author's sense: that of Oenone to Paris[1] is in Mr Cowley's way of imitation only. I was desired to say that the author, who is of the fair sex, understood not Latin. But if she does not, I am afraid she has given us occasion to be ashamed who do.

For my own part, I am ready to acknowledge that I have transgressed the rules which I have given, and taken more liberty than a just translation will allow. But so many gentlemen[2] whose wit and learning are well known being joined in it, I doubt not but that their excellencies will make you ample satisfaction for my errors.

J. DRYDEN.

[1] By Mrs Aphra Behn (1640-89).
[2] Including Nahum Tate, Thomas Rymer, Elkanah Settle, Thomas Otway, and Samuel Butler.

TO THE RIGHT HONOURABLE JOHN,
LORD HAUGHTON

Prefixed to *The Spanish Friar* (1681)

Text: 4°, 1681.

Dryden's most Protestant play, first performed in March 1680, was
appropriately dedicated to John Holles (1662-1711), son of the third
Earl of Clare, and later created Duke of Newcastle in 1694 for his
services to William III. The tone of its preface is marred by a certain
complacency and an abundance of false modesty concerning the play;
but it defines Dryden's mature attitude to the dramatist's craft with
all its professional disdain for popular taste. Dryden's middle-aged
contempt for his audiences had long since ended his early preoccupa-
tion with the principles of drama; in his few remaining years as a
dramatist he consulted only popular fashion and the inclination of the
moment—'for this time I satisfied my own humour'.

MY LORD,

WHEN I first designed this play, I found, or thought I found,
somewhat so moving in the serious part of it, and so pleasant
in the comic, as might deserve a more than ordinary care in
both. Accordingly, I used the best of my endeavour, in the
management of two plots,[1] so very different from each other,
that it was not perhaps the talent of every writer to have made
them of a piece. Neither have I attempted other plays of the

---

[1] Dryden's self-congratulation over his technical success was accepted by
both Addison and Johnson at its face value. Addison compared *The Spanish
Friar* to *Paradise Lost* (*Spectator*, no. 267), its fall of man matched by
the fall of the angels; and Johnson, more aptly, compared it to *The Merchant
of Venice* in his edition of Shakespeare (1765): 'Dryden was much pleased
by his own address in connecting the two plots of his *Spanish Friar*, which
yet, I believe, the critic will find excelled by this play.'

same nature, in my opinion, with the same judgment; though
with like success.[1] And though many poets may suspect themselves for the fondness and partiality of parents to their youngest
children, yet I hope I may stand exempted from this rule,
because I know myself too well to be ever satisfied with my own
conceptions, which have seldom reached to those ideas that I
had within me; and consequently, I presume I may have liberty
to judge when I write more or less pardonably, as an ordinary
marksman may know certainly when he shoots less wide at what
he aims. Besides, the care and pains I have bestowed on this,
beyond my other tragi-comedies, may reasonably make the
world conclude that either I can do nothing tolerably, or that
this poem is not much amiss. Few good pictures have been finished
at one sitting; neither can a true just play, which is to bear the
test of ages, be produced at a heat, or by the force of fancy,
without the maturity of judgment. For my own part, I have both
so just a diffidence of myself, and so great a reverence for my
audience, that I dare venture nothing without a strict examination; and am as much ashamed to put a loose indigested play
upon the public as I should be to offer brass money in a payment. For though it should be taken (as it is too often on the
stage), yet it will be found in the second telling; and a judicious
reader will discover in his closet that trashy stuff whose glittering
deceived him in the action. I have often heard the stationer
sighing in his shop, and wishing for those hands to take off his
melancholy bargain which clapped its performance on the stage.
In a playhouse, everything contributes to impose upon the
judgment: the lights, the scenes, the habits, and, above all, the
grace of action, which is commonly the best where there is
the most need of it, surprise the audience, and cast a mist upon
their understandings; not unlike the cunning of a juggler, who
is always staring us in the face, and overwhelming us with gib-
berish, only that he may gain the opportunity of making the
cleaner conveyance of his trick. But these false beauties of the
stage are no more lasting than a rainbow; when the actor ceases
to shine upon them, when he gilds them no longer with his
reflection, they vanish in a twinkling.

I have sometimes wondered, in the reading, what was become

[1] For example *The Rival Ladies* (1664), *Secret Love* (1668), and *Marriage
a-la-Mode* (1673).

of those glaring colours which amazed me in *Bussy D'Ambois*[1]
upon the theatre; but when I had taken up what I supposed a
fallen star, I found I had been cozened with a jelly:[2] nothing but
a cold, dull mass, which glittered no longer than it was shooting;
a dwarfish thought, dressed up in gigantic words, repetition in
abundance, looseness of expression, and gross hyperboles; the
sense of one line expanded prodigiously into ten; and, to sum
up all, uncorrect English, and a hideous mingle of false poetry
and true nonsense; or, at best, a scantling of wit which lay
gasping for life, and groaning beneath a heap of rubbish. A
famous modern poet used to sacrifice every year a Statius to
Virgil's Manes;[3] and I have indignation enough to burn a
D'Ambois annually to the memory of Jonson.

But now, my Lord, I am sensible, perhaps too late, that I
have gone too far: for, I remember some verses of my own
Maximin and Almanzor[4] which cry vengeance upon me for their
extravagance, and which I wish heartily in the same fire with
Statius and Chapman. All I can say for those passages, which
are, I hope, not many, is that I knew they were bad enough
to please, even when I writ them. But I repent of them amongst
my sins; and if any of their fellows intrude by chance into my
present writings, I draw a stroke over all those Dalilahs[5] of the
theatre; and am resolved I will settle myself no reputation by

---

[1] Chapman's tragedy (1607), which Charles Hart had revived upon the
Restoration stage in about 1675. Dryden returned to his attack upon Chap-
man by substituting his name for that of Gauthier de la Calprenède in
Soame's translation of Boileau's *Art poétique* (1683):

> Affected wits will naturally incline
> To paint their figures by their own design:
> Your bully poets bully heroes write:
> Chapman in Bussy d'Ambois took delight,
> And thought perfection was to huff and fight.
>   (ll. 553–7; cf. Boileau, III.130f.)

[2] The alga nostoc, a damp plant, was popularly thought the remains of a
falling star. Cf. Dryden and Lee, *Oedipus*, II.i: 'The shooting stars end all in
purple jellies.'

[3] According to Strada (1572–1649) in his treatise on poetics, the *Pro-
lusiones* (1617), Andrea Navagero (Naugerius) (1483–1529), a Venetian
diplomat and Latinist, used every year to sacrifice a copy of Martial to the
memory of Virgil. Dryden's confusion of Martial with Statius is the more
understandable when we realize, as Malone showed, that his quotation from
Statius, below, is from the same prolusion.

[4] In *Tyrannic Love* (1670) and *The Conquest of Granada* (1672).

[5] I.e. deceivers. Dryden may have been reminded of Samson's temptress
by the Dalila of Milton's unacted *Samson Agonistes* (1671).

the applause of fools. 'Tis not that I am mortified to all ambition, but I scorn as much to take it from half-witted judges, as I should to raise an estate by cheating of bubbles. Neither do I discommend the lofty style in tragedy, which is naturally pompous and magnificent; but nothing is truly sublime that is not just and proper. If the Ancients had judged by the same measures which a common reader takes, they had concluded Statius to have written higher than Virgil; for

> quæ superimposito moles geminata Colosso[1]

carries a more thundering kind of sound than

> Tityre tu patulæ recubans sub tegmine fagi:[2]

yet Virgil had all the majesty of a lawful prince, and Statius only the blustering of a tyrant. But when men affect a virtue which they cannot reach, they fall into a vice which bears the nearest resemblance to it. Thus an injudicious poet who aims at loftiness runs easily into the swelling puffy style, because it looks like greatness. I remember, when I was a boy, I thought inimitable Spenser a mean poet in comparison of Sylvester's *Dubartas*; and was rapt into an ecstasy when I read these lines:

> Now, when the Winter's keener breath began
> To crystallize the Baltic Ocean;
> To glaze the lakes, to bridle up the floods,
> And periwig with snow the bald-pate woods.[3]

I am much deceived if this be not abominable fustian, that is, thoughts and words ill sorted, and without the least relation to each other; yet I dare not answer for an audience, that they would not clap it on the stage: so little value there is to be given to the common cry that nothing but madness can please madmen.

[1] Statius, *Sylvae*, I.i.i: 'a mound doubled by a Colossus on its top.' Cf. p. 276n., above.

[2] Virgil, *Eclogues*, I.i: 'You, Tityrus, lie under the cover of a spreading beech. . . .'

[3] Joshua Sylvester (1563-1618), *Divine Weeks and Works* (1605, etc.), from the fourth part of the first day of the second Week. Dryden's memory has tamed the original, which has 'and periwig with wool . . .'. His first poem, the 'Heroic Stanzas Consecrated to Oliver [Cromwell]' (1659) is the only evidence we have of Dryden's early sympathies with the metaphysical style, which he promptly abandoned before he was thirty. Du Bartas's name is intruded twice by Dryden into Soame's version of Boileau (ll. 21f., 101f.), the second mention being a reference to this same passage from Sylvester, as an awful example.

and a poet must be of a piece with the spectators to gain a reputation with them. But as in a room contrived for state, the height of the roof should bear a proportion to the area; so, in the heightenings of poetry, the strength and vehemence of figures should be suited to the occasion, the subject, and the persons. All beyond this is monstrous: 'tis out of nature, 'tis an excrescence, and not a living part of poetry. I had not said thus much, if some young gallants who pretend to criticism had not told me that this tragi-comedy wanted the dignity of style; but as a man who is charged with a crime of which he thinks himself innocent is apt to be too eager in his own defence, so perhaps I have vindicated my play with more partiality than I ought, or than such a trifle can deserve. Yet, whatever beauties it may want, 'tis free at least from the grossness of those faults I mentioned. What credit it has gained upon the stage, I value no farther than in reference to my profit, and the satisfaction I had in seeing it represented with all the justness and gracefulness of action. But as 'tis my interest to please my audience, so 'tis my ambition to be read: that I am sure is the more lasting and the nobler design: for the propriety of thoughts and words, which are the hidden beauties of a play, are but confusedly judged in the vehemence of action. All things are there beheld as in a hasty motion, where the objects only glide before the eye and disappear. The most discerning critic can judge no more of these silent graces in the action than he who rides post through an unknown country can distinguish the situation of places, and the nature of the soil. The purity of phrase, the clearness of conception and expression, the boldness maintained to majesty, the significancy and sound of words, not strained into bombast, but justly elevated; in short, those very words and thoughts which cannot be changed but for the worse, must of necessity escape our transient view upon the theatre; and yet without all these a play may take. For if either the story move us, or the actor help the lameness of it with his performance, or now and then a glittering beam of wit or passion strike through the obscurity of the poem, any of these are sufficient to effect a present liking, but not to fix a lasting admiration; for nothing but truth can long continue; and time is the surest judge of truth. I am not vain enough to think I have left no faults in this which that touchstone will not discover; neither indeed is it possible to avoid them in a play